IMAGES
of America

AROUND BRADFORD

IMAGES
of America

AROUND BRADFORD

Sally Ryan Costik
and the Bradford Landmark Society

ARCADIA
PUBLISHING

ISBN 978-0-7385-9700-3

Published by Arcadia Publishing
Charleston, South Carolina

Printed in the United States of America

For all general information contact Arcadia Publishing at:
Telephone 843-853-2070
Fax 843-853-0044
E-mail sales@arcadiapublishing.com
For customer service and orders:
Toll-Free 1-888-313-2665

Visit us on the Internet at www.arcadiapublishing.com

Contents

Acknowledgments

The Bradford Landmark Society would like to thank the following people for their help in researching the information contained in this book: Larry Richmond, whose investigative ability is unmatched; Dick Robertson, whose knowledge of railroads, houses, and general history is invaluable; George Kish; Pat Schessler; and of course, Jane Stack, who put the photographic collection of the Landmark on its feet and whose knowledge and love of the history of Bradford is unequaled.

Introduction

"It was the world unknowing, by the world unknown," wrote John J. McLaurin in his 1896 book *Sketches in Early Oildom*. He was referring, of course, to Bradford. A young, lumber-town Bradford, which had not yet seen the tremendous effects that the simple discovery of oil in the earth under its feet would bring. It literally changed the "Rip-Van Winkle cross-roads village of 1875 into a thriving, bustling, get-up-and-get metropolis."

Like all towns, Bradford has its own history, characters, stories, and memories. The Bradford Landmark Society is the keeper of many of these memories through photographs, documents, newspapers, and personal scrapbooks and papers. As guardians of the past, we collect, conserve, and preserve the history of Bradford for the coming generations and future historians.

The goal of this book is to educate, entertain, and enlighten those who proudly call Bradford their home. Our focus was not on the oil industry, but on the common man, the everyday workday, and the interesting events that have occurred over the past one hundred or so years, from the earliest Bradford to the city that stands today. Primarily, we focused on those years when Bradford was "booming"—from the discovery of oil in the late 1870s to the 1940s. Its a nostalgic look at the past that most people still hold in fond remembrance.

The history of Bradford is a tale well told. In 1837, the United States Land Company of Boston hired a young land agent, Colonel Levitt Little, to journey to their land holdings in the wild forests of northern Pennsylvania, and establish a town. He did so. Arriving by boat, down the Tunagwant Creek from Olean, he took with him his bride and two stepsons, Charles and P.L. Webster. The trip must have seemed like an adventure to the two young Webster boys, who were under twelve years of age. The Littles arrived in a rough lumber settlement, and began to build. Within a year, Little and a man named Leech had surveyed and laid out the town, which was appropriately called Littleton. Homes were built, schools and churches established, rude roads cut through the woods, a bridge laid across the Tuna, and lumber mills built to run day and night. From just four houses in 1839, a town was growing.

Then, in 1850, the United States Land Company sold 50,000 acres to Daniel Kingsbury. Said to be a rival of Colonel Little, Kingsbury established his own lumber operations and mill in the town, and when Little died in 1854, the village name Littleton died, too. Bradford became the new town's name.

In the early 1870s oil exploration was underway. The success of Titusville to the south had fired the entrepreneurial imagination. The first well was drilled in 1861, but the lack of oil and the outbreak of the Civil War caused its abandonment. Others followed. Job Moses drilled just off Seward Avenue and found a small pool, and his success encouraged others. The first major well was struck in 1875, and the rest, as they say, is history.

These photographs are an attempt to illustrate that history. Most have never been published, and some have been forgotten. We resurrect them now, for your enjoyment.

To the shopkeepers, the trolley drivers, the oil producers, the railroad men, the soldiers, the firemen, the police, the schoolchildren and their teachers, the oil field workers, and every man, woman, and child, we dedicate this collection in hopes that your lives and livelihoods will not be forgotten. We owe it to the past, and to the future.

Sally Costik, Curator
Bradford Landmark Society

One

Early Bradford

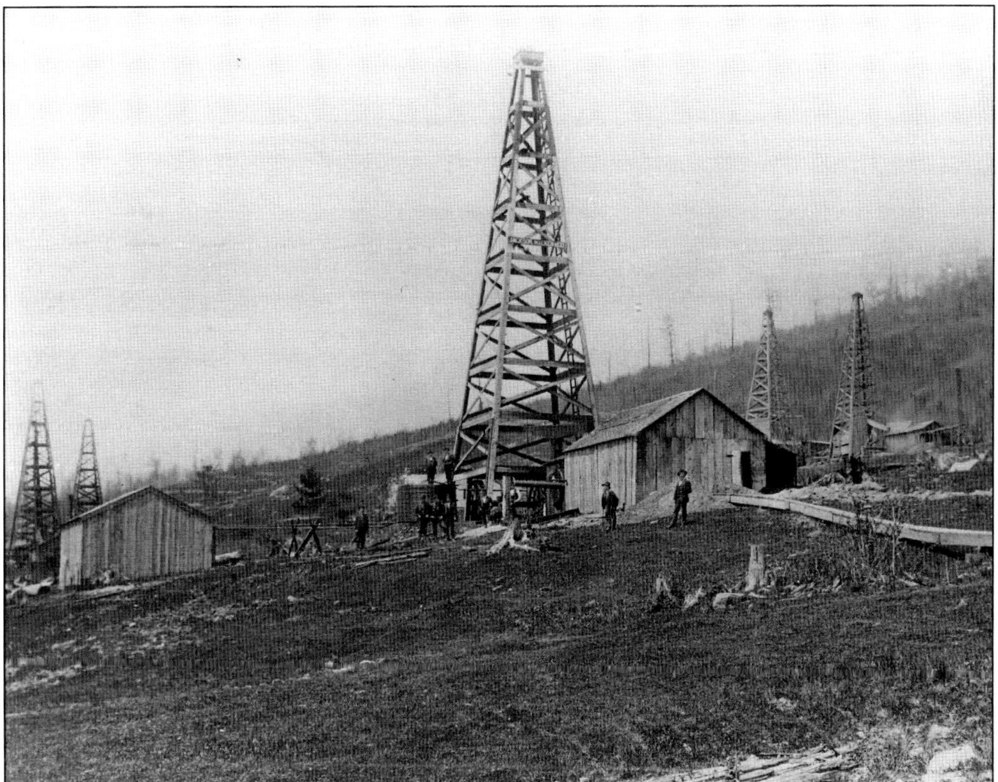

The first oil well struck, July 14, 1875. This oil well, designated as the Jackson & Walker Co. Well No. 1, was the first to successfully strike substantial amounts of oil, flowing in 85 barrels a day for the first 30 days. It was located above Jackson Avenue. By the turn of the century, it was estimated that there were 15,000 oil wells in the Bradford field. No other event has had as much impact on the history of Bradford.

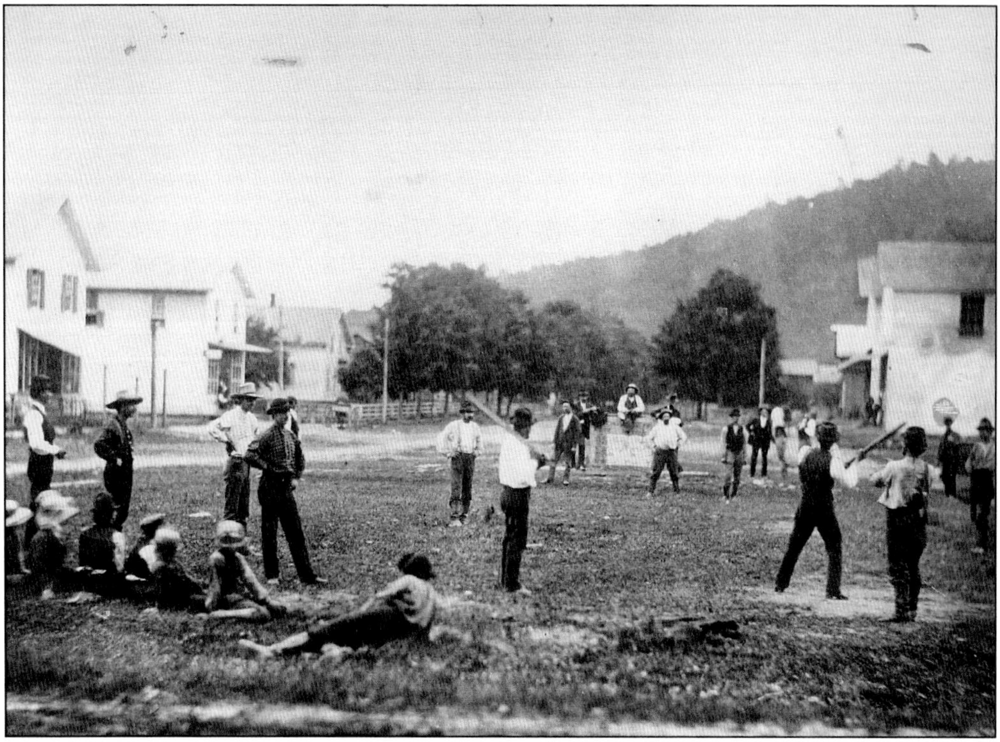

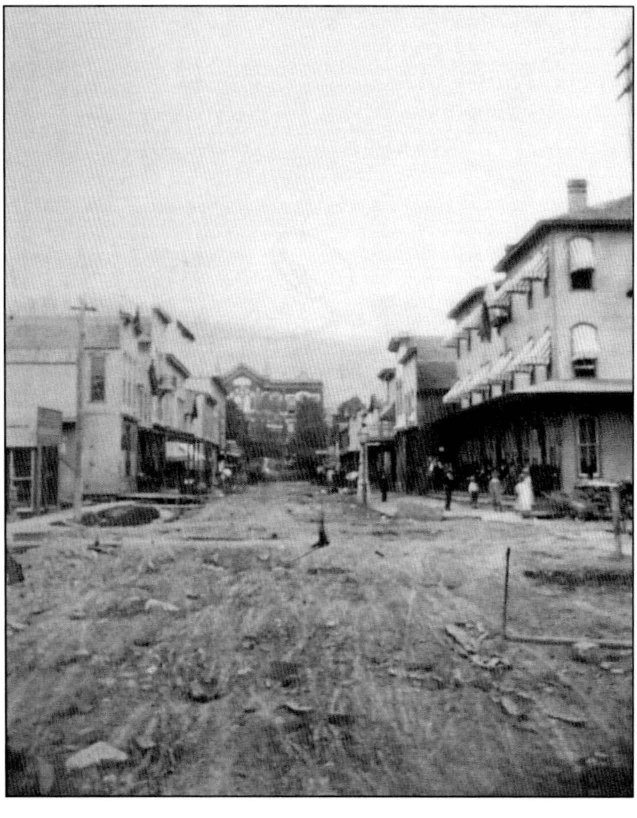

Men and boys playing baseball, 1870. Later, this site will become Bradford's public square. Bradford was still just a backwoods lumber town in 1870, but the coming oil boom would force many changes on the small town and games of baseball on Main Street would come to an end.

Congress Street, looking toward Main Street, 1879. The oil exchange is seen at the far end. The large hotel in the front right foreground, the Tuna Valley House, burned in 1880. The second city hall was built on this site, although it burned as well, in 1894. At present, Carnegie's Restaurant stands on this spot, and the Northwest Savings Bank occupies the site of the old oil exchange.

Barnabas Pike, early Bradford settler and lumberman. Born in 1793, he came to this area in the 1820s, building a log cabin near the corner of Sherman and Clarence Streets. In 1829 he married Mary Ann Colegrove of Smethport and raised ten children.

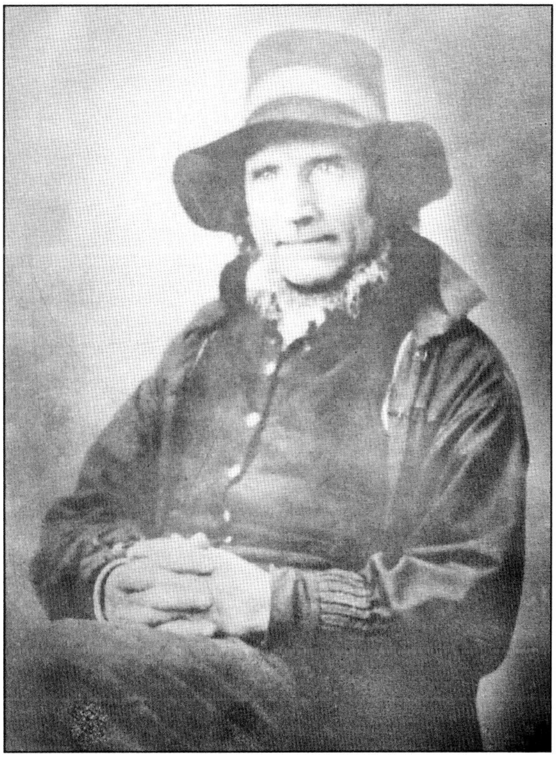

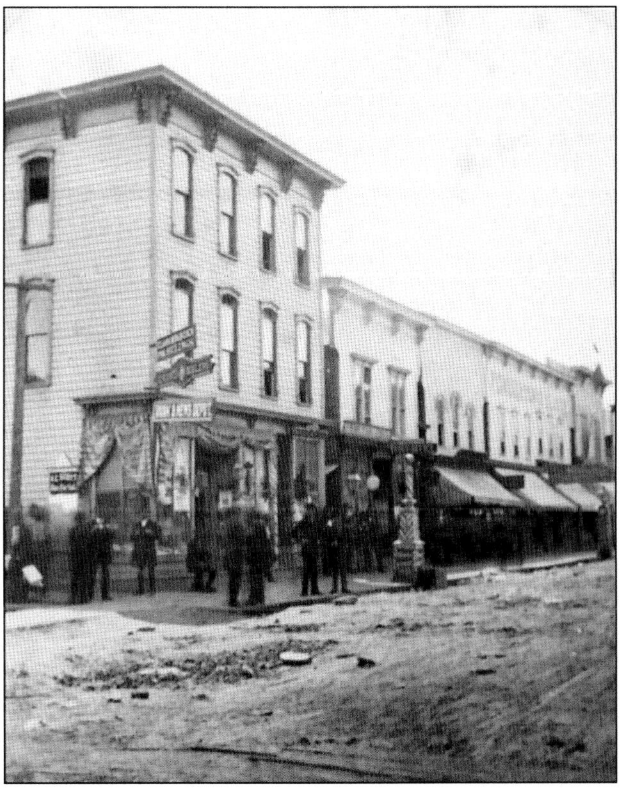

The corner of Pine and Main Streets, *c.* 1876. Main Street is as yet unpaved and the sidewalks are plank boards. The F.W. Davis building occupied this location by 1881.

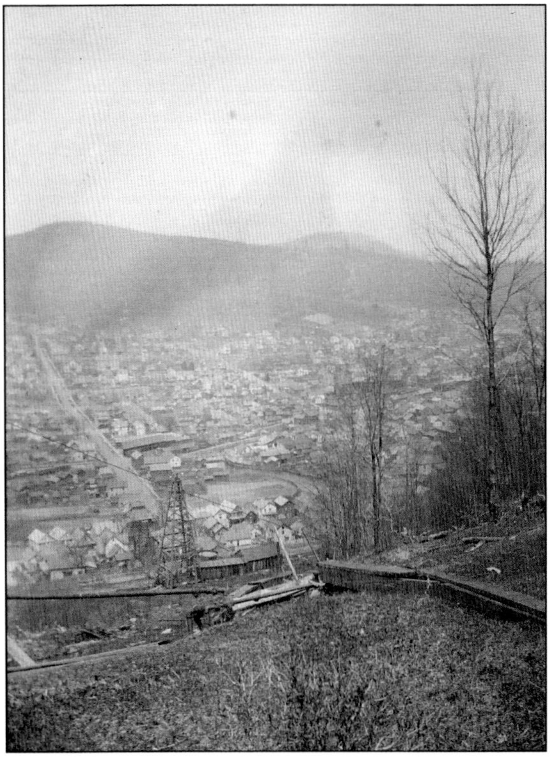

A view of Bradford, *c*. 1890, photographed from Mt. Raub at the east end of Main Street. The rough boxes in the foreground are sections of Bradford's water supply system and contain wooden water pipes used to carry water into the city.

Thompson & Wood, Main Street. Established in 1878, it employed six registered pharmacists and contained a deluxe soda fountain as well.

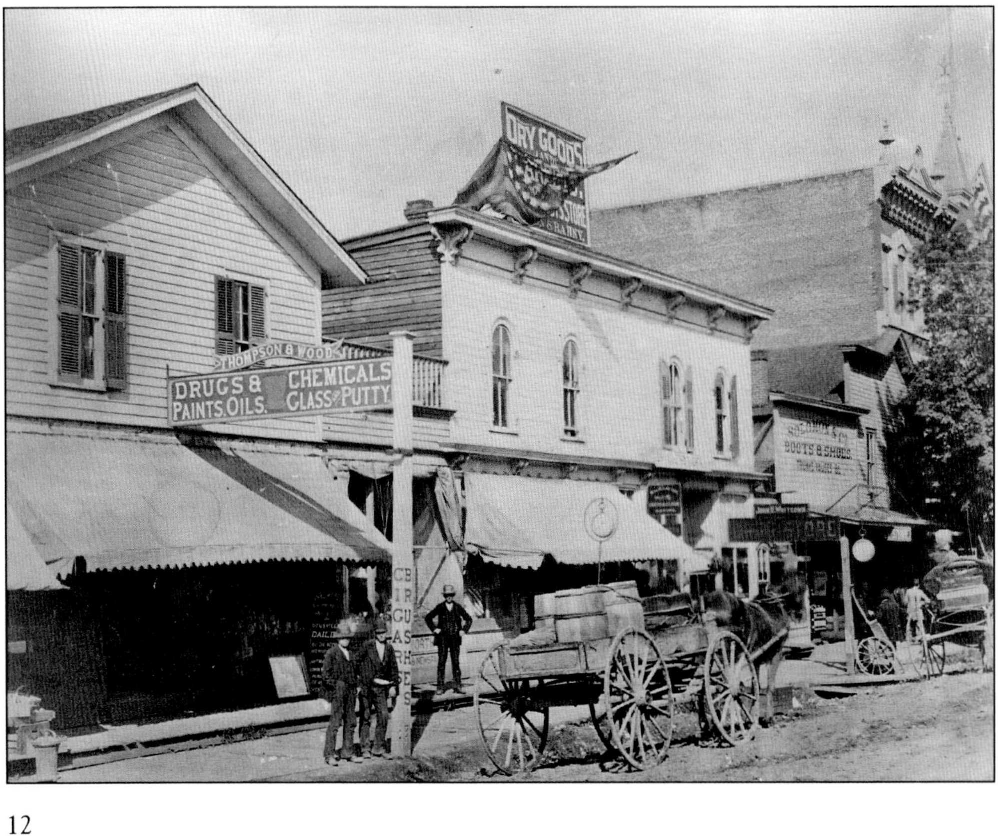

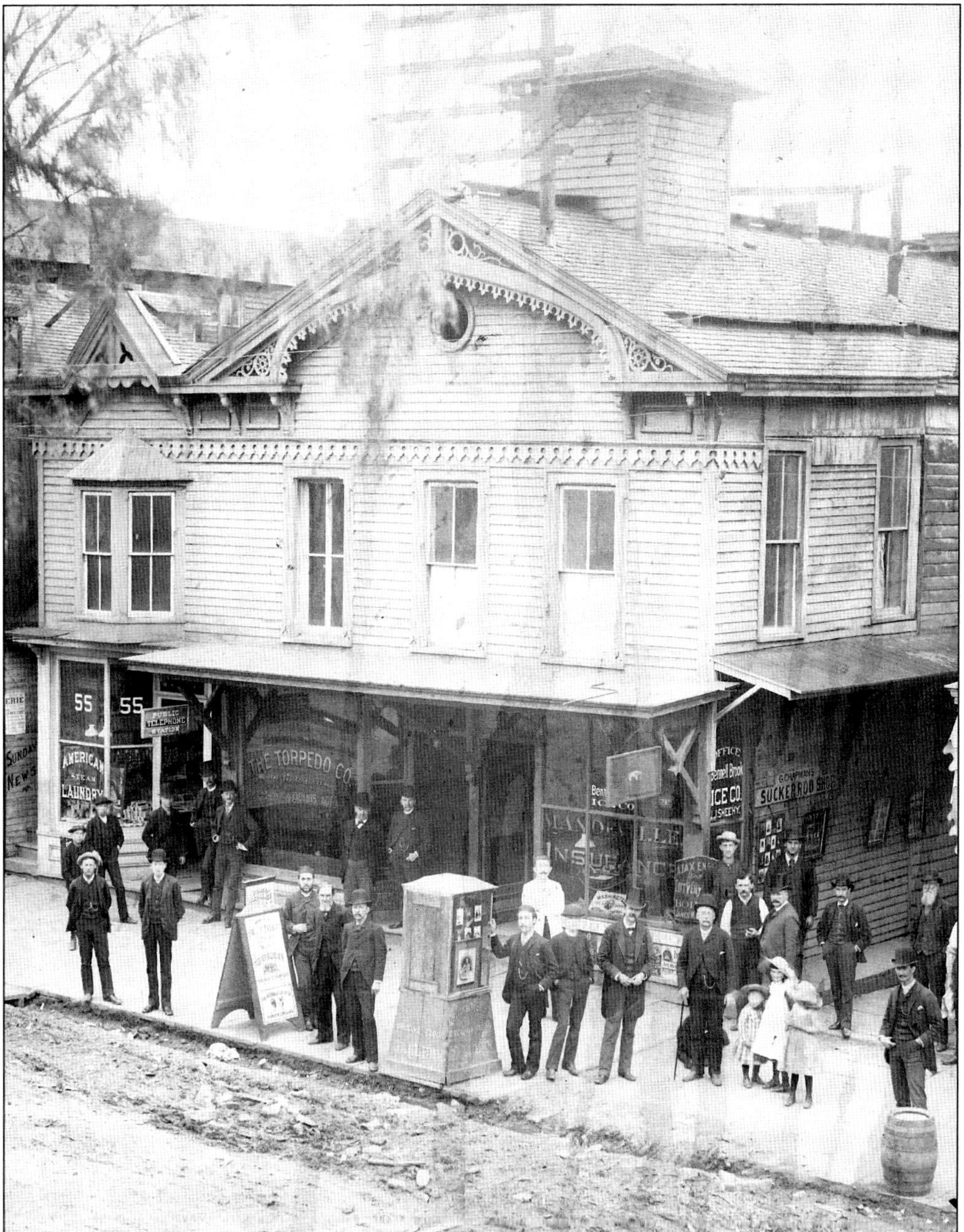

Main Street, 1882. This attractive building housed the American Steam Laundry, the Torpedo Company, the Sheehy Ice Company, the *Bradford Sunday News* office, the Mandeville Insurance Company, and a public telephone station. Main Street is as yet unpaved.

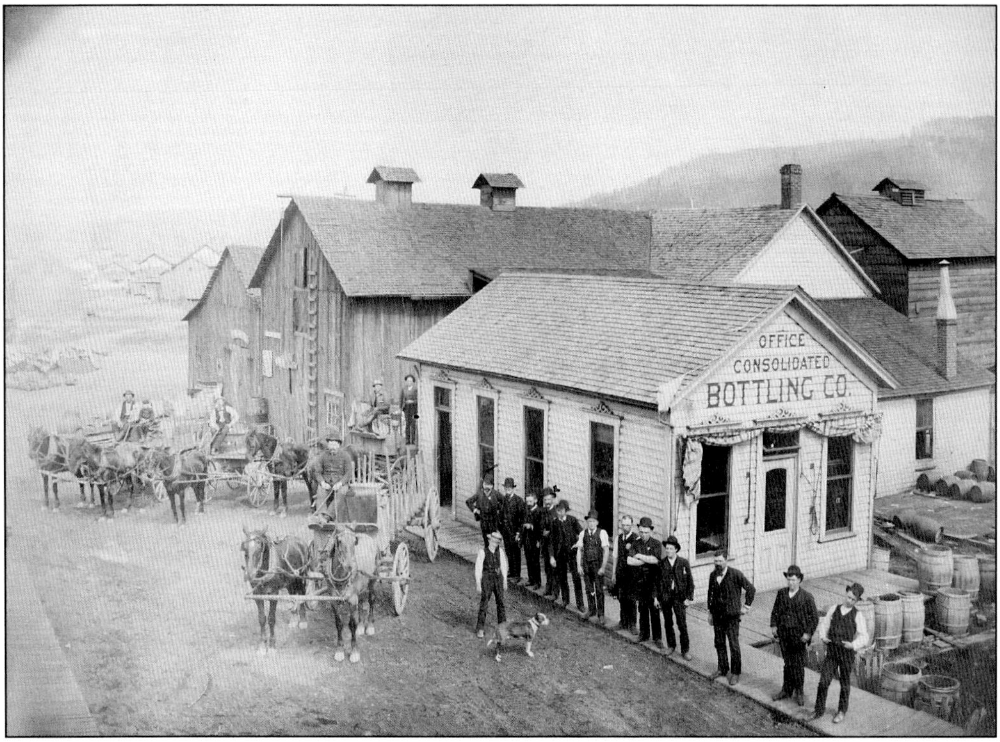

The Consolidated Bottling Company office and workplace, *c.* 1880s. An early industry in Bradford, it was located on Mechanic Street, near the present-day Grace Lutheran Church.

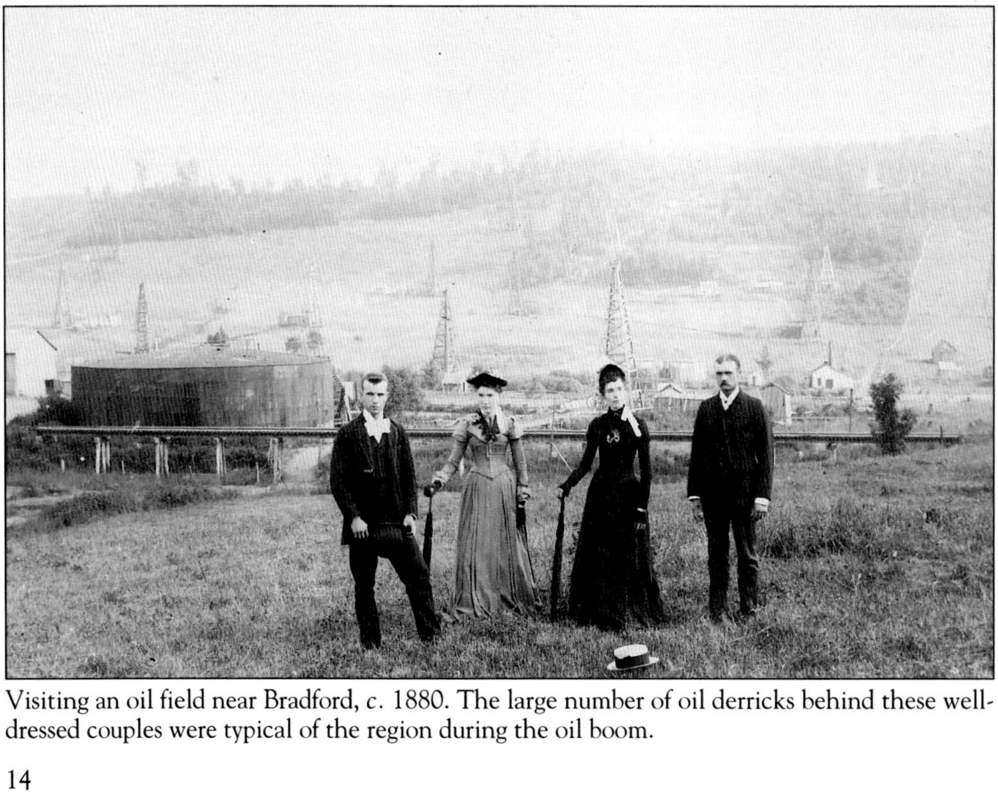

Visiting an oil field near Bradford, *c.* 1880. The large number of oil derricks behind these well-dressed couples were typical of the region during the oil boom.

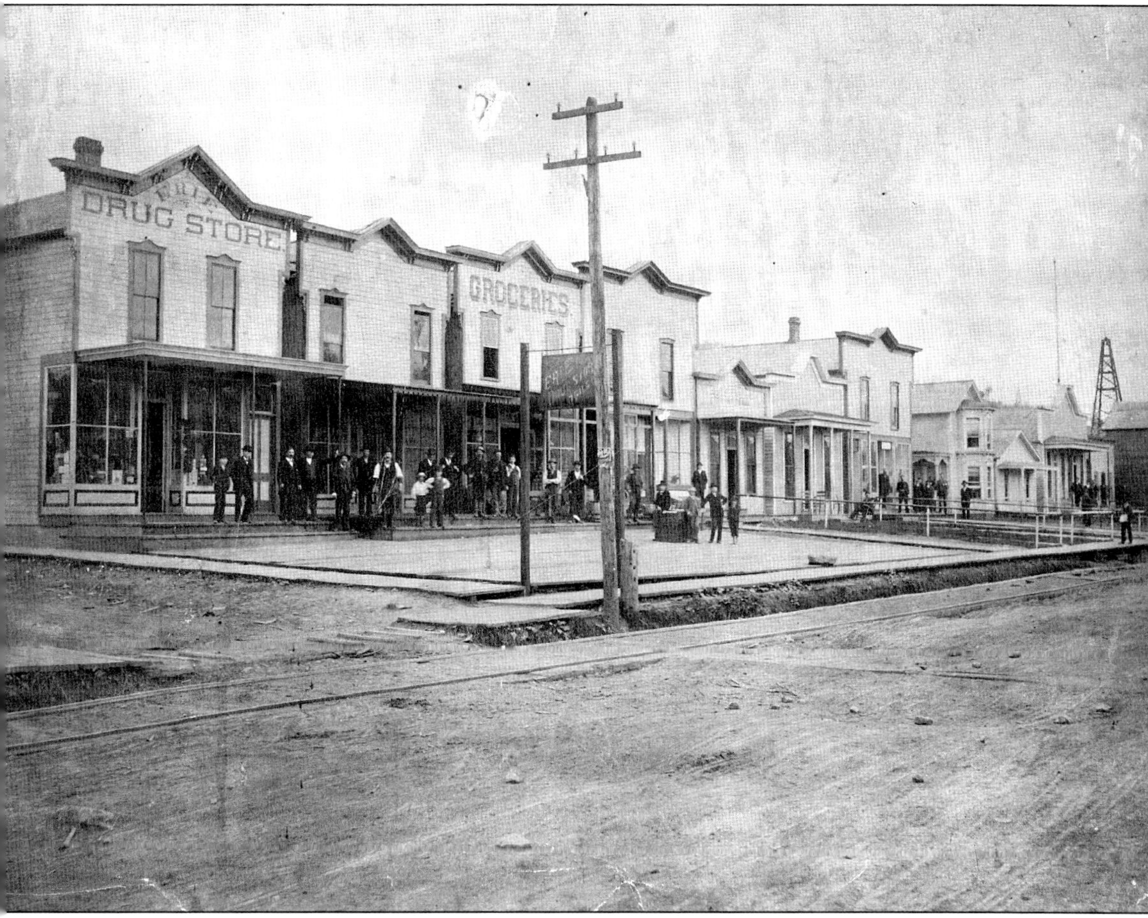

Tarport, now East Bradford, 1880. This group of buildings, with their wide front boardwalks, was located where Togi's Restaurant now stands. The eighth house from the left is the only building of this scene still standing.

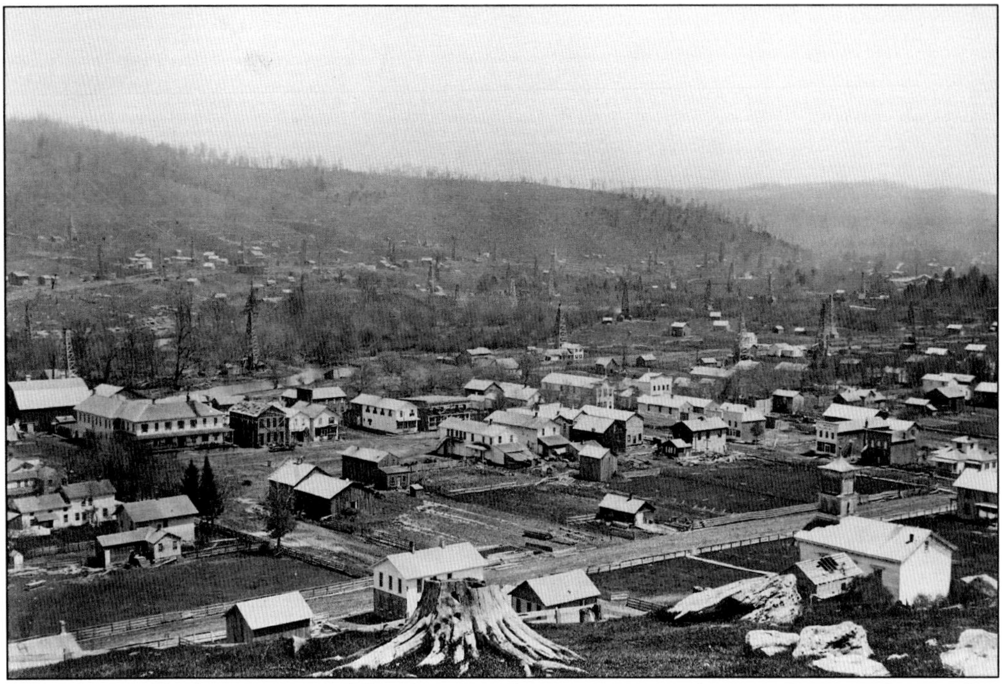

A young Bradford. In 1876, and for the next three years, an unknown photographer took a series of historic photographs from the same location, high on Quintuple Hill above West Corydon Street. These photographs recorded the effect on Bradford of the early days of the oil boom.

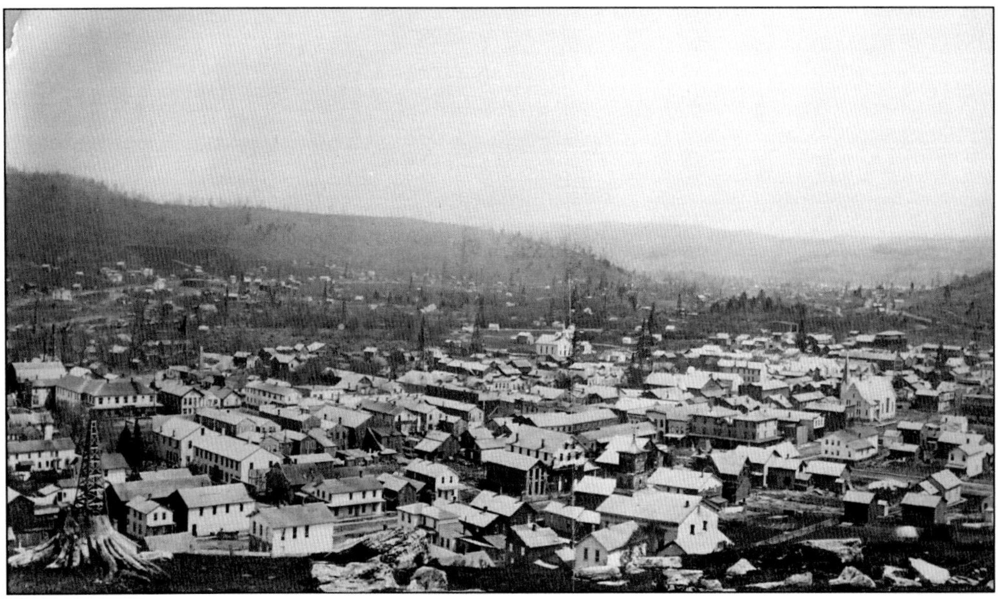

Two years later, in 1878. In just a short time Bradford had become a major player in the oil industry, and the town filled with people, new buildings, and streets. Within a year, in February 1879, the town was incorporated into the City of Bradford.

Two

Streets and Buildings

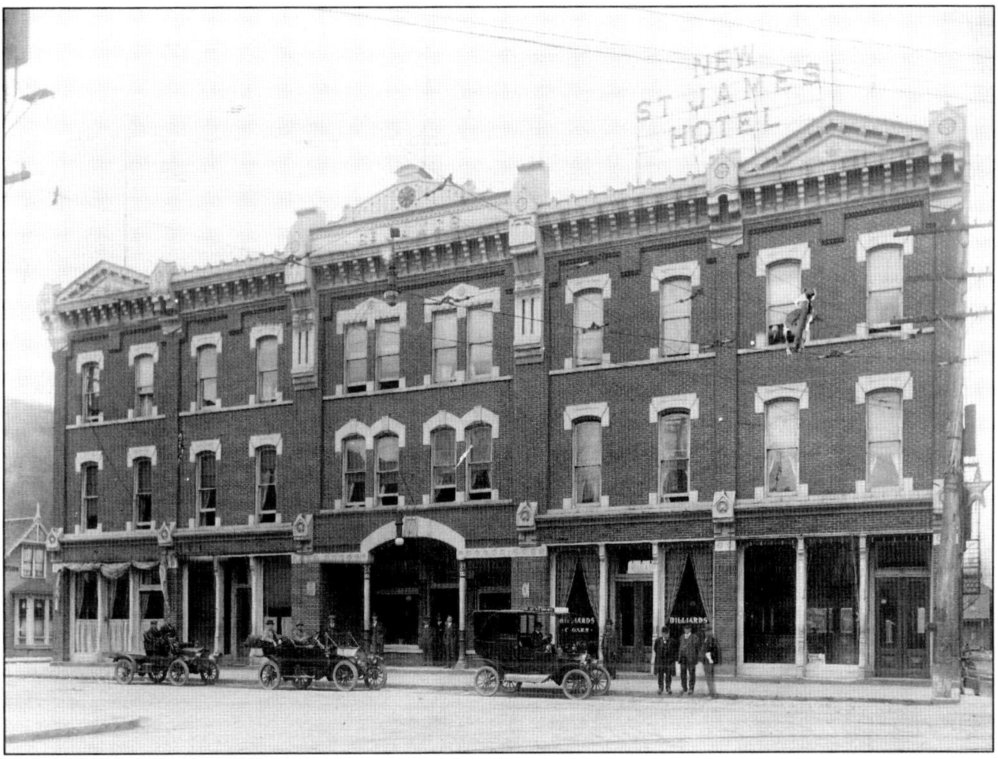

St. James Hotel, 1920. A luxurious hotel at the head of Main Street, it was replaced in 1929 by the Hotel Emery. It boasted free service to all trains, running water in every room, and was known for its huge bar which featured a brass railing.

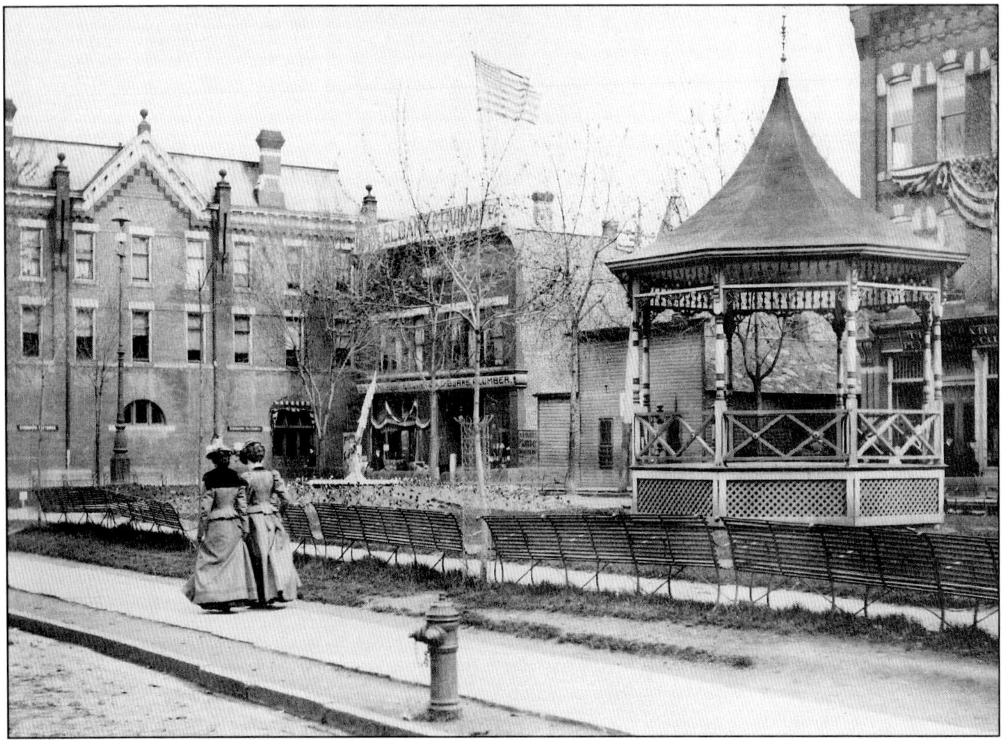

Fashionable women in the town square, *c.* 1898. There has been a town square in Bradford since the early days of its settlement.

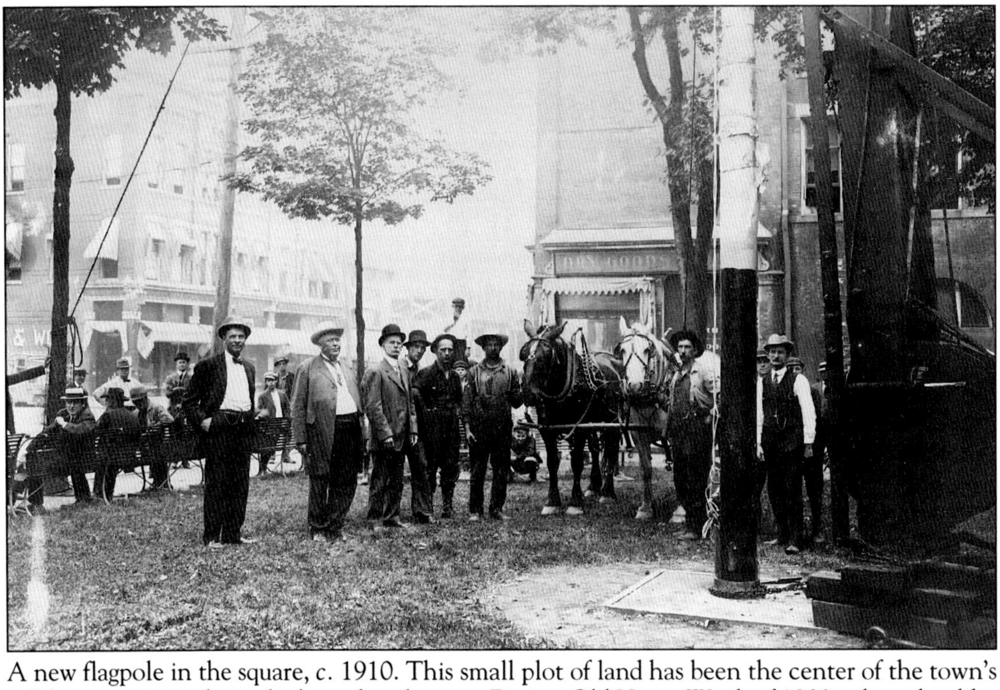

A new flagpole in the square, *c.* 1910. This small plot of land has been the center of the town's celebrations since the early days of settlement. During Old Home Week of 1909, a large boulder and tree taken from Thomas McKean's estate in Annin Township were placed in the square.

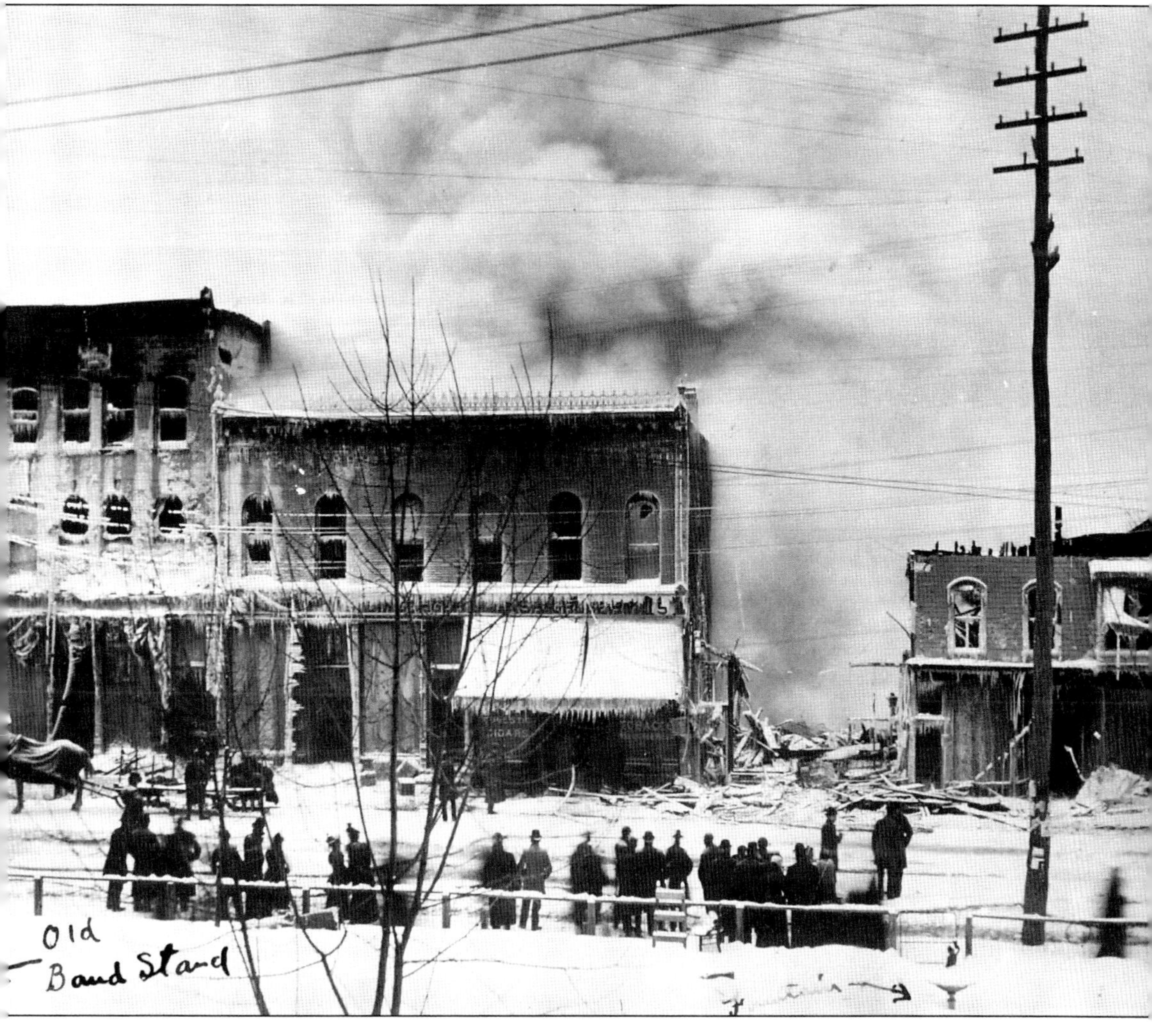

The Smith Bros. Fire, Main Street, 1897. A terrible fire in below freezing temperatures nearly burned the entire north side of Main Street across from the square. It began in a rooming house on Mechanic Street, and spread rapidly around the corner and through the neighboring buildings. Although no one was killed, several people lost all their belongings, and due to the high cost of insurance in the 1890s, many buildings were either underinsured or had none at all. Fires such as this were common in Bradford, where buildings thrown up in haste during the oil boom were mostly of wooden frame construction. After the turn of the century, all buildings on Main Street were required to be made of brick, and such disastrous fires became less common.

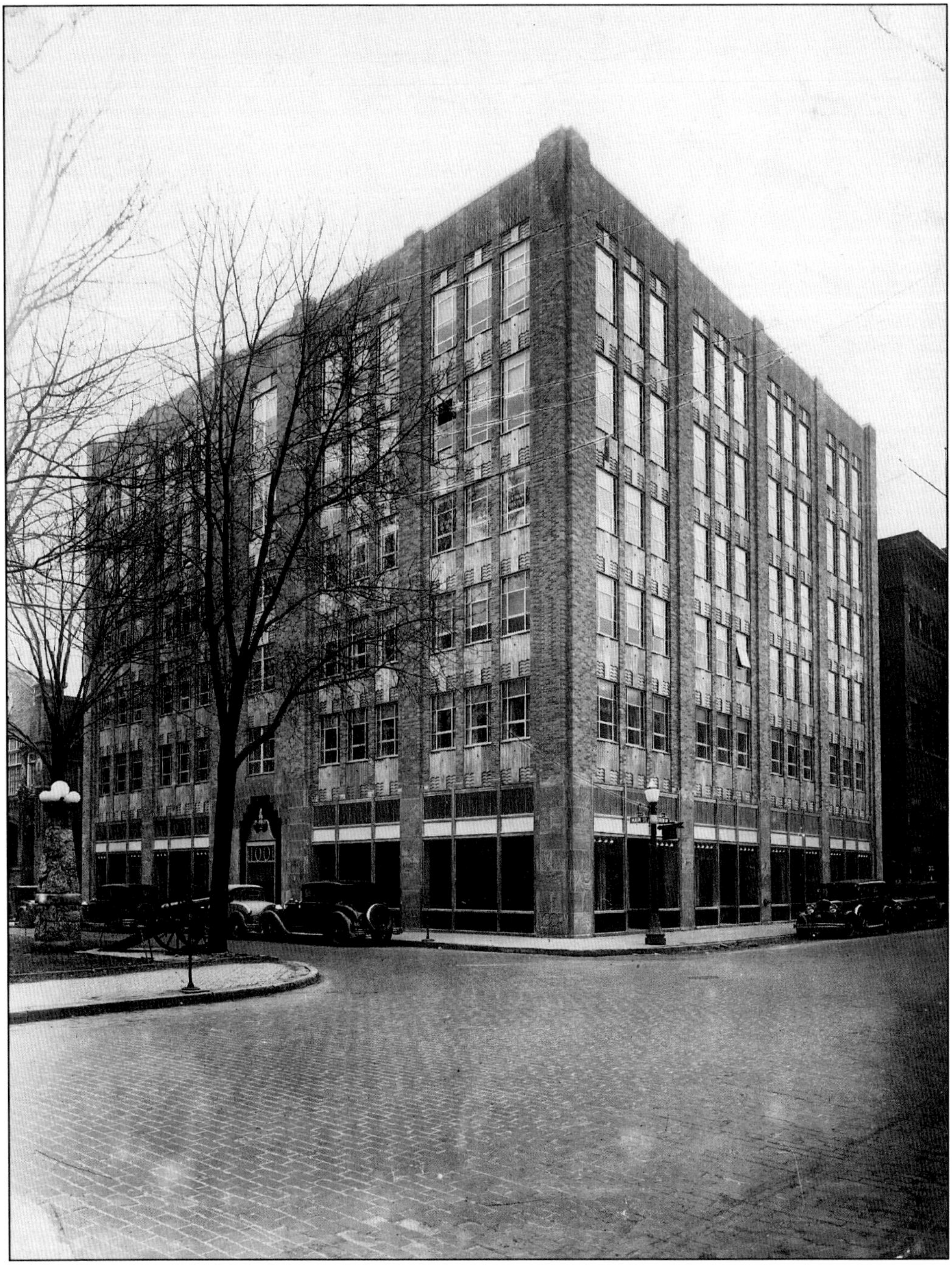

The IOOF Building, *c.* 1930. This is the third structure built on this site by the International Order of Odd Fellows. The first was destroyed by fire in 1902; the second was razed. Shea's Theater is in the background to the right, and the Elks Club House sits to the left. Note the cannons in the square—they were donated to a scrap metal drive during World War II. At present this building is known as the Seneca Building.

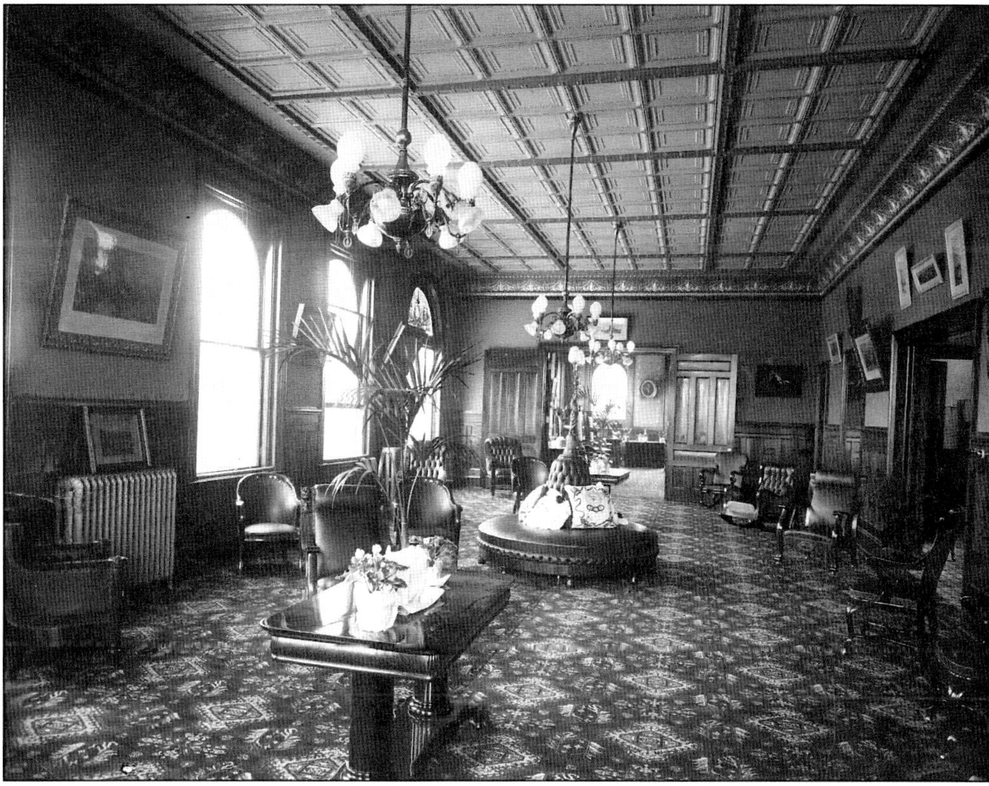

The Club Room of the Odd Fellows Building, *c*. 1930s.

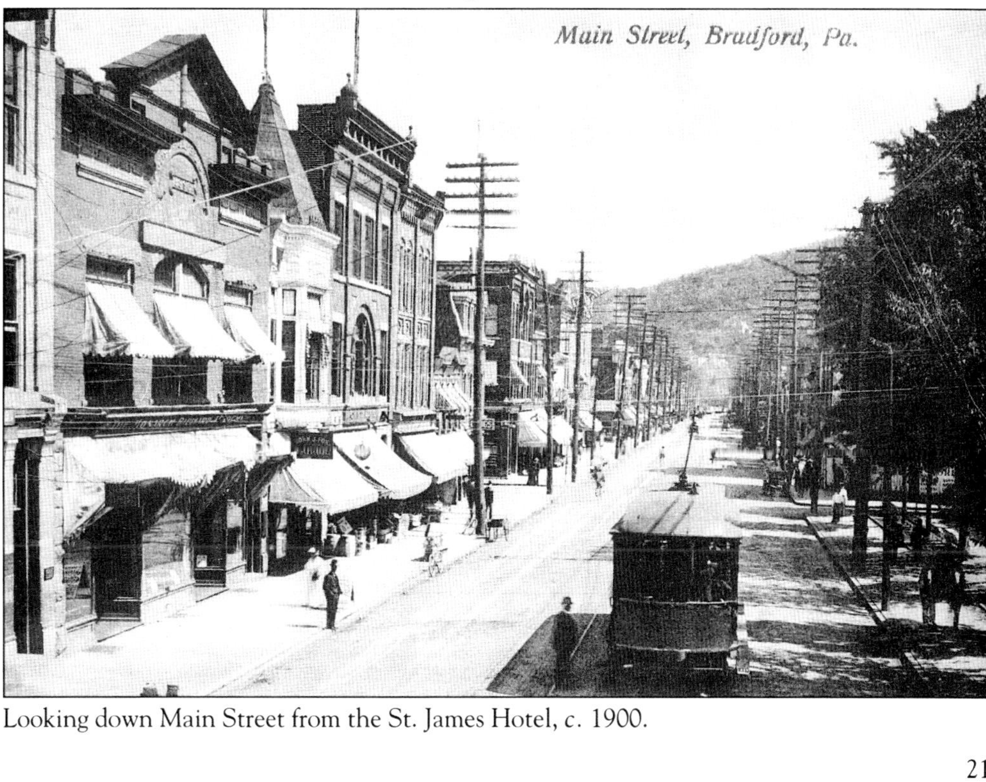

Looking down Main Street from the St. James Hotel, *c*. 1900.

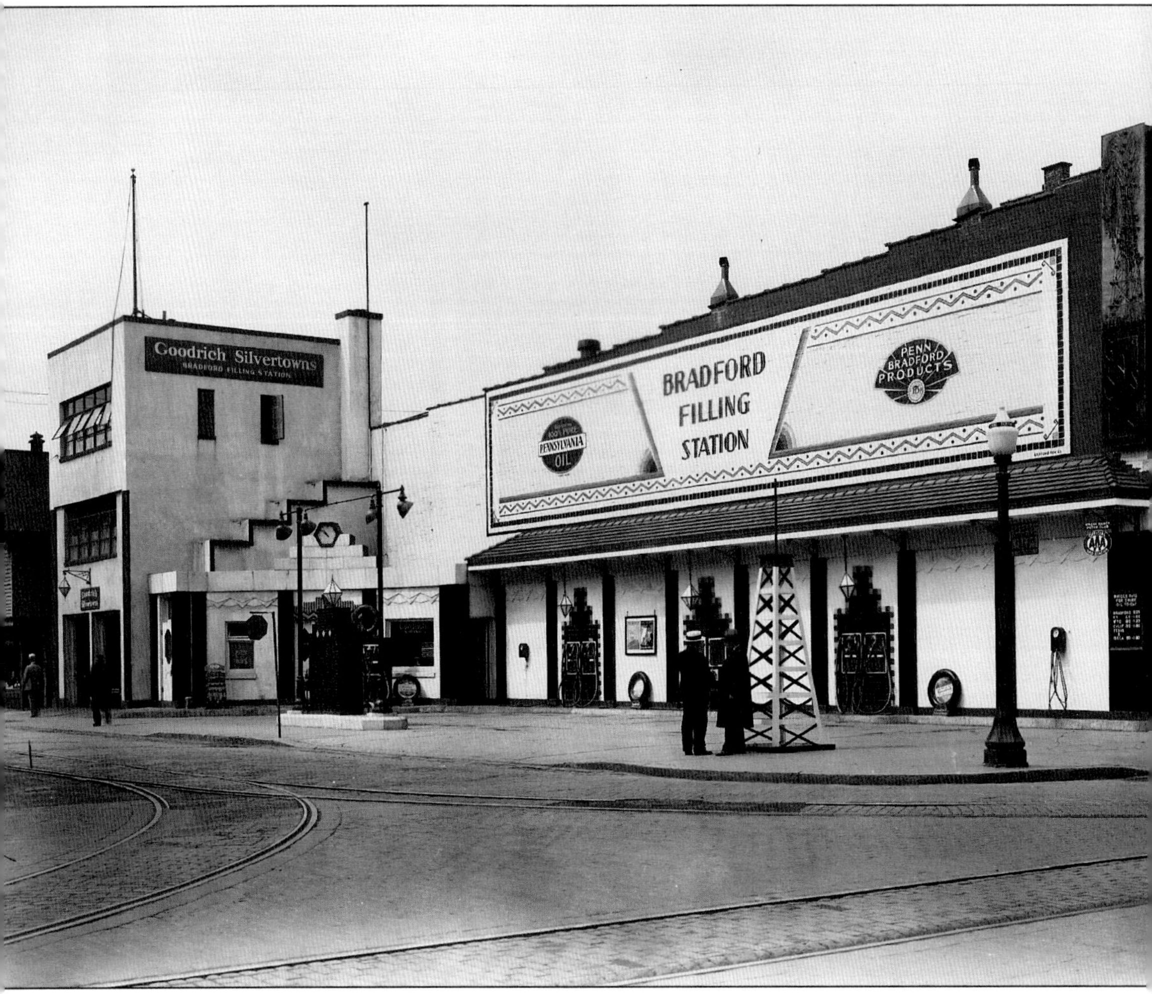

The Bradford Filling Station, c. 1930. It officially opened for business on May 2, 1929, against much opposition from local citizens who believed that it would be detrimental to the appearance of Main and Congress Streets. Gasoline was 15¢ a gallon, and due to the narrowness of the lot, the gas pumps were mounted directly into the rear wall. The small sign at right lists the daily crude oil prices in Kentucky, Wyoming, California, Texas, Oklahoma, and Bradford. The two men seen here wearing fashionable "boater" straw hats are perhaps discussing the latest oil field discovery.

The F.W. Davis Building, 1881, at the corner of Pine and Main Streets. Still standing today, its first tenants were O'Donnells' general store and the Thompson & Wood Drug Store. Davis, a Civil War veteran, also donated the money to erect the Civil War Monument in Oak Hill Cemetery.

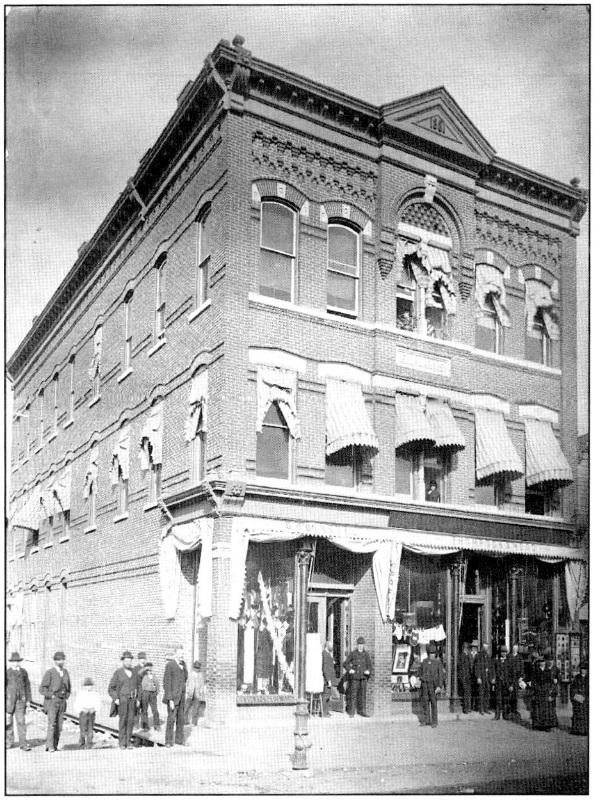

The Grand Theater, 1910. Now known as the McKean Theater, the Grand was a popular entertainment spot in its prime. The Exchange Lyceum, to the right of the Grand, was a large office building, housing oil company offices, telegraph offices, stock brokers, lodge rooms, a telephone company, an insurance company, and Brown's Barbershop.

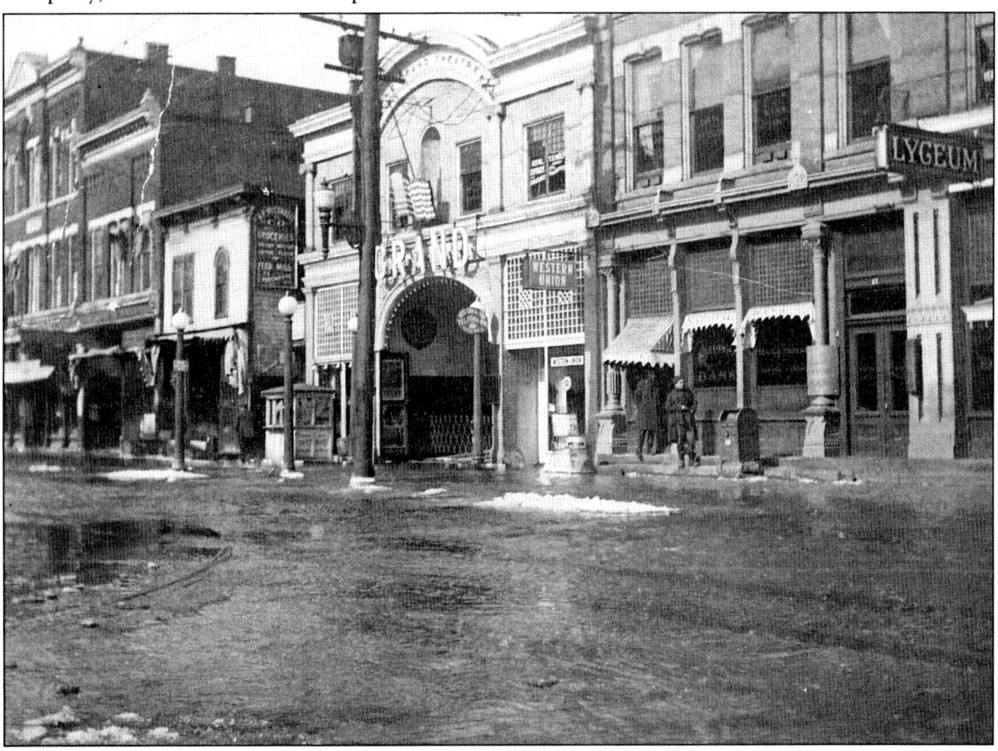

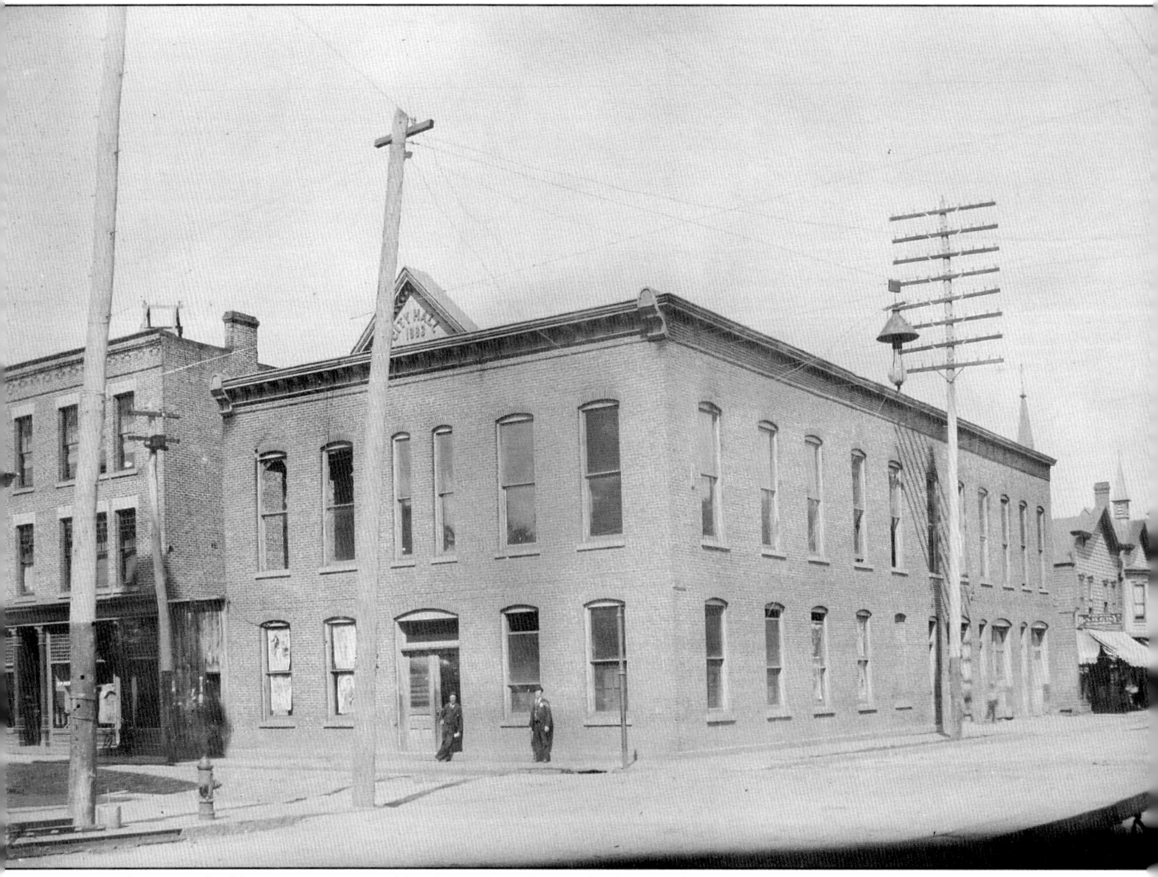

The city hall, *c.* 1893. Bradford's second city hall was built in 1883 on the corner of Corydon and Congress Streets. City offices as well as a fire company occupied the structure, which was made of brick over a wooden frame. On June 14, 1894, it was destroyed by fire. The next city hall was built on Kennedy Street.

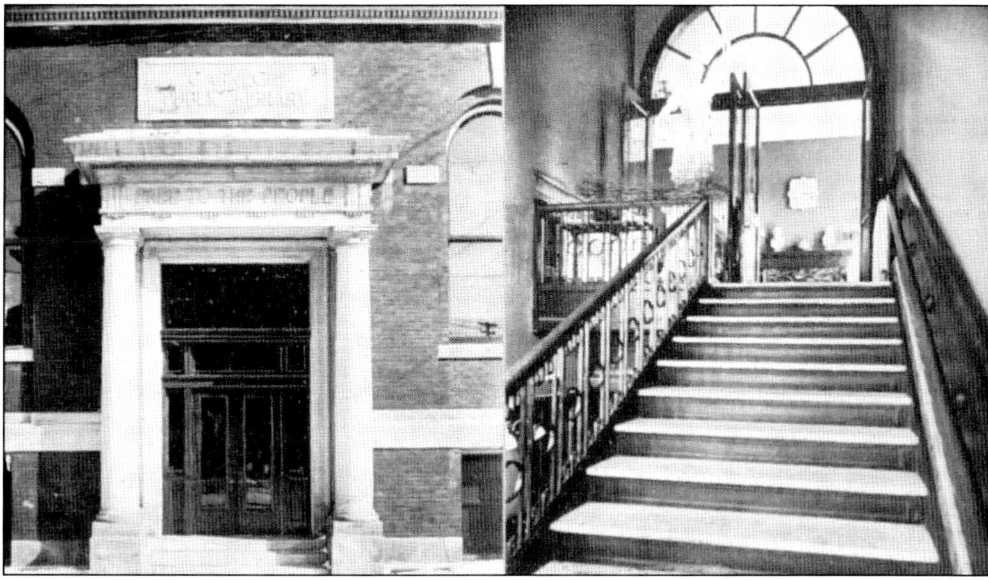

The Carnegie Public Library, on the corner of Congress and Corydon Streets. Consolidating two other, smaller libraries in Bradford, this new building was designed to accommodate 30,000 volumes. It proudly stated "Free to the People" above its entranceway.

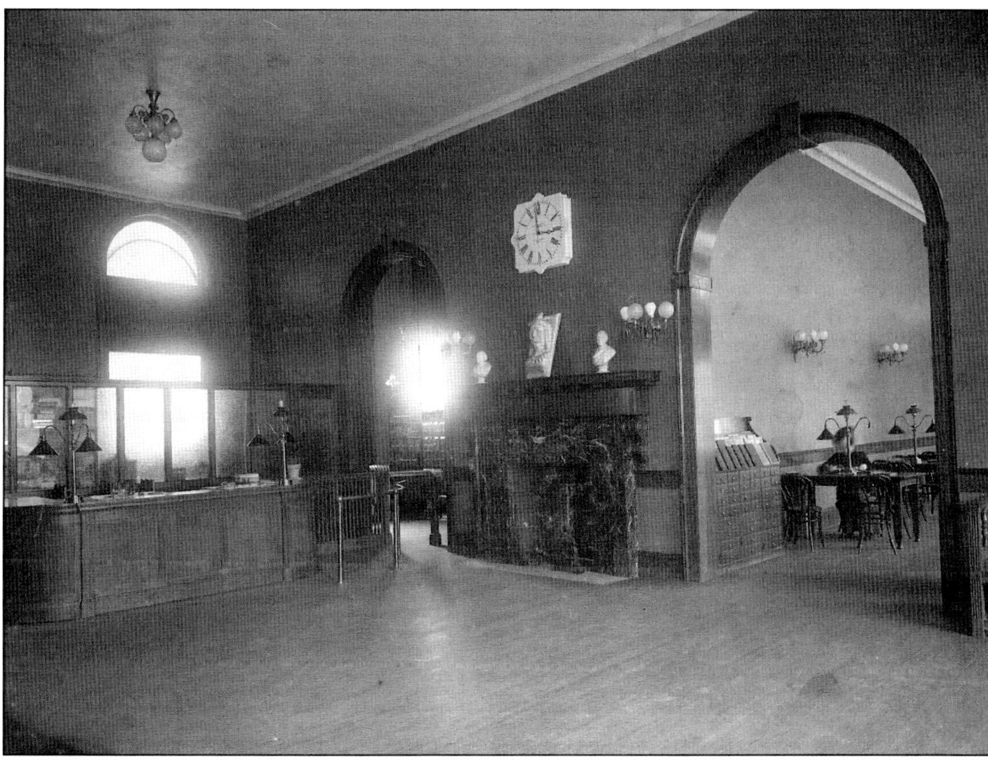

An interior view of the Carnegie Public Library, 1901. The new, well-stocked, spacious library with large bright windows was primarily financed through a $30,000 gift from Andrew Carnegie, the steel millionaire and philanthropist of Pittsburgh.

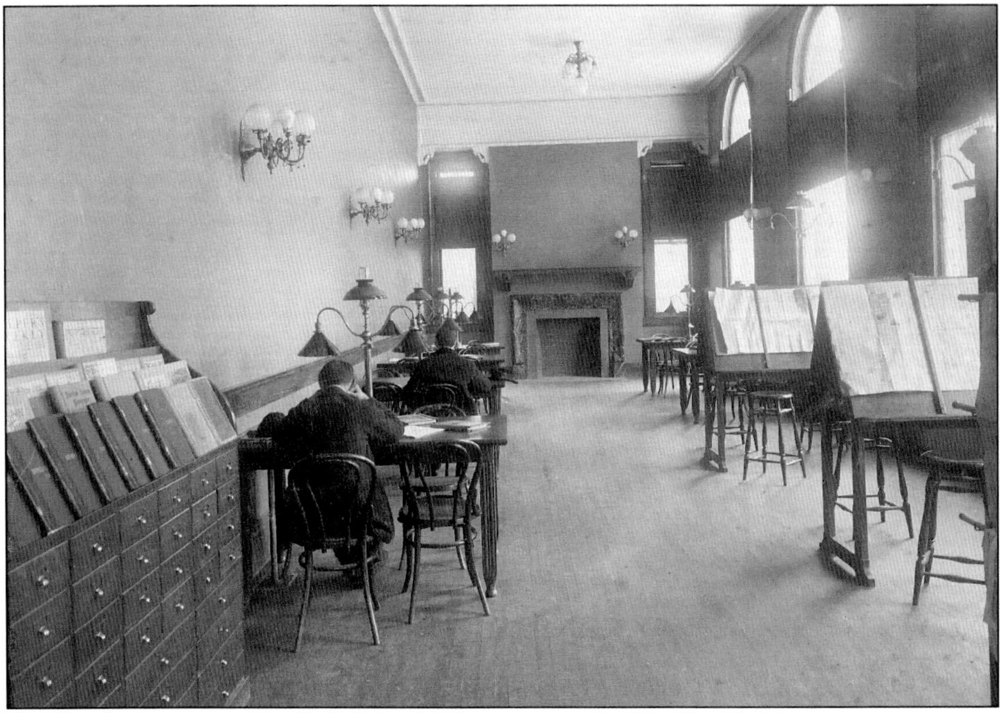

The Reading Room of the Carnegie Library, 1901. The large arched windows, as well as a variety of wall sconces, ceiling lights, and individual table lamps, guaranteed good light for reading. Later this room was converted into a children's room.

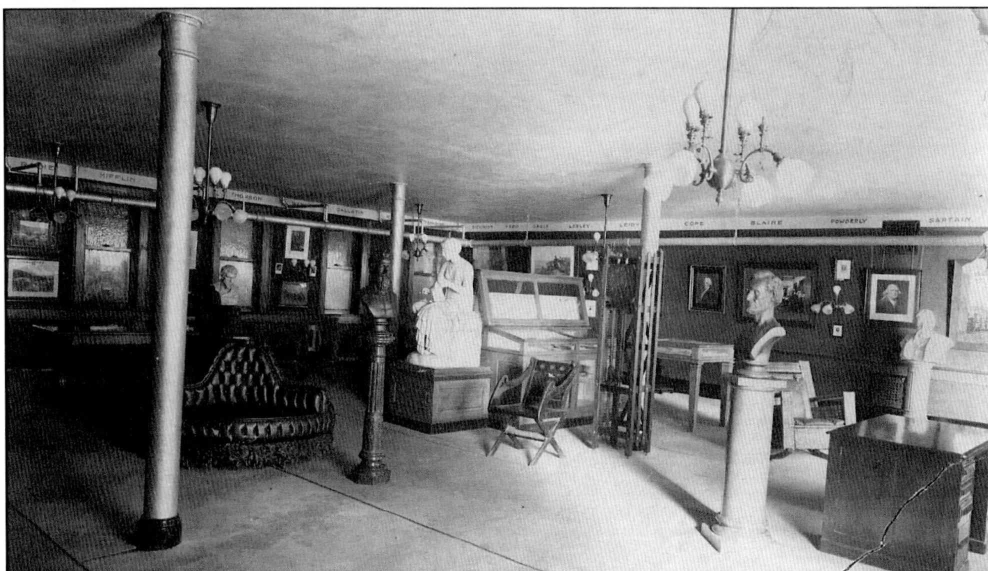

The McKean County History Room, c. 1930. Located in the basement of the Carnegie Public Library and under the direction of historian and lawyer Rufus Stone, it was Bradford's first museum. The collection was removed to the McKean County Courthouse in Smethport in the early 1940s and became the basis for the McKean County Historical Society, which still maintains the collection in the county museum.

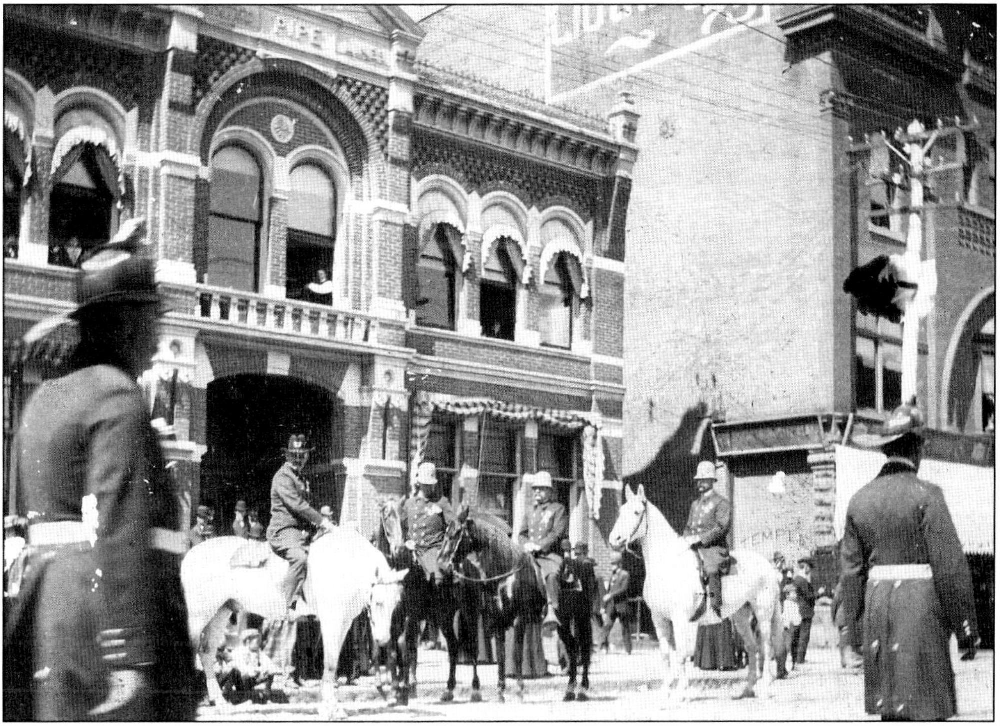

The firemen's convention parade, 1897, in front of the United Pipe Company Building (owned by Standard Oil). This building eventually became the Bradford Club. Currently, the site is the parking lot for National City Bank.

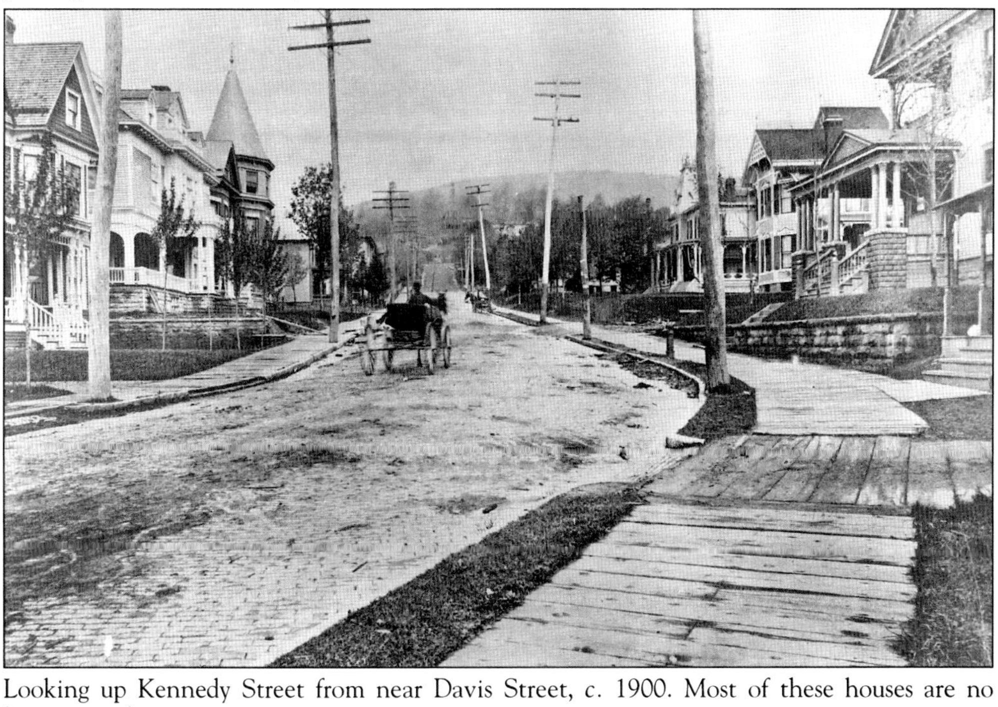

Looking up Kennedy Street from near Davis Street, *c.* 1900. Most of these houses are no longer standing.

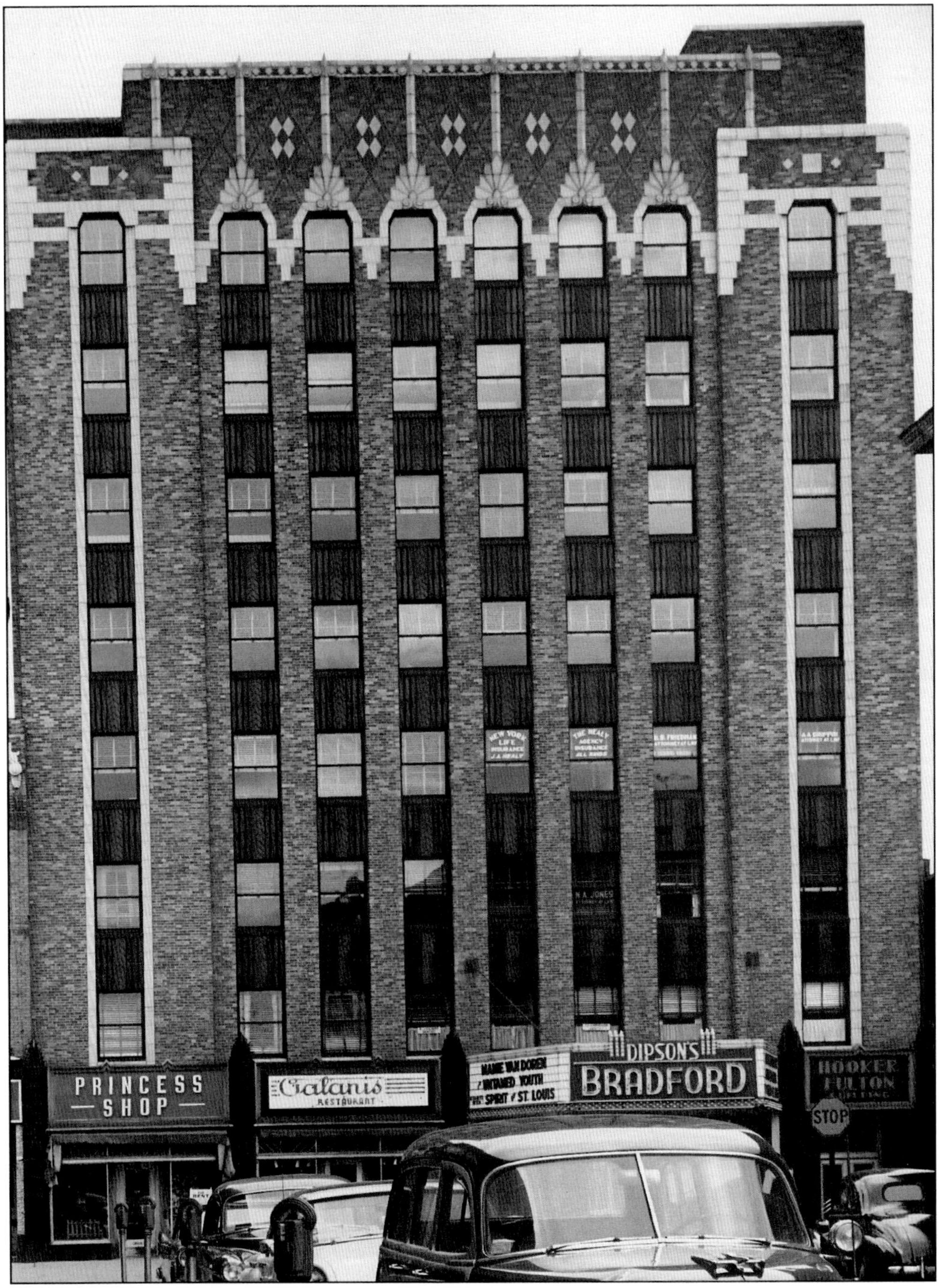

The Hooker-Fulton Building. Opened in May 1931 by Clarence Hooker and Robert Fulton, its construction employed hundreds of men during the Depression.

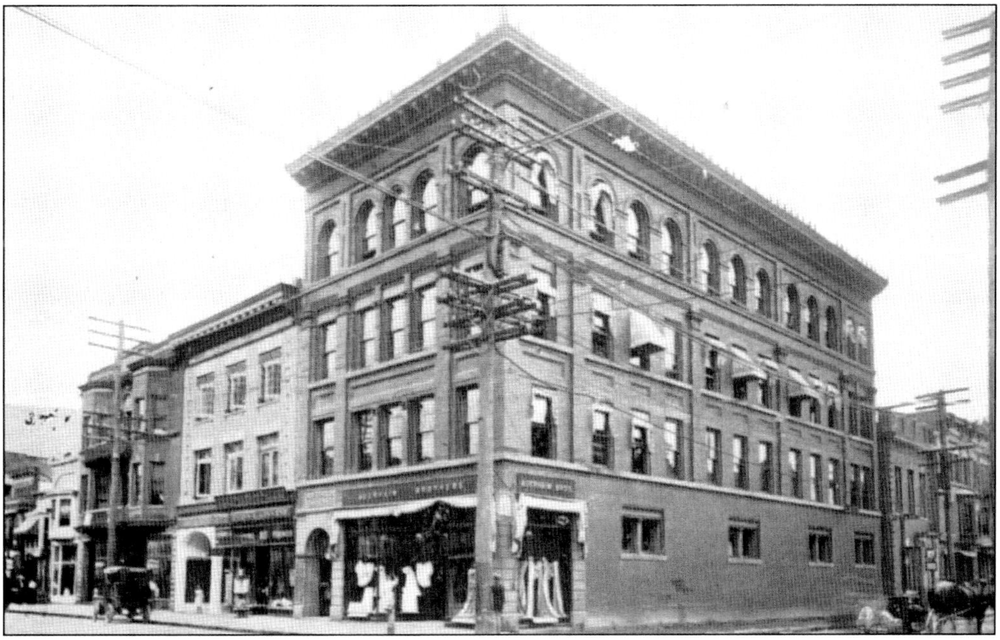

The Auerhaim Brothers Building, c. 1900. Currently modified as the Forest Oil Building on the corner of Main and Chestnut Streets, Auerhaims' was Bradford's leading department store at the turn of the century. The third building from the right with the large bay windows is the Bay State Hotel, a popular and prosperous hotel that is also still standing.

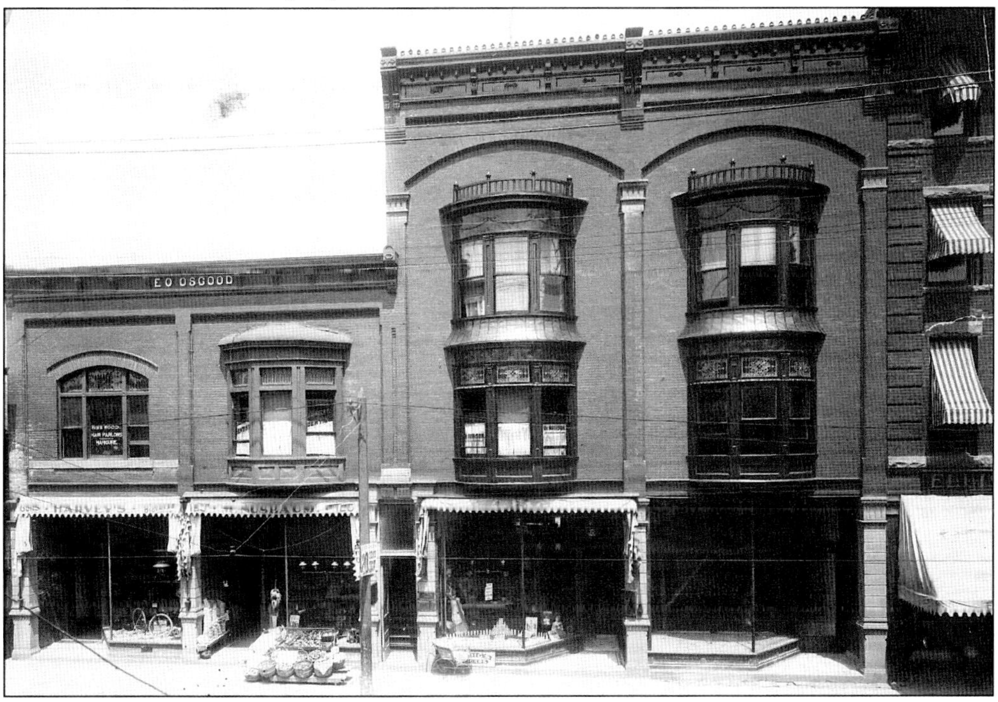

The George Fagnan Building at 125 Main Street, 1903. Fagnan, mayor of Bradford from 1896 to 1898, operated a drugstore at this location for many years. The building is on the site of a present-day McDonald's Restaurant.

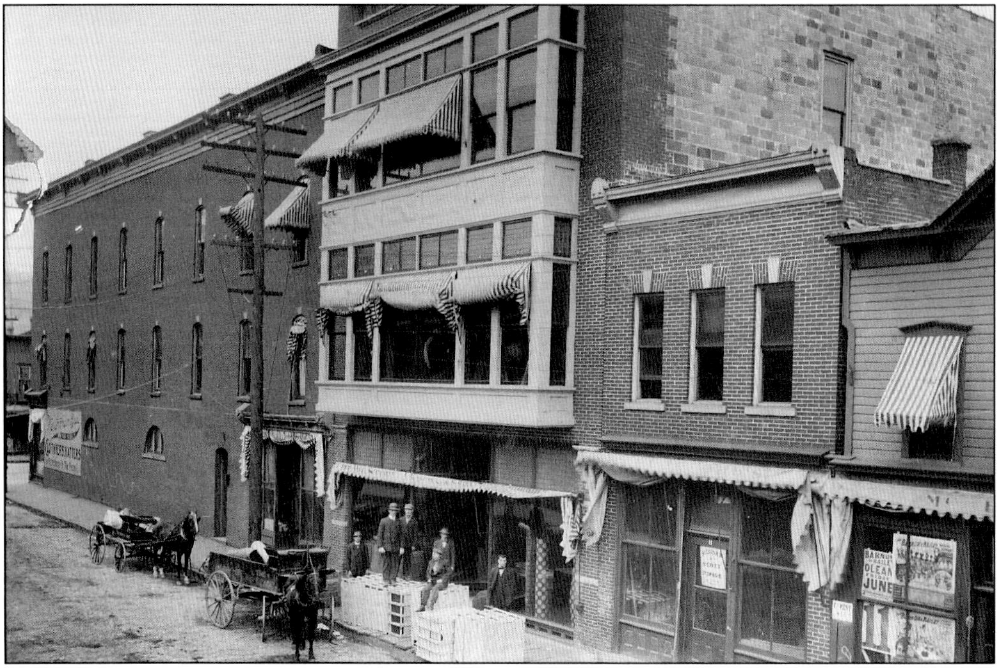

Krienson's store, Webster Street, 1909. These employees appear to be unloading freight.

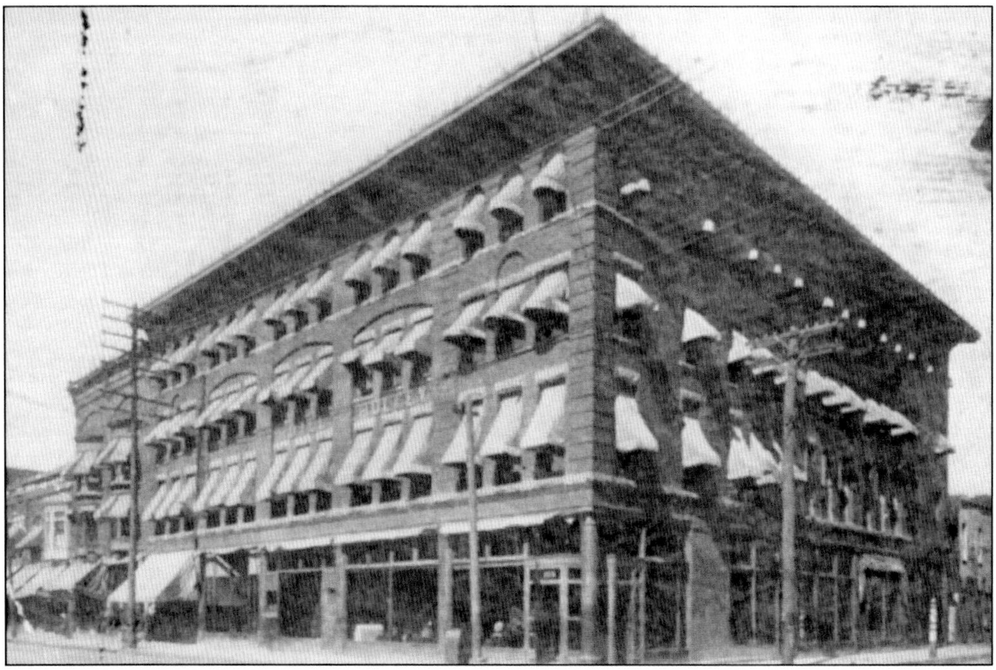

The Hotel Holley, Main Street, 1907. Built on the site of the old Riddell House, the Holley was designed by E.N. Unruh, a prominent Bradford architect, and completed in 1902. It had ninety rooms, fifty of them having connecting baths, brass beds with the finest covered box springs and hair mattresses, Italian marble throughout, and a modern kitchen "entirely covered with white tile." A billiard hall, reading room, barbershop, and bar were located on the ground floor. It is still standing today, but its name has been changed back to the original Riddell House.

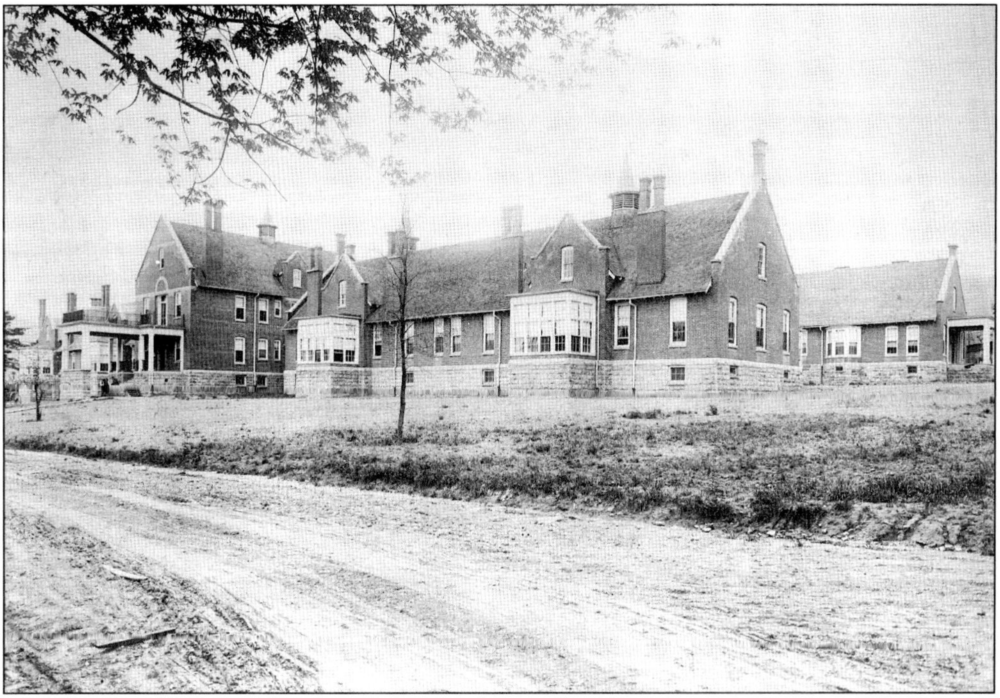

The Bradford Hospital, *c.* 1910. Located on Bennett Brook Road (now Interstate Parkway), it was built in 1906, replacing a farmhouse which had served as the first hospital. It boasted an administration wing, men's ward, women's ward, surgical wing, and a kitchen. Certain sections remained in use until the 1950s.

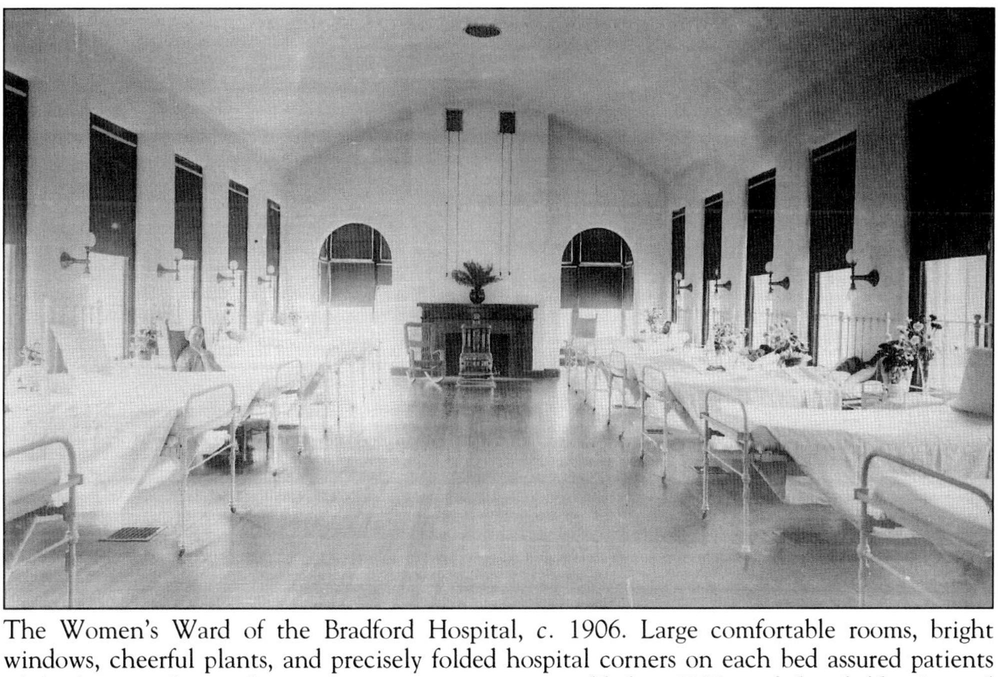

The Women's Ward of the Bradford Hospital, *c.* 1906. Large comfortable rooms, bright windows, cheerful plants, and precisely folded hospital corners on each bed assured patients of the latest in hospital care. A maternity wing was added in 1908, and the children's ward in 1914.

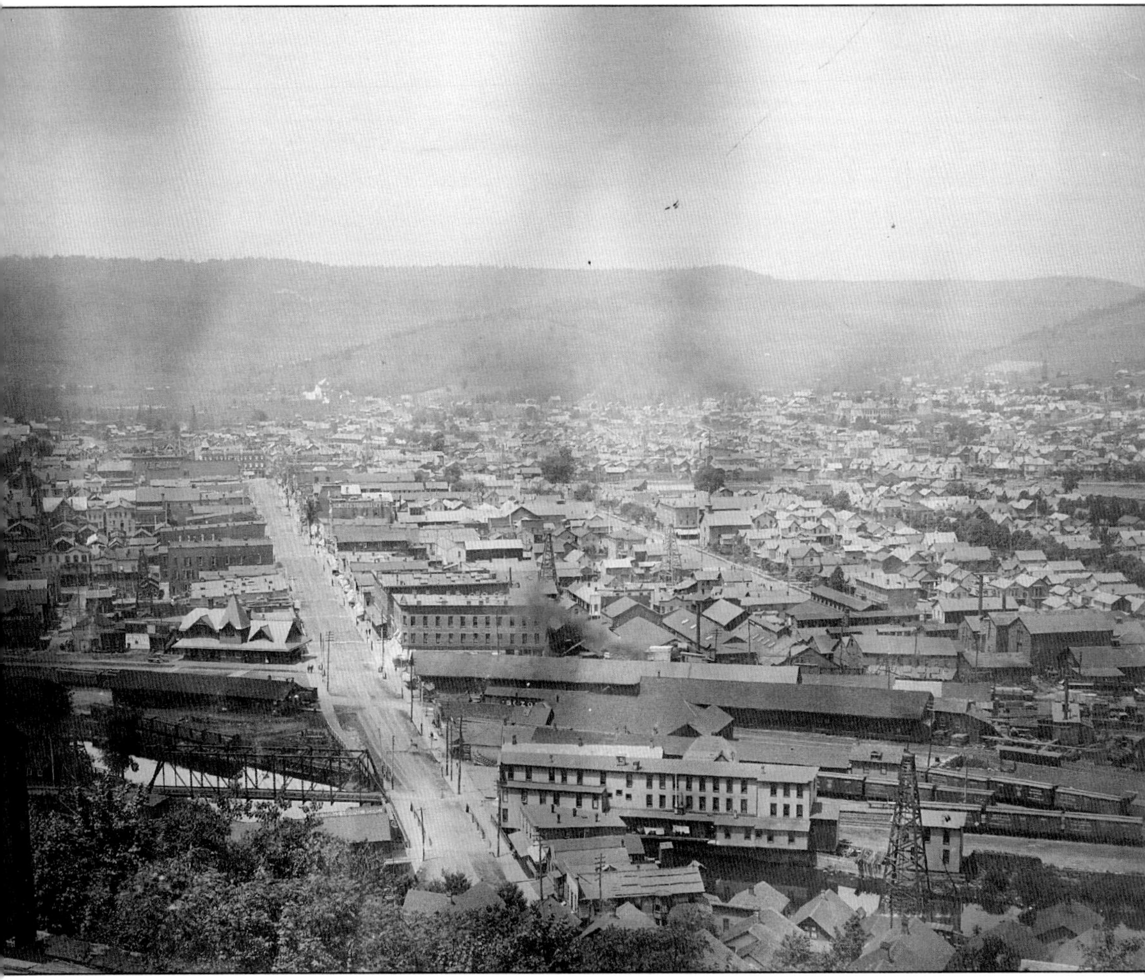

A bird's-eye view of Main Street in Bradford. This image was taken from Mt. Raub about 1915.

Three

Transportation

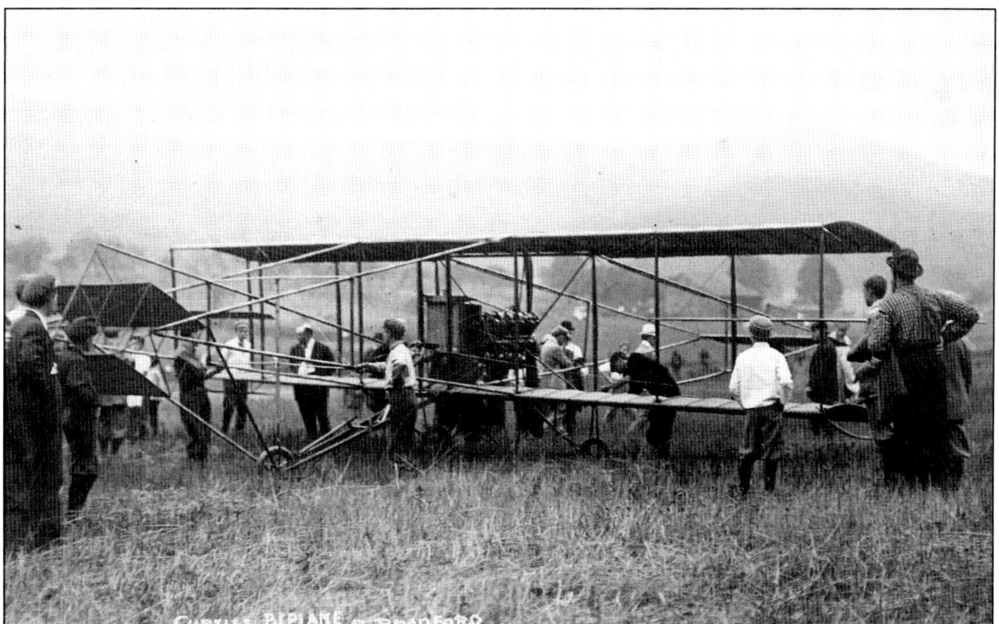

The first airplane in Bradford, July 4, 1919. As a child, Parker "Shorty" Cramer vowed to be the first to fly a plane into Bradford. He succeeded. Piloting his 8-cylinder Curtis biplane from Buffalo, he landed the craft on the B.F. Hooker farm near the Tuna Crossroads. His co-pilot and friend, Harri Emery, accompanied him on his historic flight.

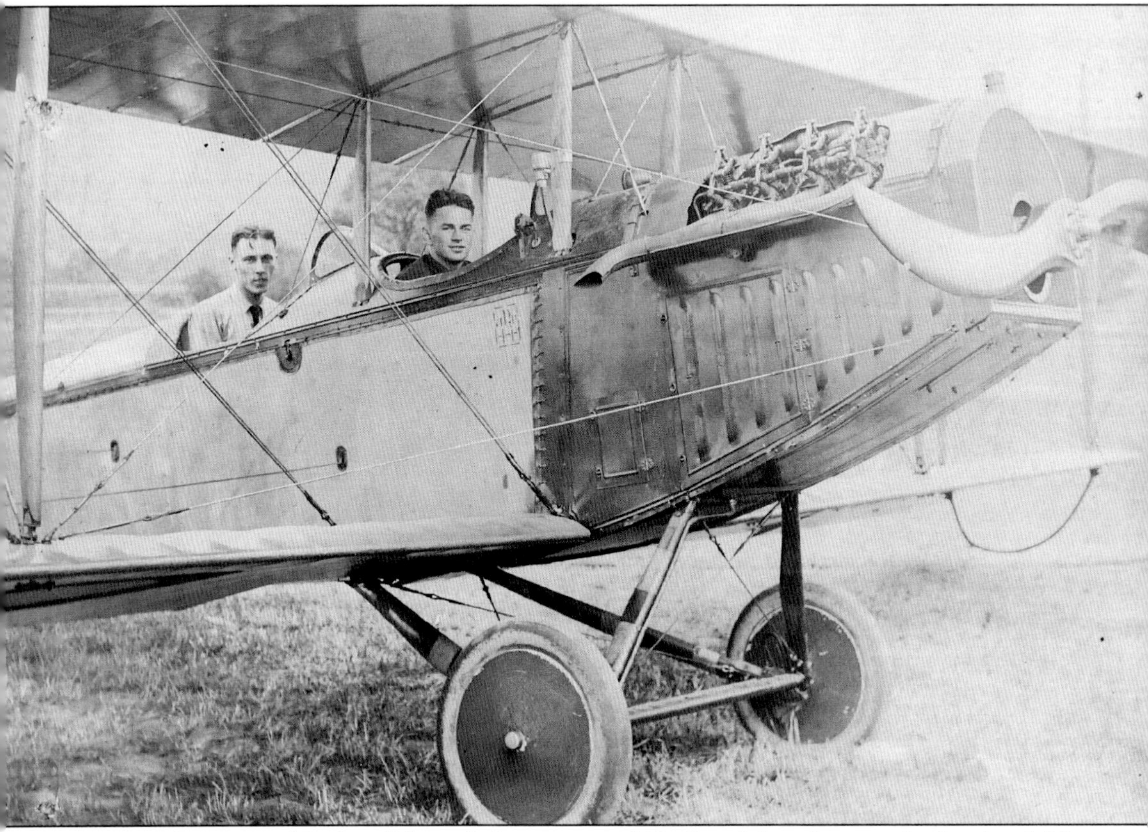

Harri Emery and Parker "Shorty" Cramer, *c*. 1919. Good friends since high school (they played on the 1914 Bradford High School football team), both had a love of aviation. Both joined the Air Corps during World War I, and each achieved the rank of lieutenant. Ironically, both would be killed in air crashes. Emery was killed in an air crash near Kane in 1929; his grave is located in Oak Hill Cemetery. Cramer, while attempting to fly to Copenhagen from Detroit by a northern route, was lost off the coast of Norway on August 9, 1931. His body was never recovered.

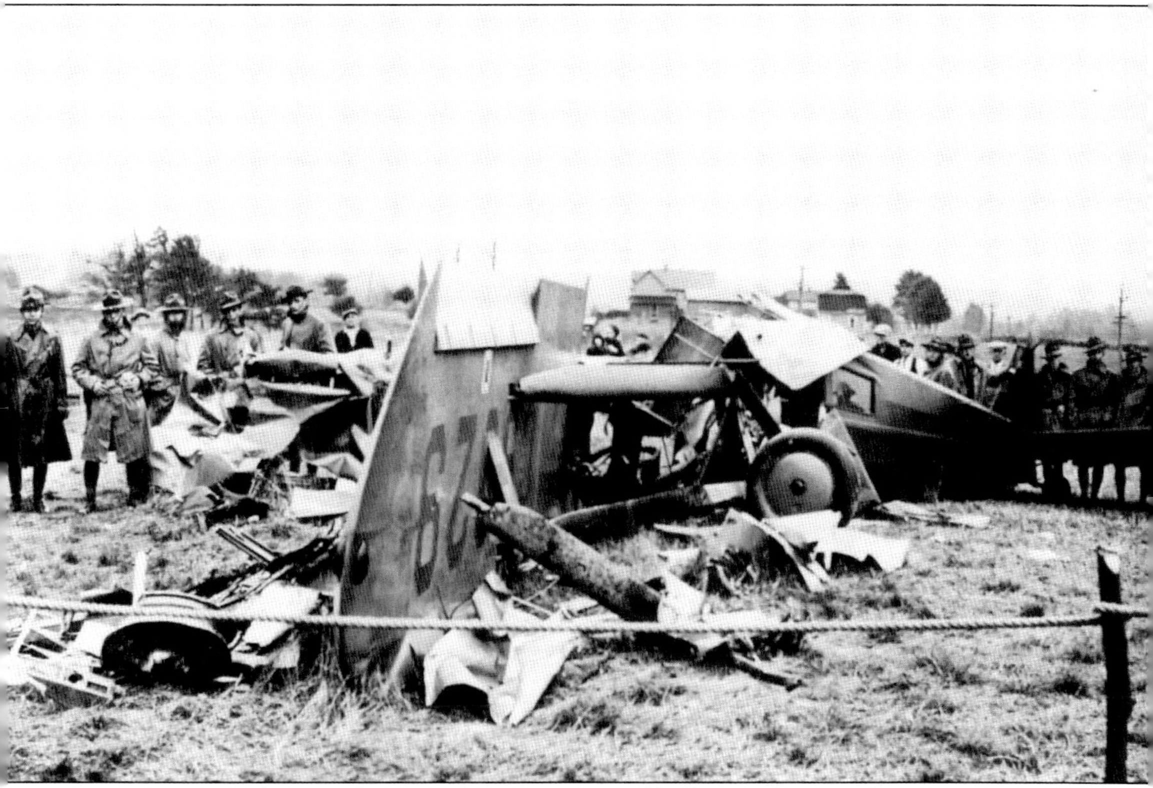

Harri Emery's Travel Air crash, September 29, 1929. Bradford's most famous pilot, Harri Emery, was killed when his airplane was lost in heavy fog near Kane. Emery (age thirty-three), his brother Leon (age forty-eight), Ella Davis (age thirty-five), and Ellis Michaels (age thirty-four) had been returning from an aerial circus show in St. Marys. All three men were killed instantly; Ella Davis was taken to the Kane Memorial Hospital, but died en route. Upon hearing of the accident, hundreds of onlookers flocked to the crash site. State troopers, shown here, maintained control of the crowds. On the morning of his funeral, the Bradford Airport was renamed the Harri Emery Airport in his memory. The wooden propeller from this crash is in the collection of the Bradford Landmark Society.

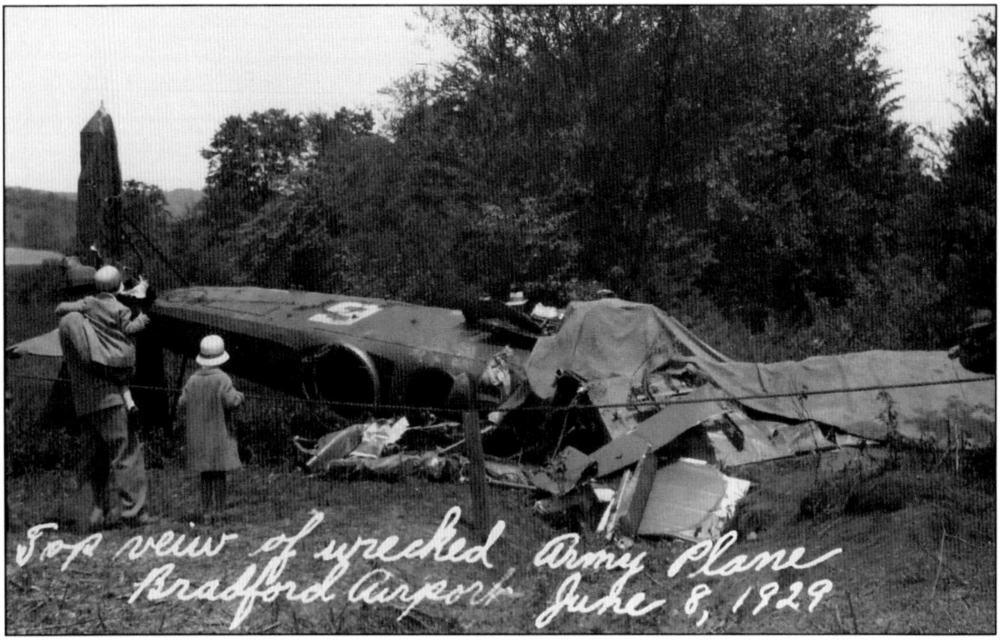

The army plane crash at Bradford Airport, June 8, 1929. The illegal parking of automobiles on the runway caused the airplane to hit a "dinky" engine that was on a nearby track and crash into trees 300 yards away. Pilot Fay Updegrove was uninjured, but an eleven-year-old Custer City boy, Joseph Kassick, stepped on a high tension wire that had fallen and suffered a burn on his foot. The plane, a total loss, was valued at $60,000.

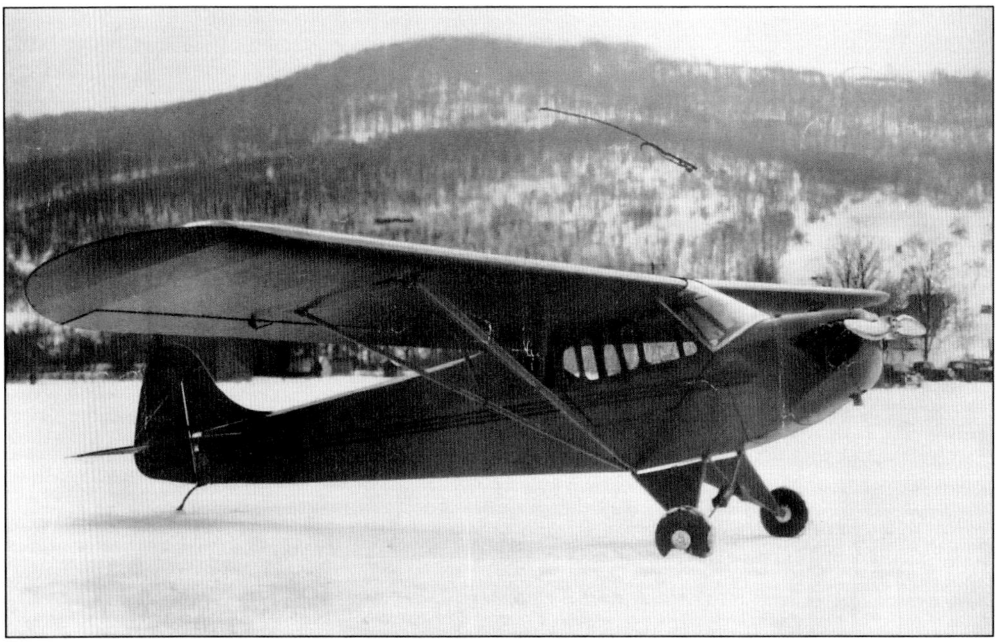

The new Cub. Possibly the most famous light airplane in the world, the Taylor Cub (later, the Piper Cub) was designed at the Taylor Aircraft Co. in Bradford. Sold in 1936 to William Piper, the aircraft factory was completely destroyed by fire on March 17, 1937. Choosing not to rebuild here, the manufacturer were moved to Lock Haven.

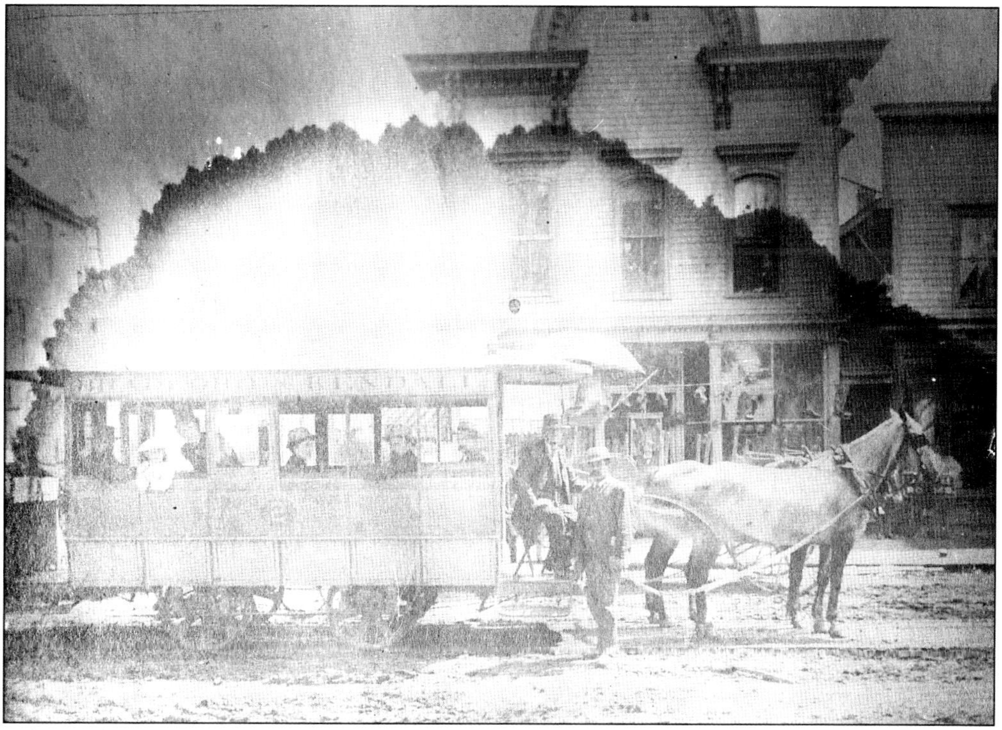

A horse-drawn trolley on Main Street, 1879. Such trolleys were replaced by an electric traction system in the early 1890s.

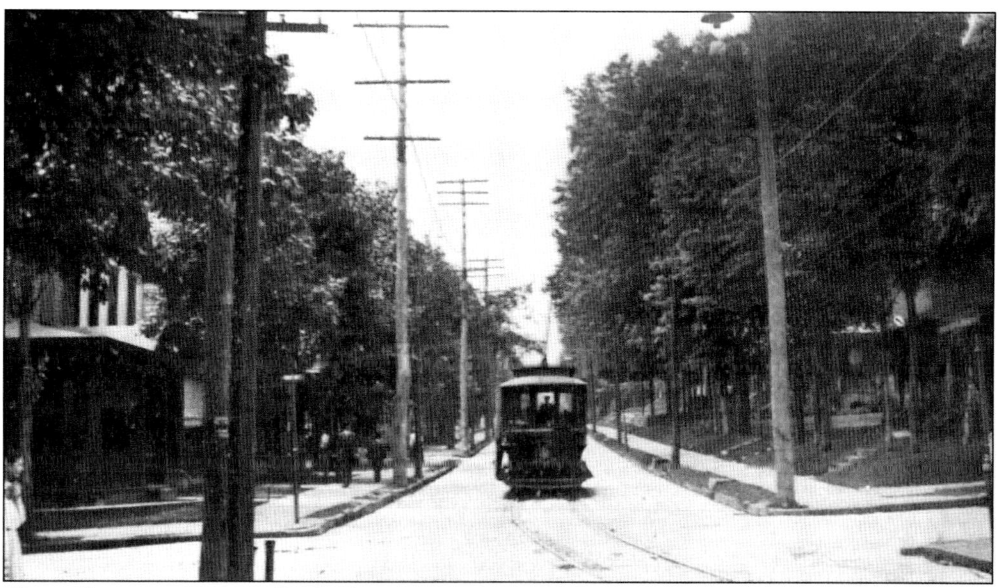

The trolley system in Bradford. This was the main mode of transportation for nearly forty years. The trolley is headed down Congress Street from Elm Street, possibly on its way to Custer City.

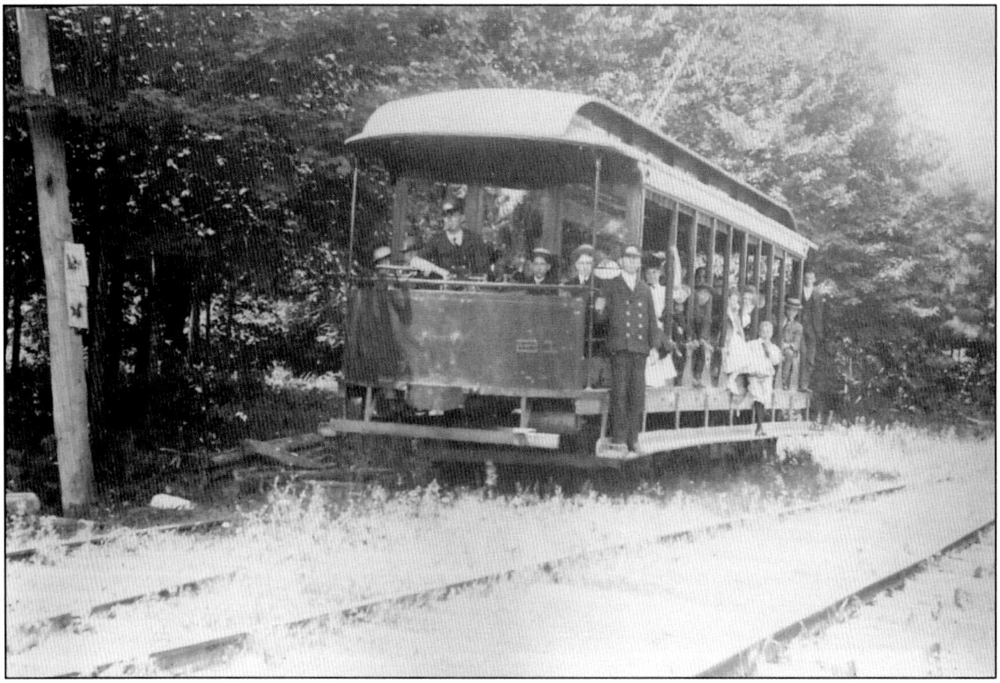

An open-sided trolley car, *c.* 1915. Belonging to the Western NY & Penna Traction Company, the trolley line ran adjacent to the Erie Railroad tracks. Here, the trolley is seen passing through the Foster Brook "Clarksville" area. This system was in operation from around 1908 to 1927.

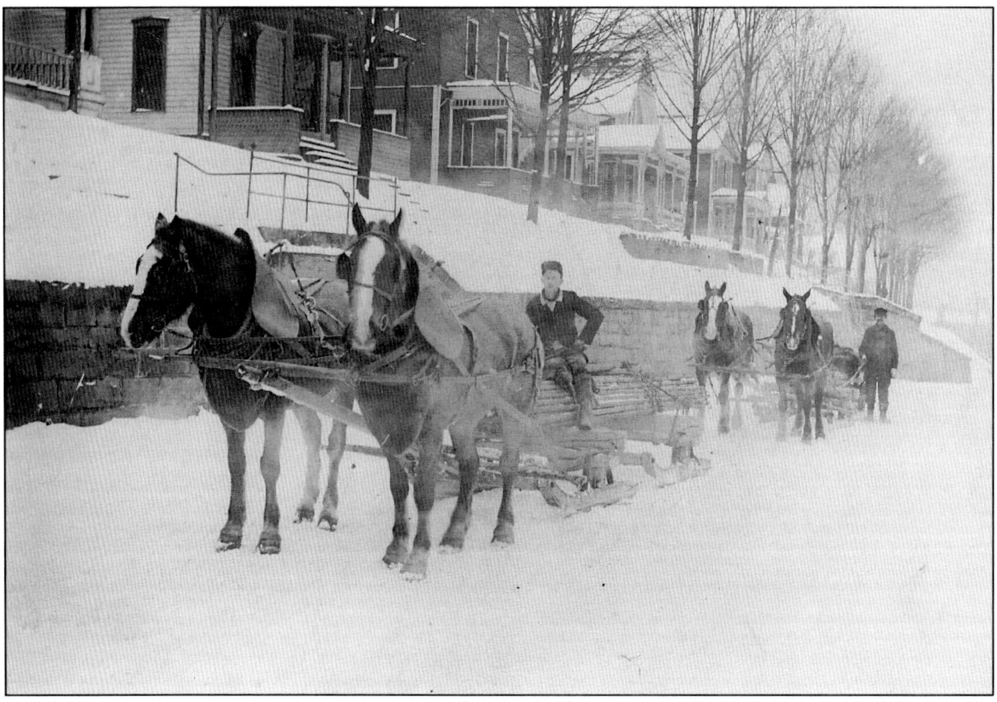

South Avenue, winter 1905. These horse-drawn sleds appear to be hauling iron rods for the oil fields.

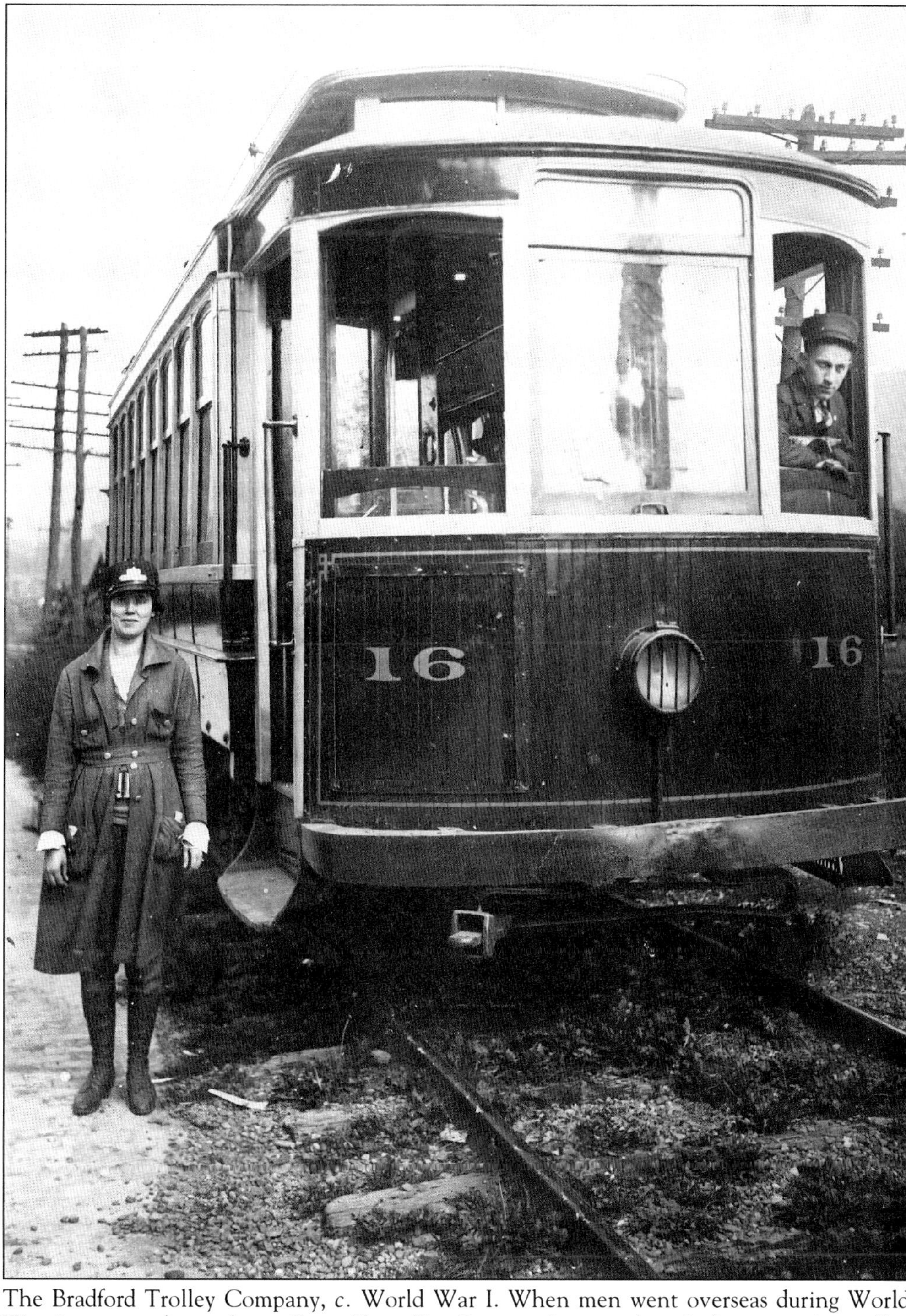

The Bradford Trolley Company, *c*. World War I. When men went overseas during World War I, women drove the trolleys. Here, Eva Bova and an unidentified man at the trolley window stop for a moment on the Jackson Avenue run. Women drivers were discontinued after the war.

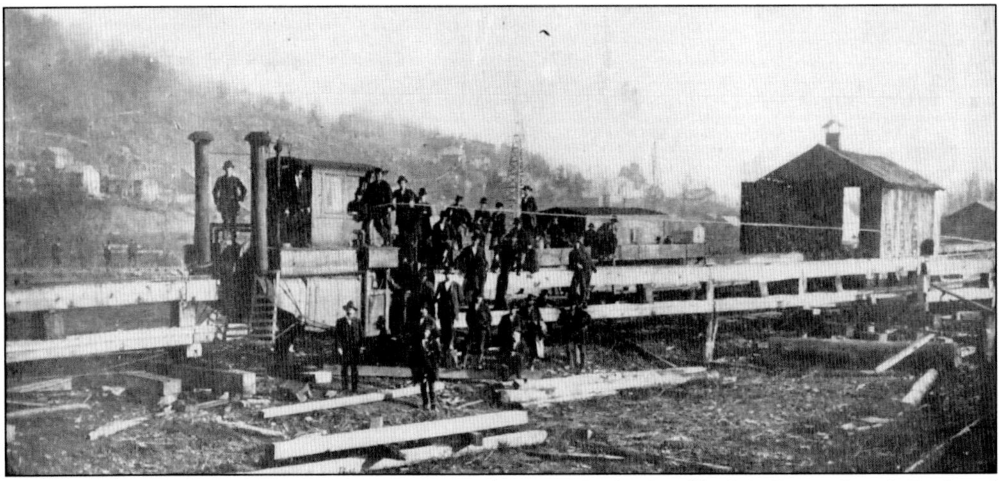

The Peg Leg Railroad, Engine No. 1, 1877. Built in 1877, the Bradford & Foster Brook Railroad was known locally as the "Peg Leg" and was one of the first monorails to be tried commercially in the world. Following a series of accidents, it was abandoned in 1880.

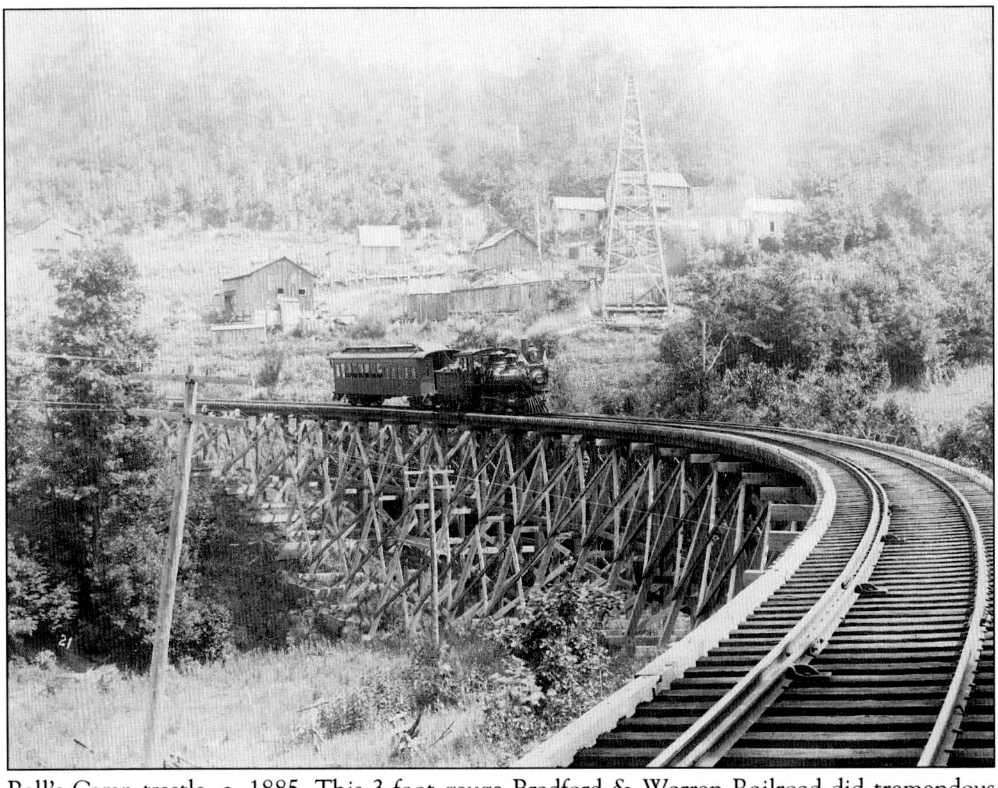

Bell's Camp trestle, *c.* 1885. This 3-foot gauge Bradford & Warren Railroad did tremendous business during the oil boom. Here, an engine is seen rounding the curve at Bell's Camp.

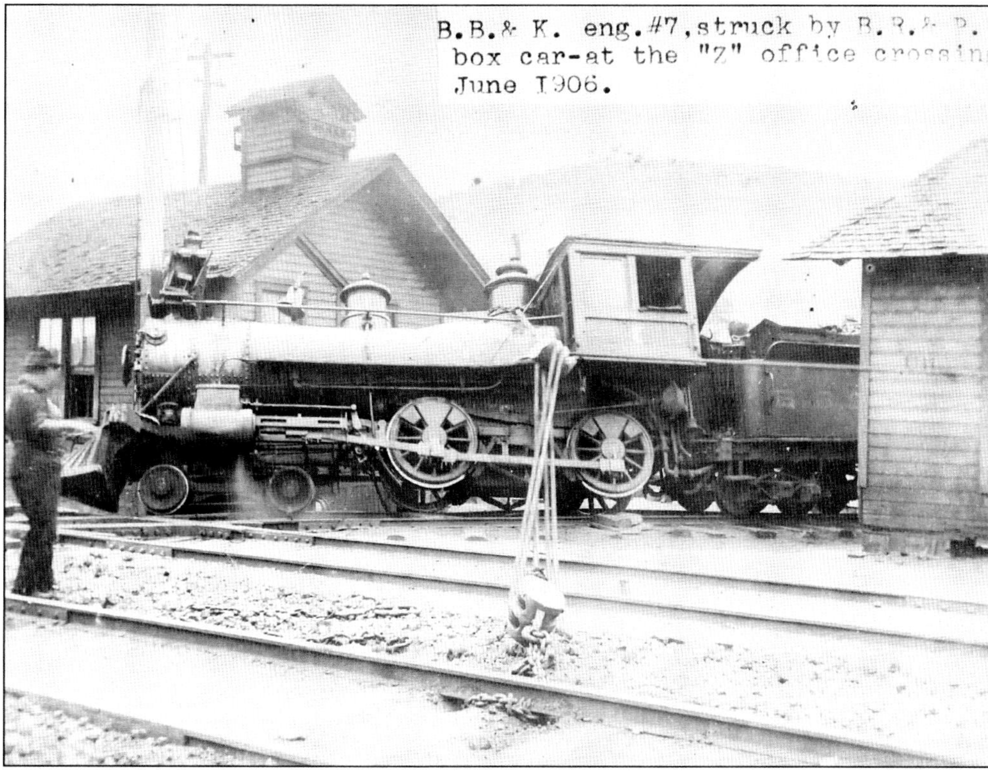

An accident at the B.R. & P. crossing at Bradford, June 14, 1906. Engine No. 9 of the B.B. & K. collided with a boxcar from the Bradford, Rochester, & Pittsburgh line (B.R. & P.) with such force that the little engine was tilted off its wheels. Wrecking crews were called in, and the engine was soon righted.

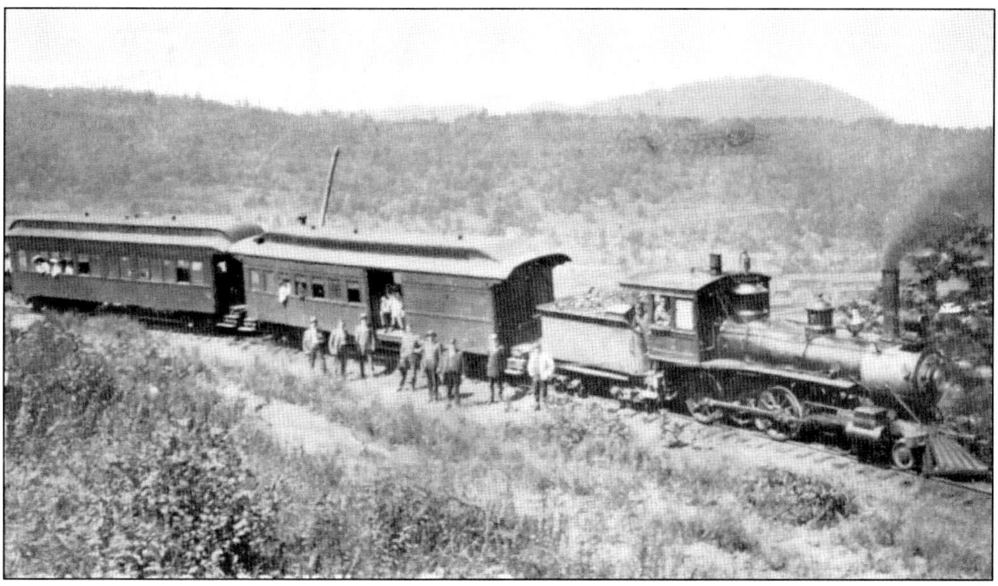

The last train over the Bradford, Bordell & Kinzua (the B.B. & K.) narrow gauge railroad. On July 23, 1906, the railroad was sold for $85,000 to the B.R. & P.

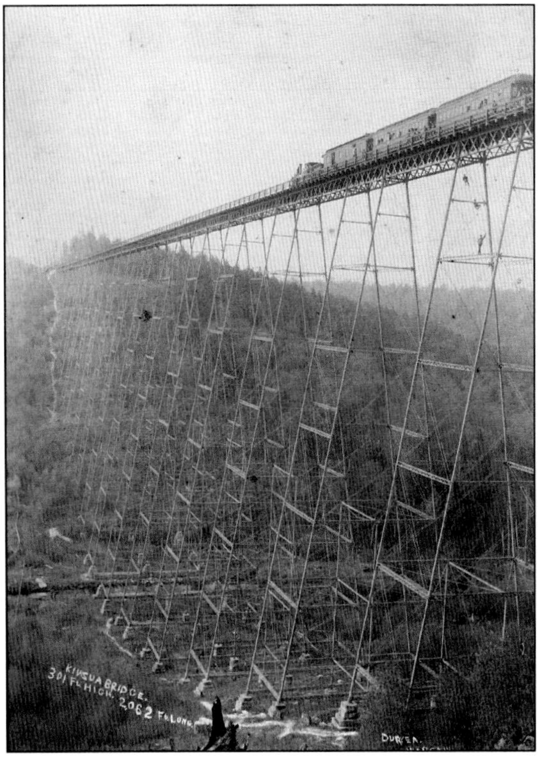

The Kinzua Bridge, 1882. The first Kinzua Bridge was built of iron, and at 301 feet, it was the highest railroad viaduct in the world. It was rebuilt of steel in 1900 and is currently a tourist attraction at the Kinzua Bridge State Park near Mt. Jewett. Note the men standing on the bridge supports.

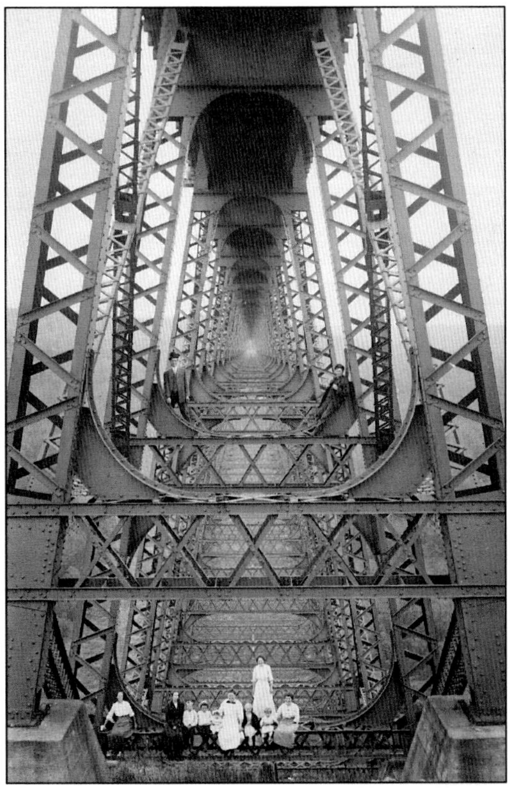

The Kinzua Bridge, 1910. Ever since its construction, people have been fascinated by the bridge and often traveled by train to picnic and view the scenery from atop the 301-foot structure. Countless photographs have been taken in this exact spot as people dare to sit on the cross supports. One of the bridge's most famous visitors was former President Ulysses S. Grant in November 1883.

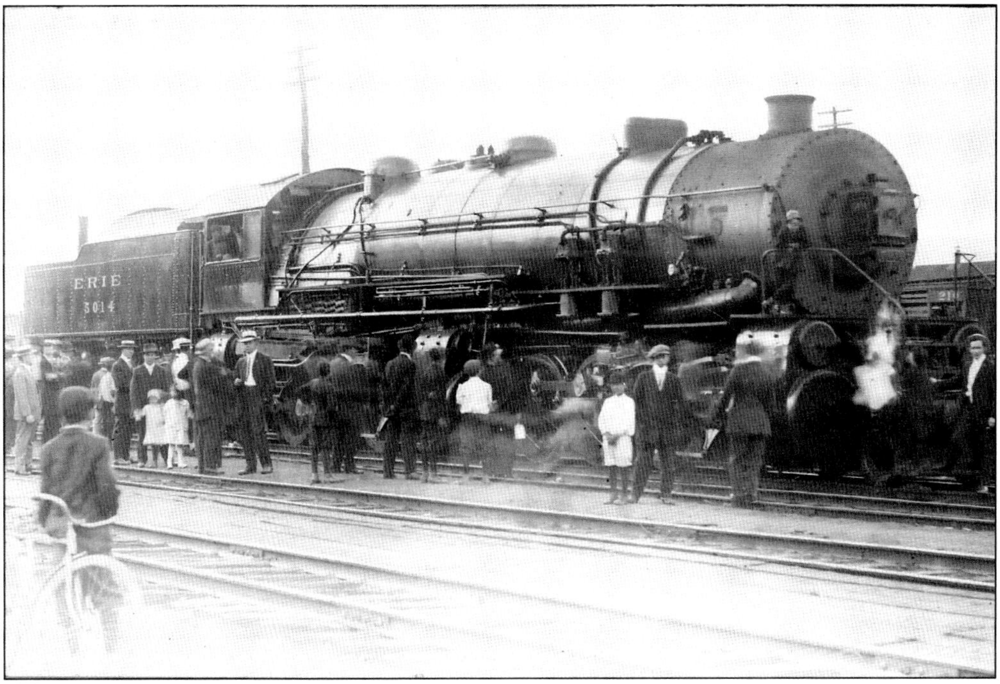

An Erie Railroad locomotive, *c*. 1930s.

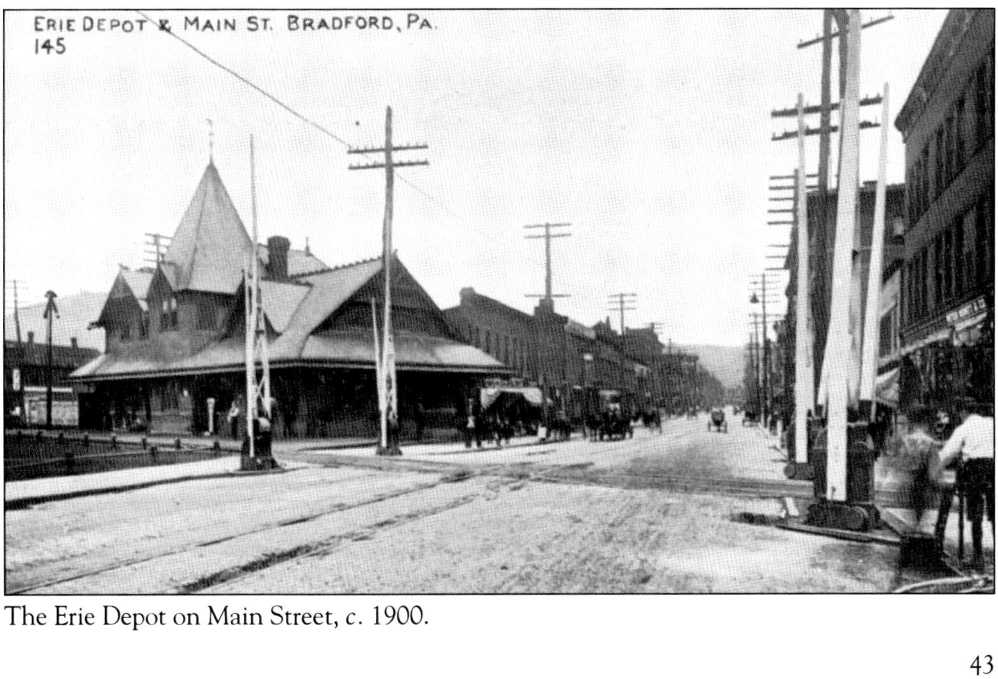

The Erie Depot on Main Street, *c*. 1900.

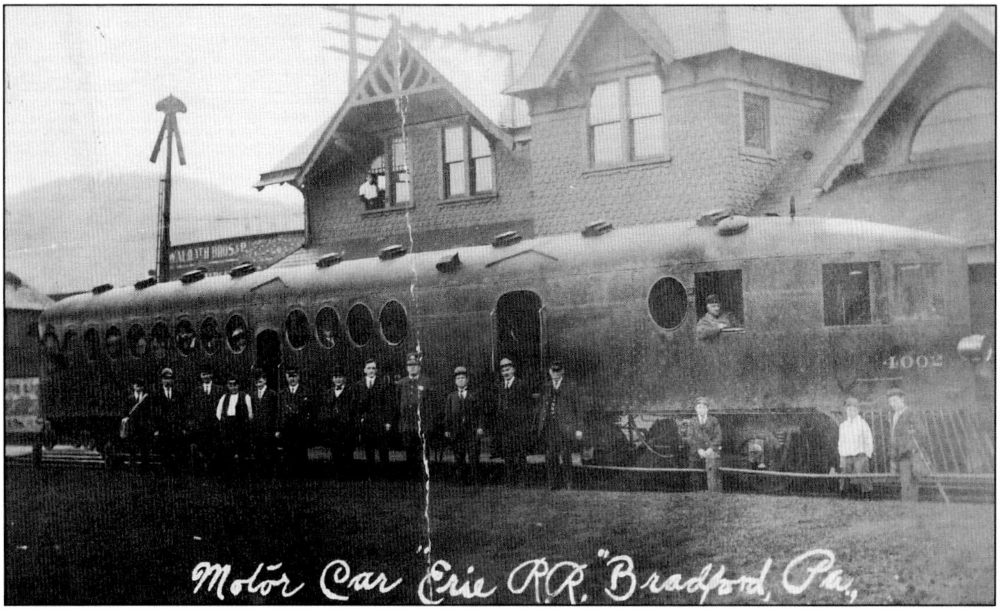

A motor car on the Erie Railroad, "wind splitter" class, at the Erie Station, 1907. Such unique engines provided faster service but at the expense of carrying fewer passengers.

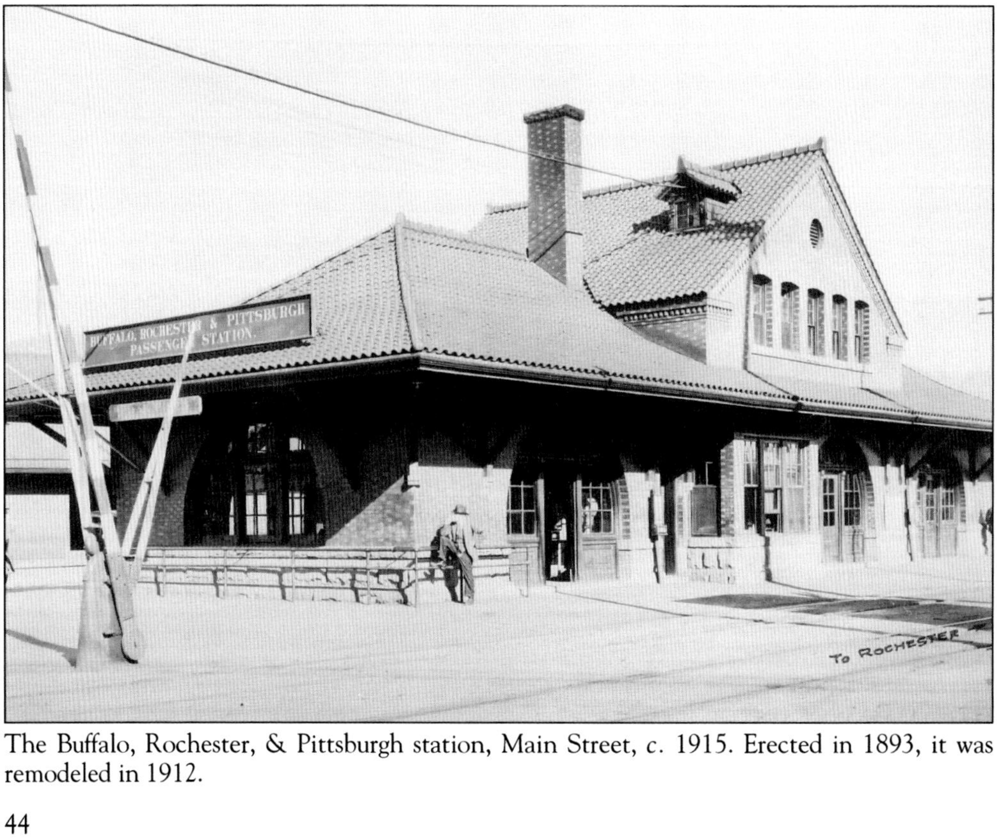

The Buffalo, Rochester, & Pittsburgh station, Main Street, *c.* 1915. Erected in 1893, it was remodeled in 1912.

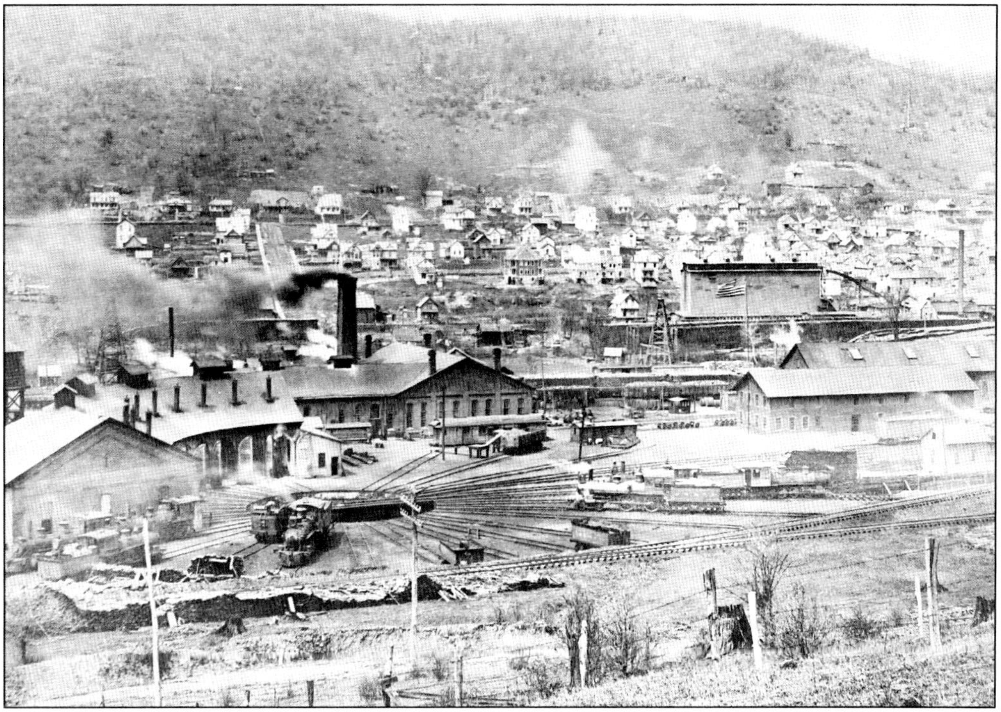

The Buffalo, Rochester, & Pittsburgh Railroad roundhouse, *c.* 1900, as seen from High Street. This roundhouse operation was phased out by 1906.

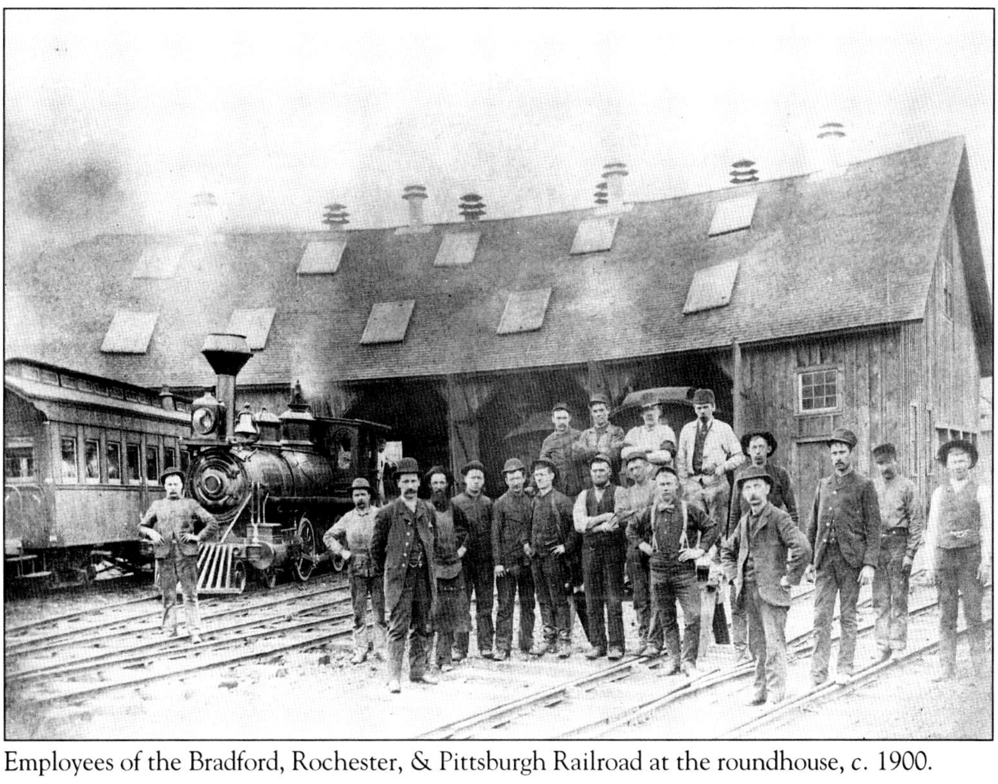

Employees of the Bradford, Rochester, & Pittsburgh Railroad at the roundhouse, *c.* 1900.

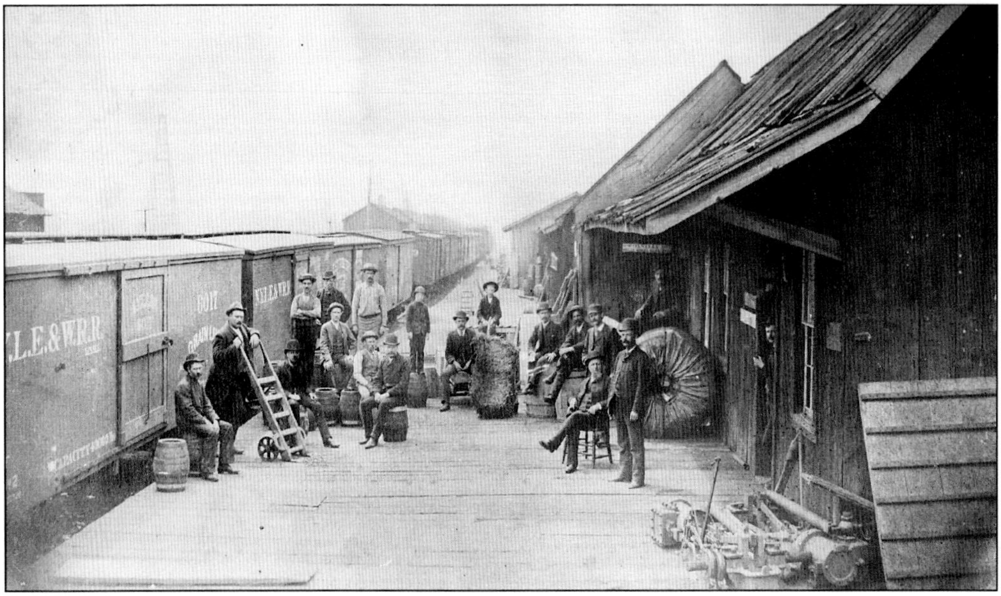

Freight depot employees of the New York, Lake Erie, and Western Railroad, mid-1880s. The large wrapped bundle of bull rope leaning against the front freight office is probably destined for the oil fields.

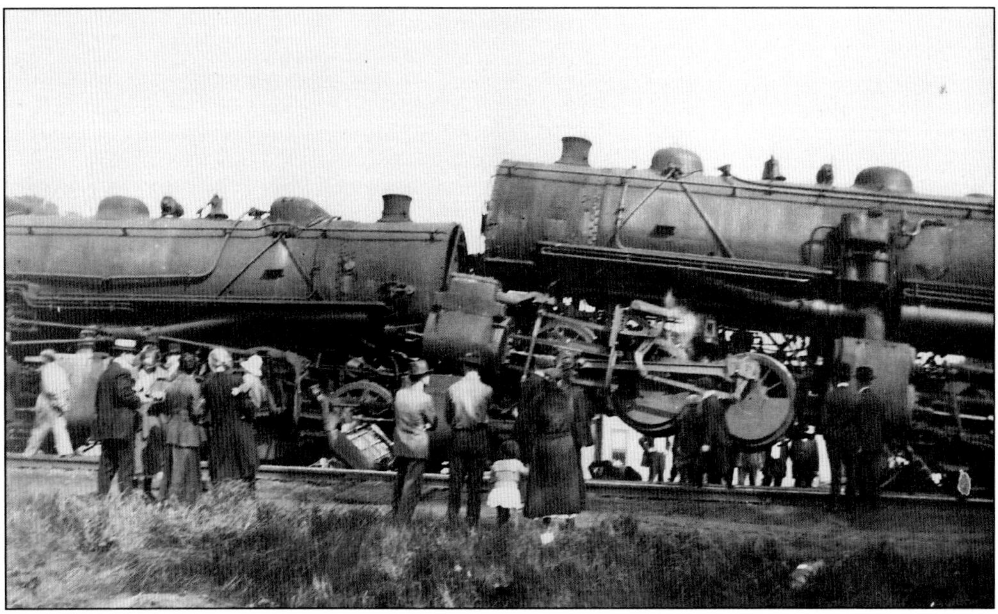

A freight train collision on Kendall Avenue. Neighbors heard the crash at 5:05 am on September 13, 1920, as Engine No. 716 and Engine No. 729 of the B.R. & P. met in a head-on crash at 20 mph. Thankfully, both crews jumped as the trains approached each other, and there were only minor injuries.

Four

Those Who Serve—Firemen and Police

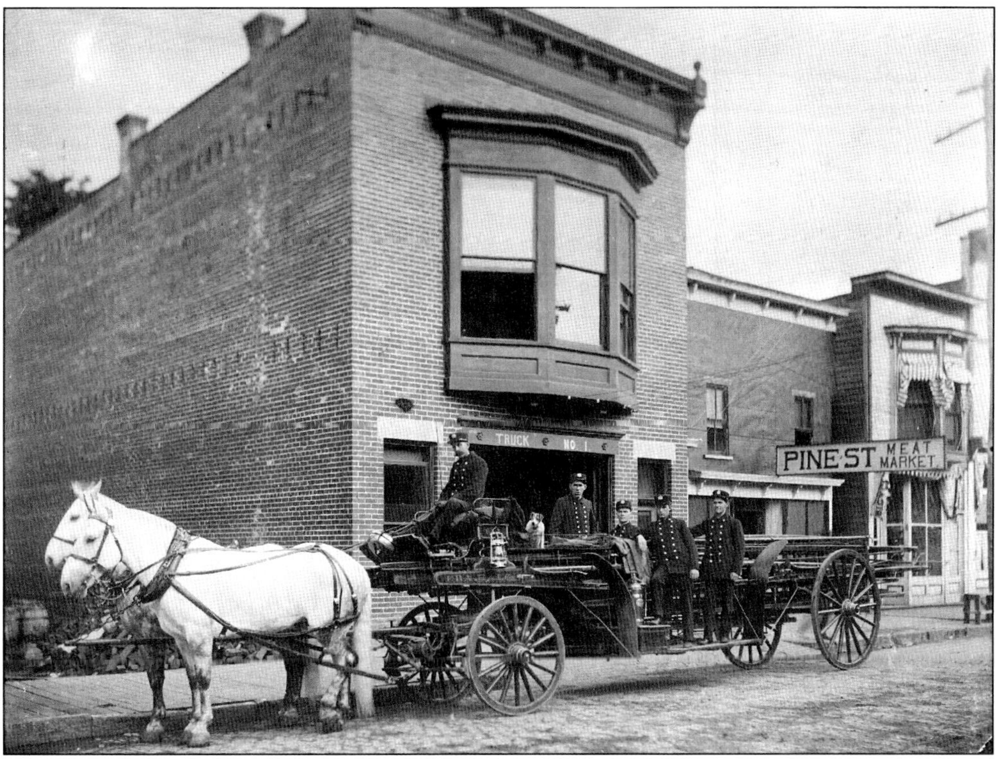

The Era Hook & Ladder Fire Company, Pine Street, *c.* 1890s. This company was organized in June 1878 by volunteers who purchased a hand-drawn hook and ladder truck with their own funds. Al Grimes is identified as the driver in this photograph. The other men are unknown. The Era Hook & Ladder was just one of nine volunteer fire companies in Bradford before 1903. Firemen were highly respected for their civic service to the community, and their loyalty to their own fire companies.

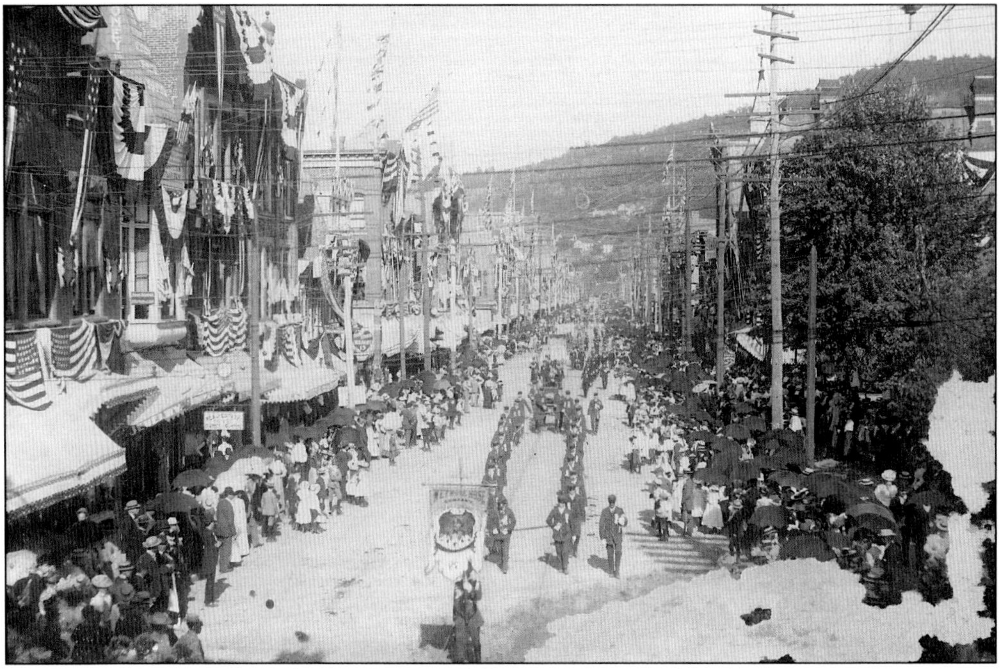

The 1897 Firemen's Parade. With nine different volunteer fire departments operating in Bradford before the turn of the century, the firemen's convention held that year was a great success. Here, a visiting fire department from Wetmore Township near Kane parades down Main Street.

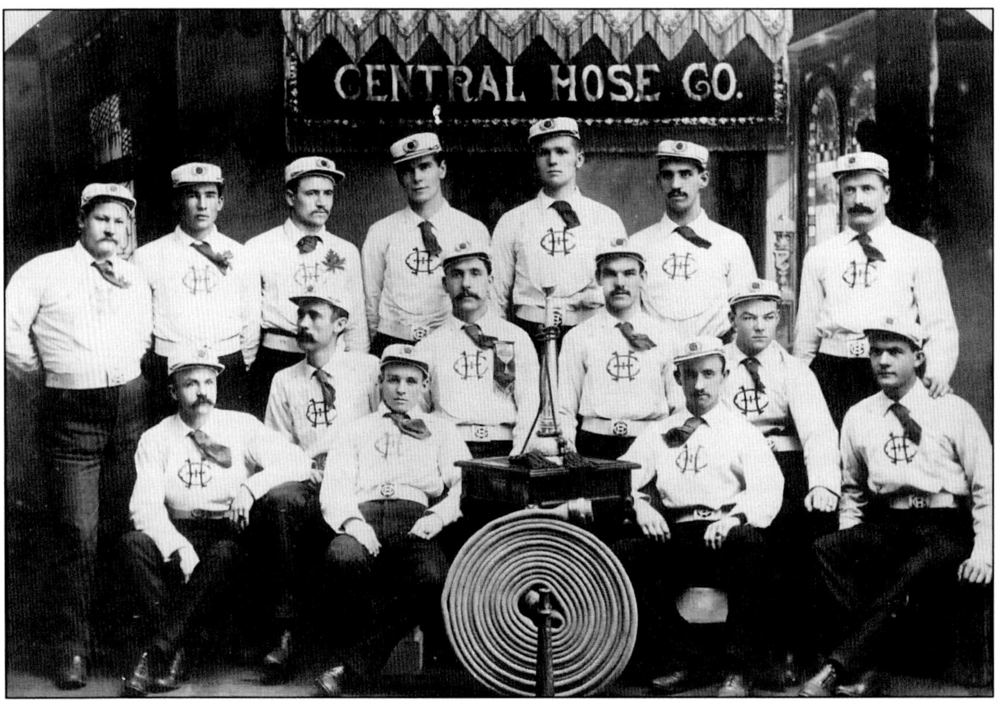

Central Hose Fire Company firemen, in dress uniform, 1890s. The Central Hose was organized in September 1885 by the employees of the Bovaird and Seyfang plant.

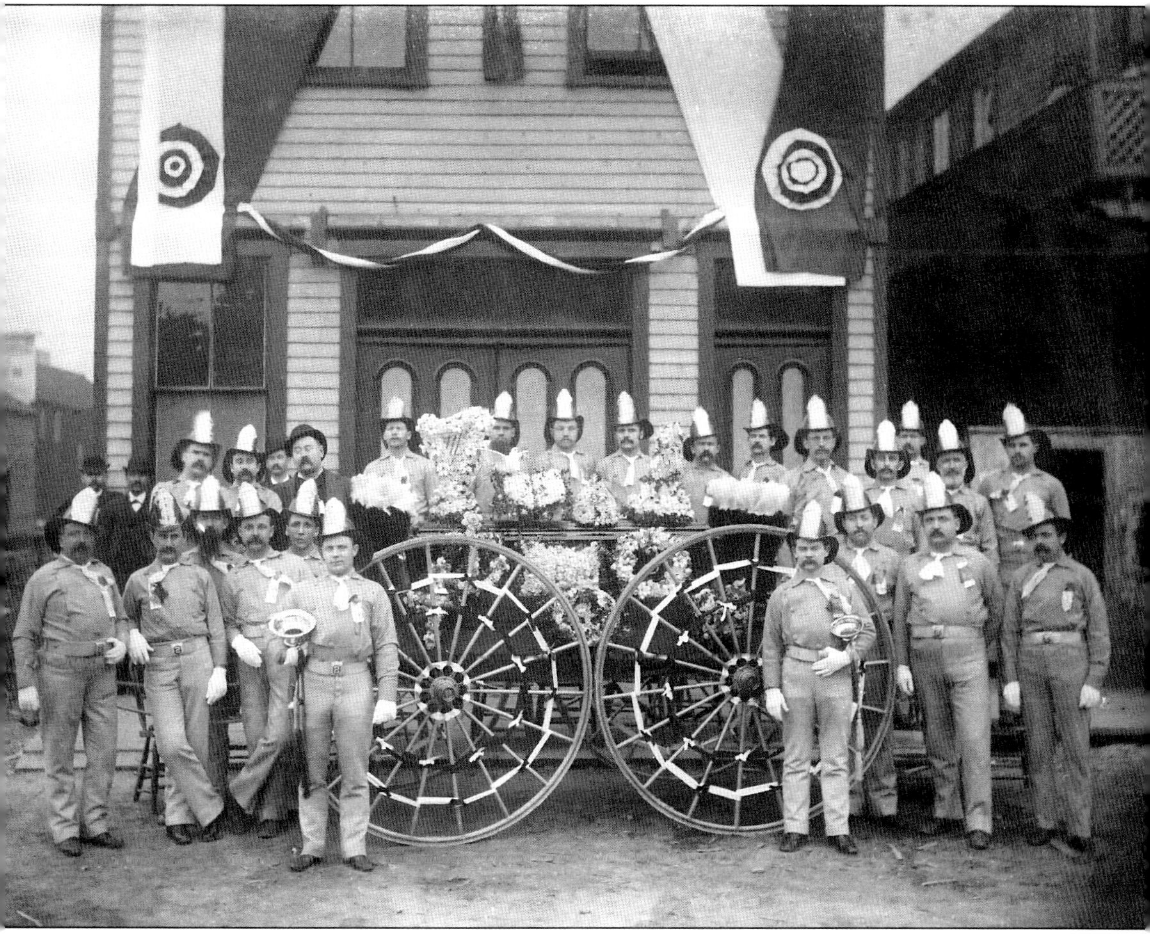

Members of the Citizens Hose Fire Company, 1897. Attired in full dress uniform, these firemen pose at attention during Firemen's Convention Week. This fire company house was located on Kennedy Street.

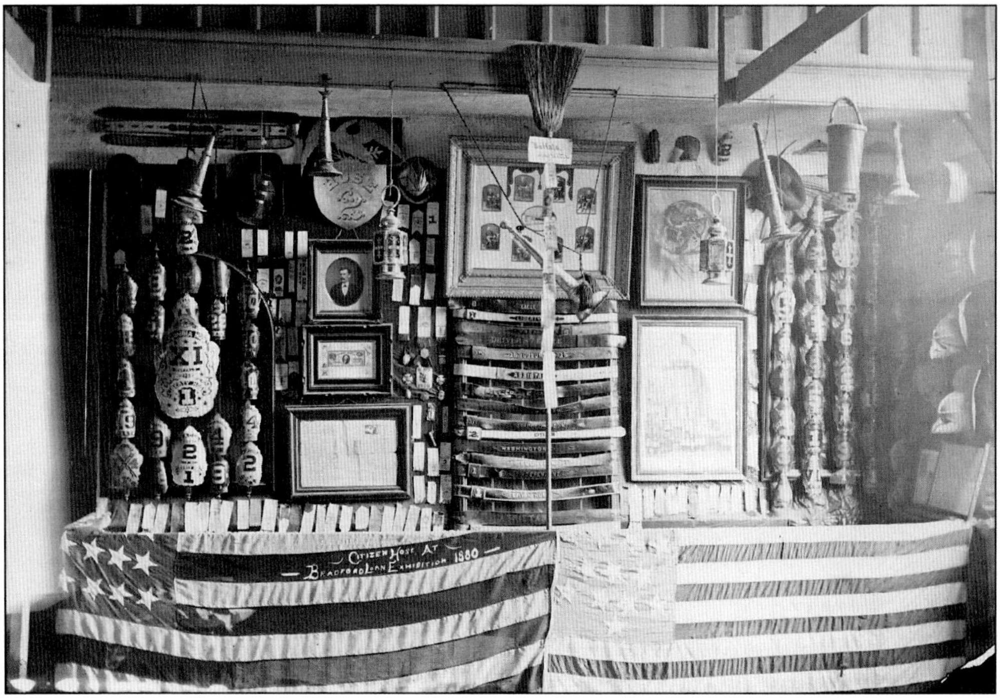

Firemen's memorabilia, on exhibit at the Bradford Loan Co., 1880. Organized in 1875 by a group of men formerly from Buffalo, the Citizen Hose Company displayed various ribbons, shields, awards, photographs, flags, cornets, and medals owned by these men.

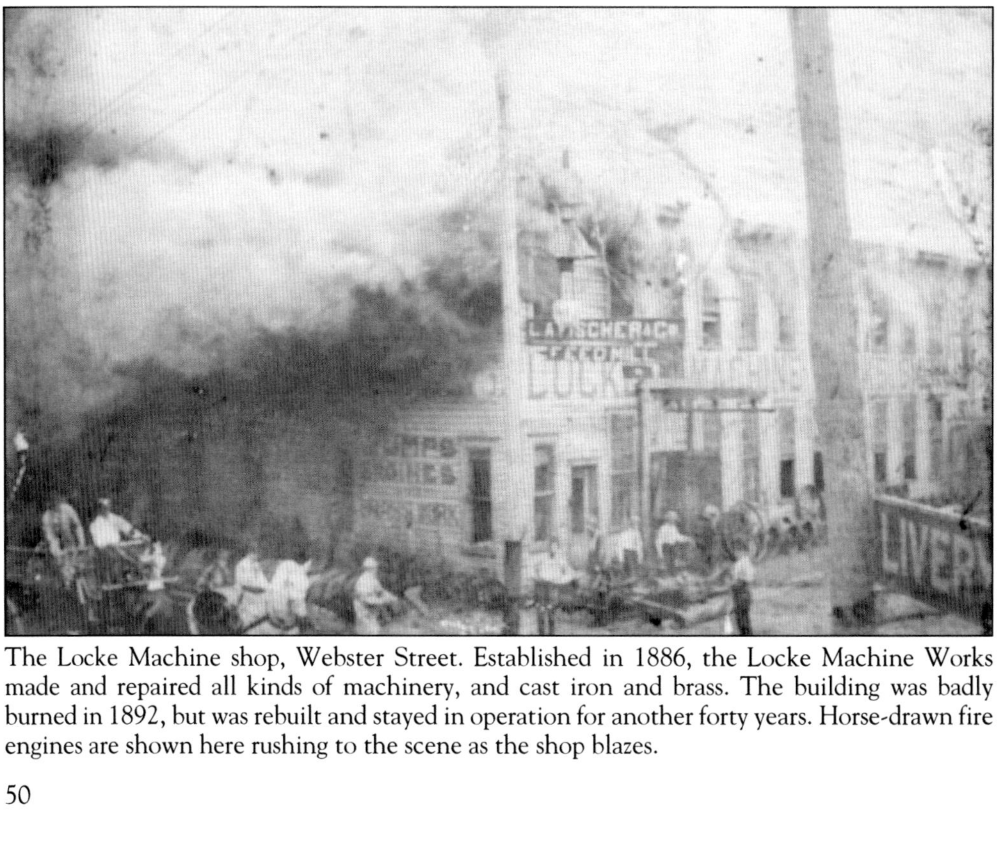

The Locke Machine shop, Webster Street. Established in 1886, the Locke Machine Works made and repaired all kinds of machinery, and cast iron and brass. The building was badly burned in 1892, but was rebuilt and stayed in operation for another forty years. Horse-drawn fire engines are shown here rushing to the scene as the shop blazes.

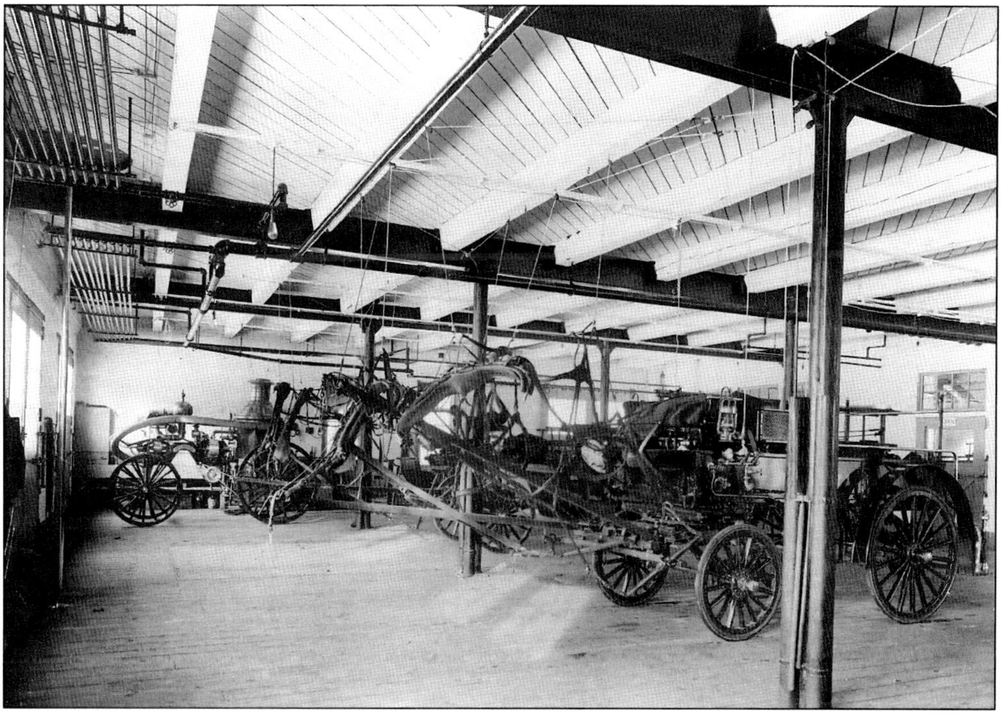

The interior of the Central Fire Department on Chestnut Street, *c.* 1905. Horse-drawn fire engines, with each team's harness suspended from the ceiling, stand ready for action. The steamer, the "Lewis Emery," one of two used by the fire department, stands in the left rear.

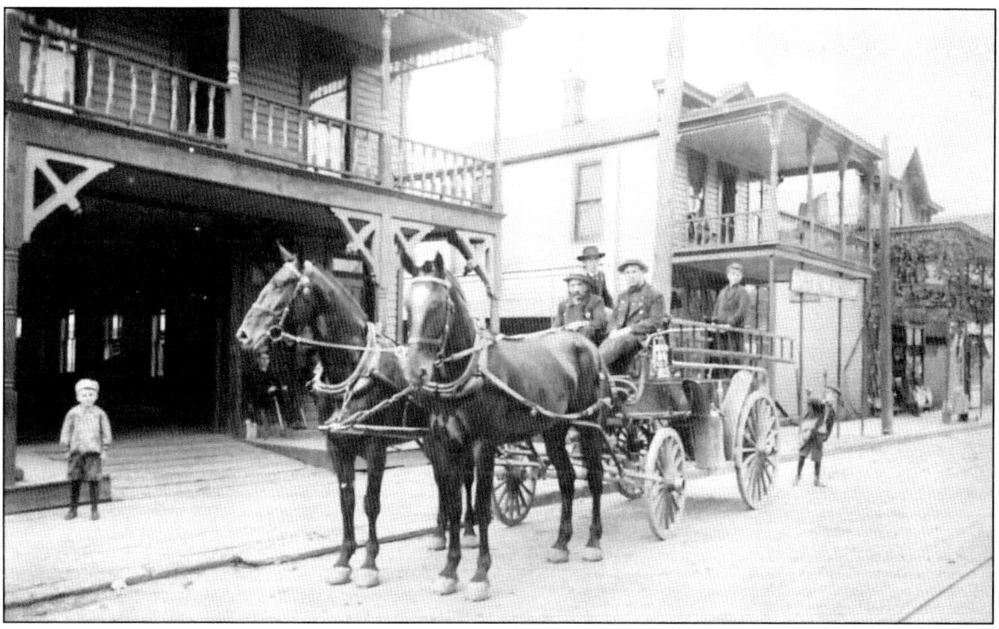

The Cornen Hose Team, *c.* 1900. Organized on March 2, 1881, it was named after the Cornen brothers (prominent oil producers) and was located in Kendall Borough, now East Main Street. The building to the right of the firehouse is the Tuna Valley House, which was in existence from 1894 through 1909.

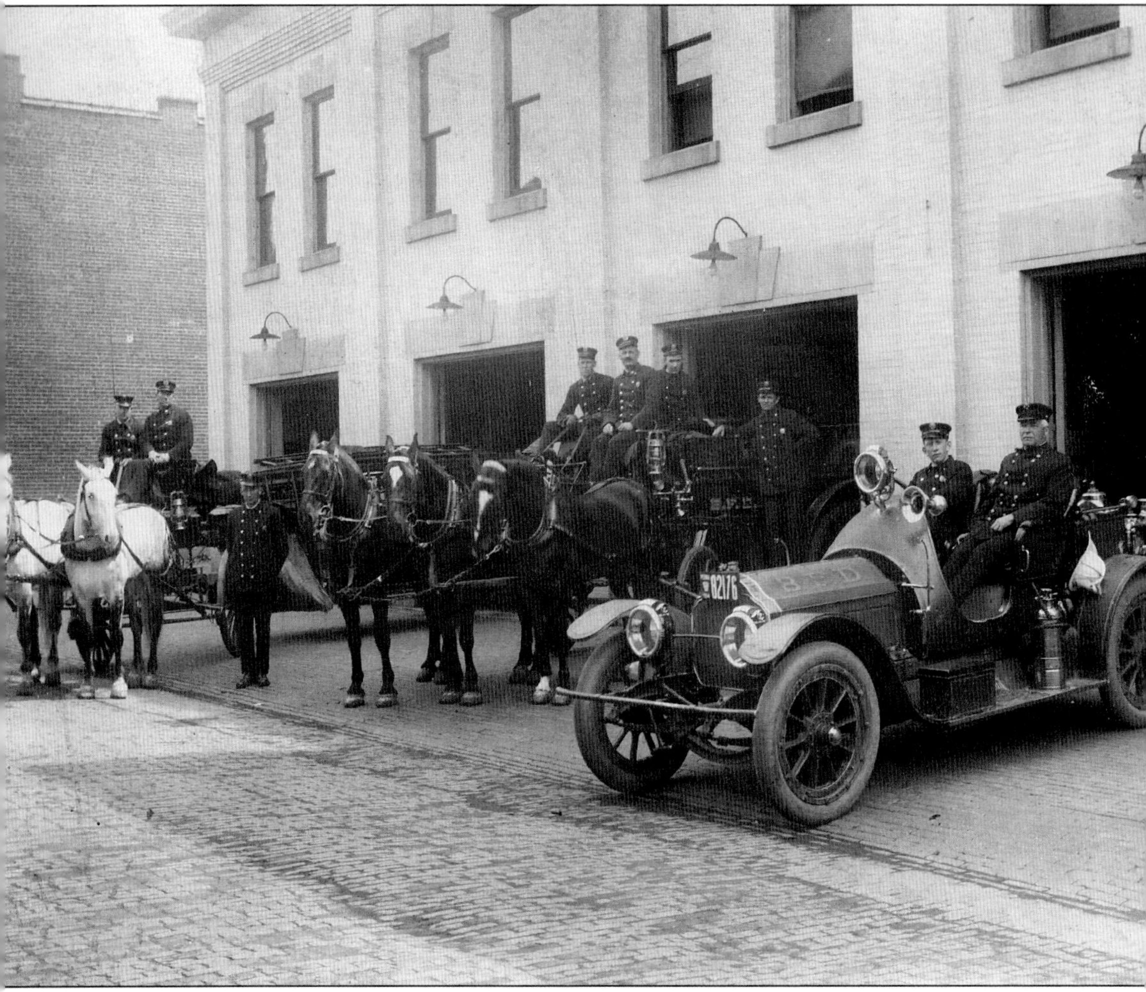

The Bradford Central Hose Fire Department, 1916. A new era dawned as horse-drawn engines were slowly replaced by motor-driven fire trucks. Chief Charles Henderson and his driver, Edward Ryan, seem quite comfortable behind the wheel of the chief's car. Notice the right-hand drive on the car. This building, on the corner of Chestnut and East Corydon Streets, is still used today by Bradford's fire department.

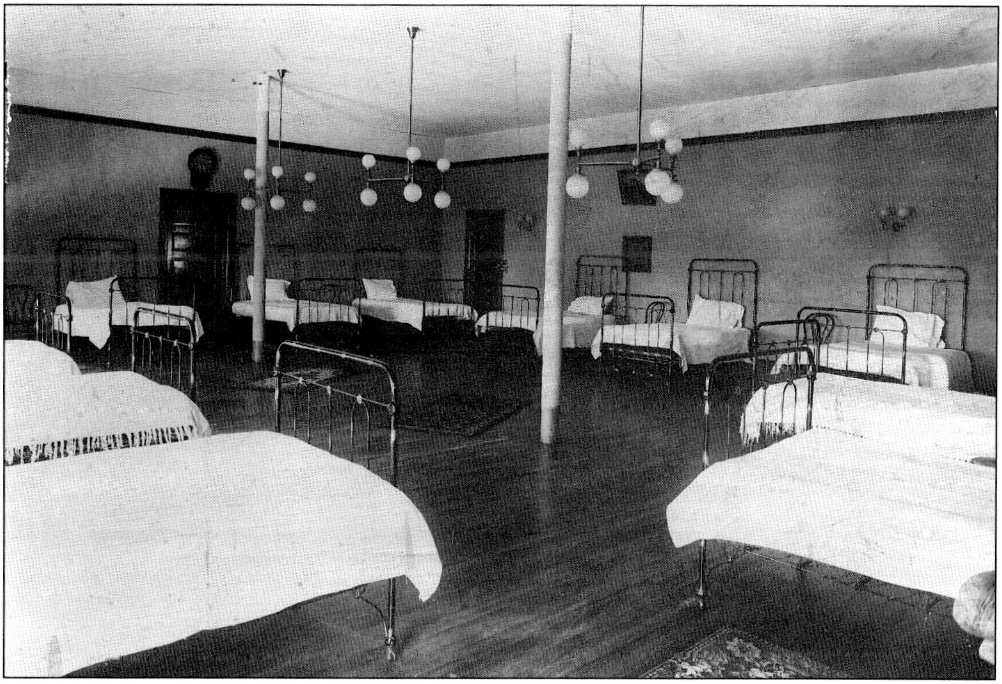

Firemen's bunk room, 1910. These beds on the second floor of the Central Hose Company on the corner of Chestnut and Corydon Streets stand ready to receive tired firemen. This fire company was the first in Bradford to have paid firemen.

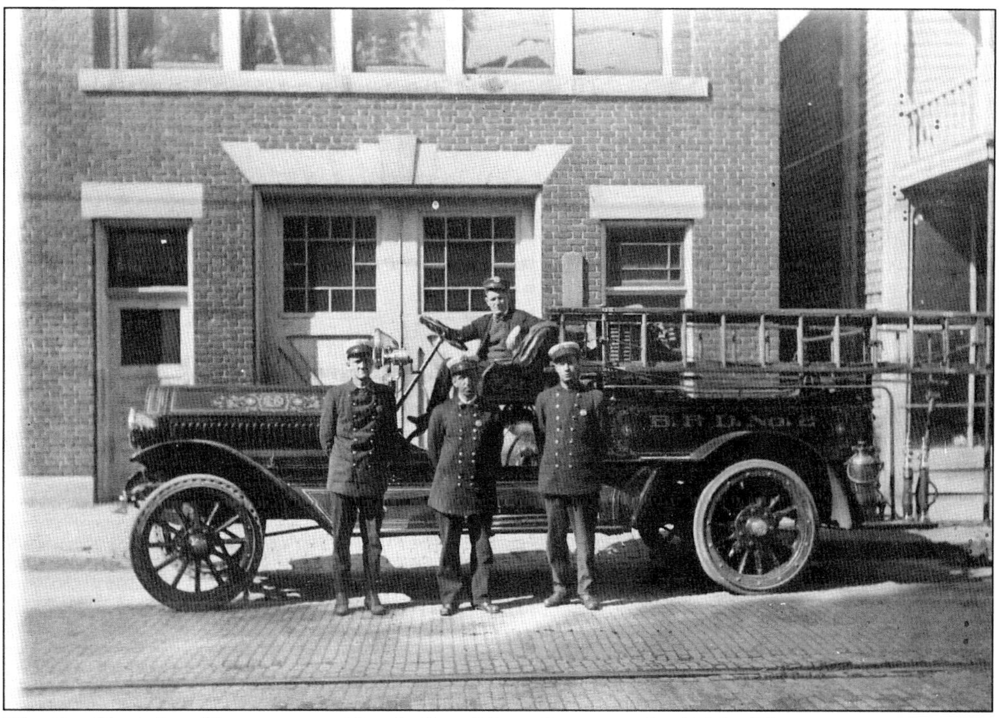

The Bradford Fire Department, No. 2, East Main Street, early 1920s. The men standing are, from left to right, unknown, Hank Crandall, and Harry Grant. The driver is Jim Martin.

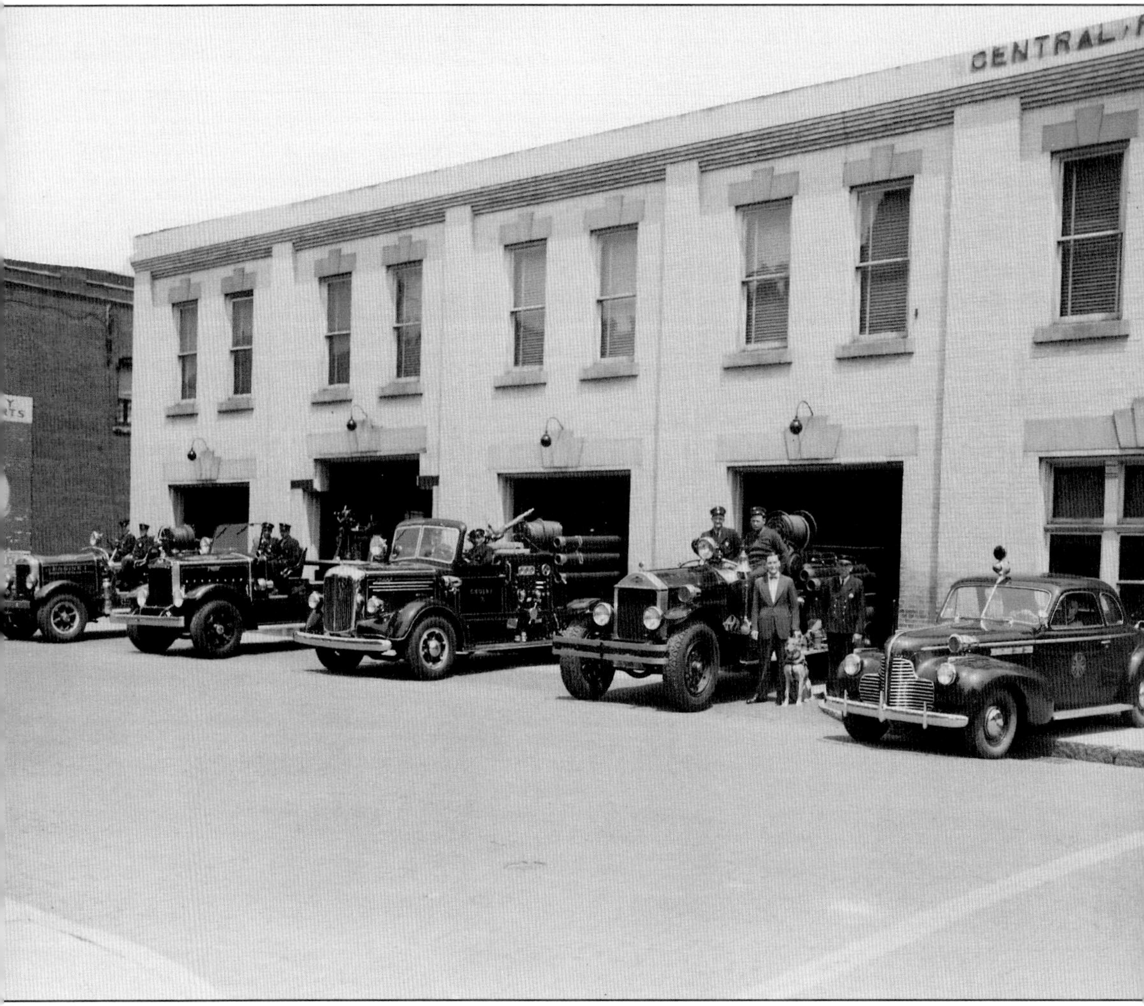

The Central Fire Co., *c.* 1940. Firemen proudly show off their modern equipment. The man with the seeing eye dog is James Butterworth, city councilman.

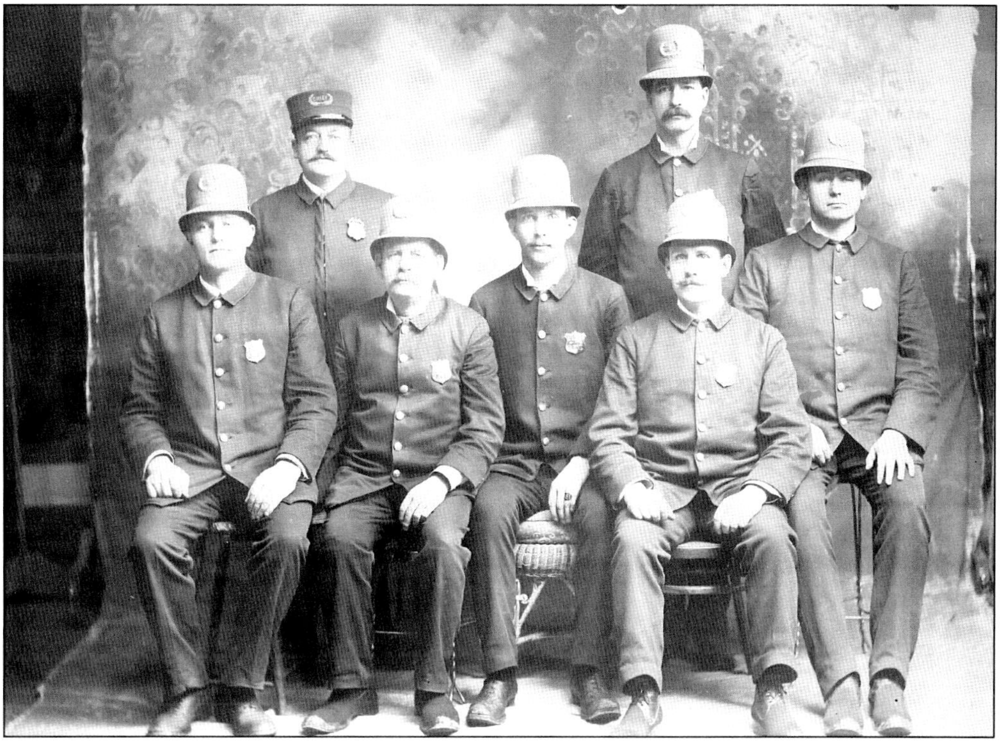

The Bradford Police Force, 1900. This seven-man department was headed by Chief M.D. Murray. Other members of the force are, from left to right, as follows: (front) Matthew Bain, F.P. Sculley, N.G. Case, H.D. Mooney, and C.L. Faust; (back) Chief Murray and R.B. Cowan.

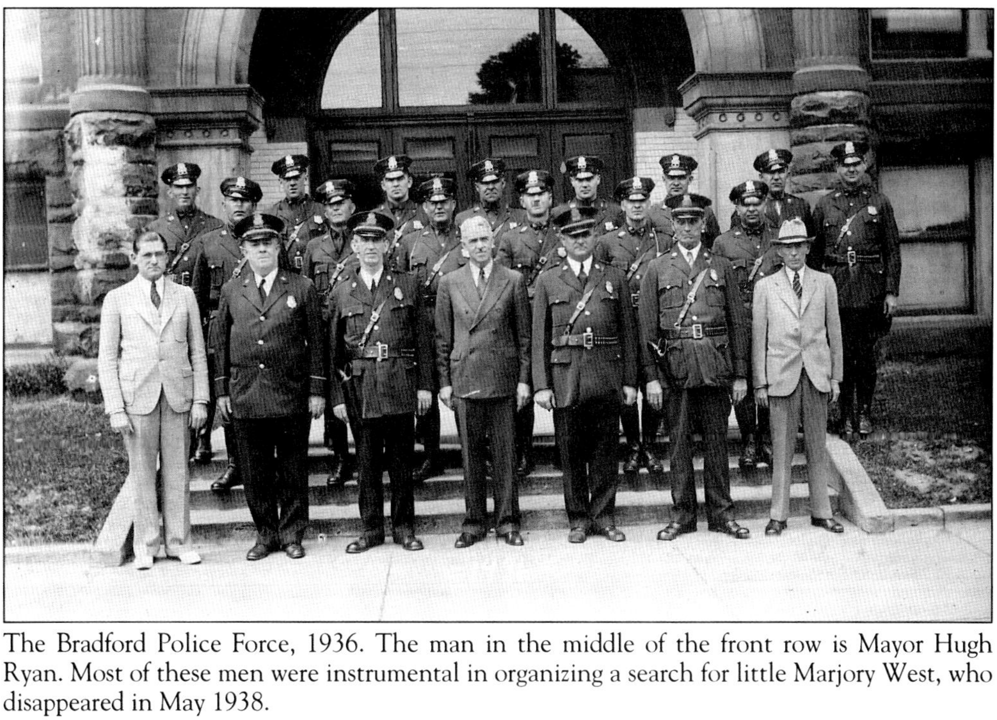

The Bradford Police Force, 1936. The man in the middle of the front row is Mayor Hugh Ryan. Most of these men were instrumental in organizing a search for little Marjory West, who disappeared in May 1938.

$2,000 REWARD!

$2,000 will be paid by the Bradford, Pa., Citizens' Reward Committee for information resulting in the safe return of MARJORY WEST, who disappeared at White Gravel, Pa., May 8, 1938.

ONE HALF THE REWARD MONEY will be paid for information resulting in the recovery of her body.

This reward expires December 15, 1938.

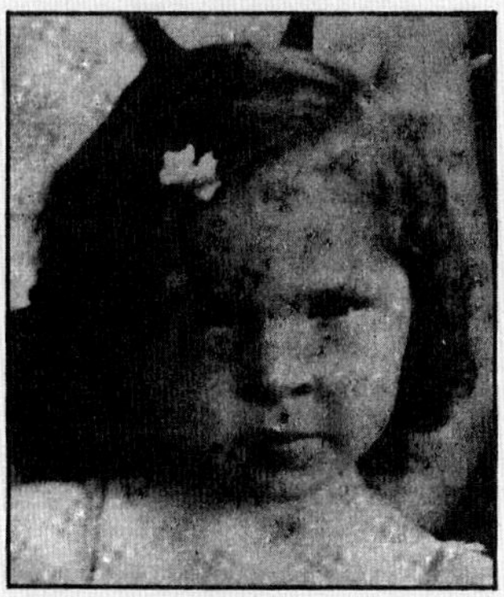

Description of MARJORY WEST

Age 4 (Four) Years. Blue Eyes. Long, Curley, Red Hair. Freckled Face. Wearing Red Shirley Temple Hat, Blue Coat, Blue Dress and Patent Leather Shoes. Talks with a Southern Accent.

Marjory West reward poster, May 1938. The most famous missing person case in local history was that of little four-year-old Marjory West, who disappeared on May 8, Mother's Day, 1938, while on a family picnic at White Gravel, near Marshburg. Wandering off to pick her mother some flowers, she never returned. Over 2,500 people eventually joined the exhaustive search through the woods. State police, high school students, local law enforcement, the American Legion, Indian trackers from the nearby Seneca Indian reservation, and even clairvoyants all joined to find her. They never did. Rewards were offered and several leads investigated, but the case remains open.

Five

Bradford Goes to War

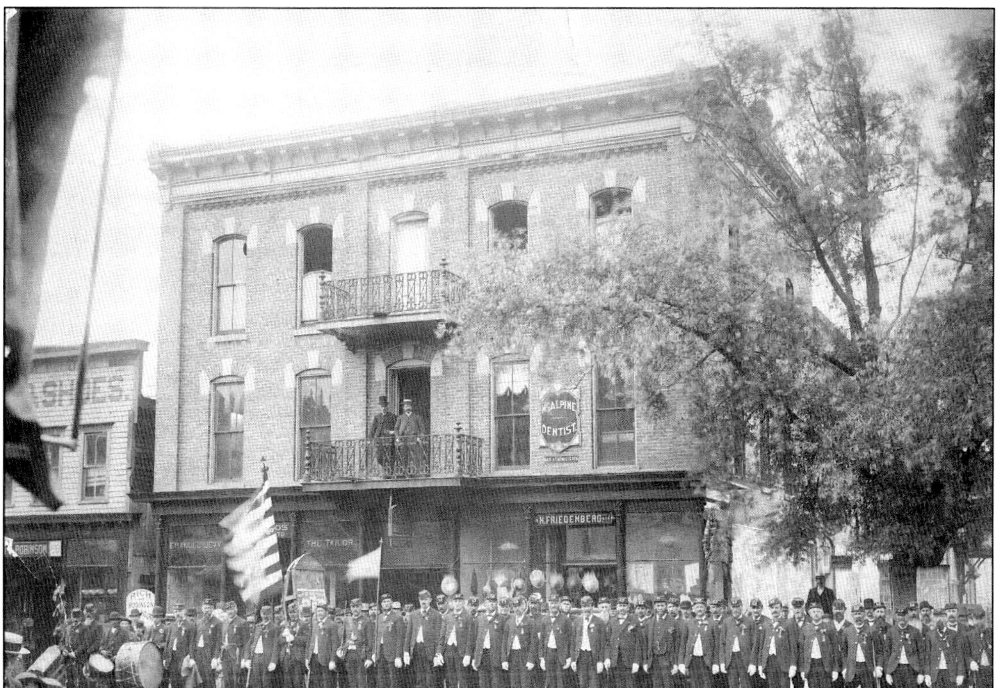

The Wagner Opera House, September 1888. The second annual reunion of the Bucktail Regiment, John S. Melvin G.A.R. Post 141, is gathered in front of this building, located at the corner of Chambers and Main Streets. Built in 1876, it is the oldest standing brick building still in continuous commercial use in Bradford. Today it is known as Poppys.

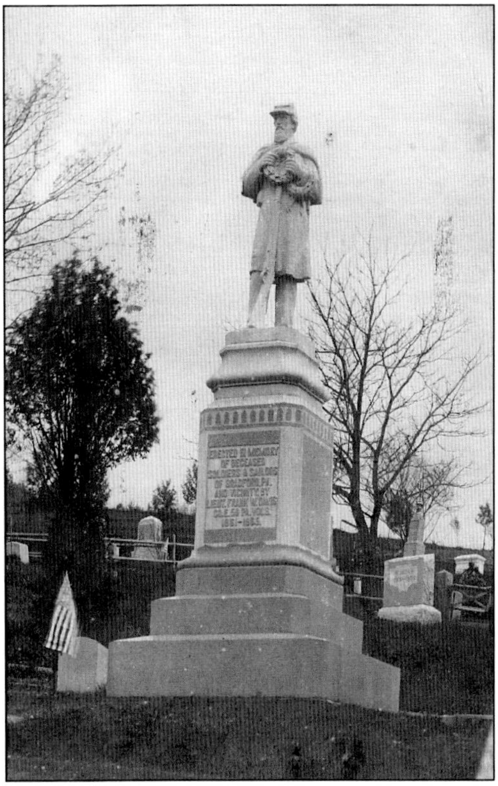

The Civil War Monument in Oak Hill Cemetery. Dedicated on Memorial Day 1907, this statue was donated by Frank W. Davis, a local businessman and Civil War veteran "in memory of the deceased soldiers of Bradford." Constructed of 14 tons of Barre Granite, and built by Hodges & Hastings of Bradford, it represents an American soldier in uniform, musket near his heart, with a laurel wreath clasped in his hands. Still standing today in Oak Hill, the monument is surrounded by the graves of approximately 375 Civil War veterans.

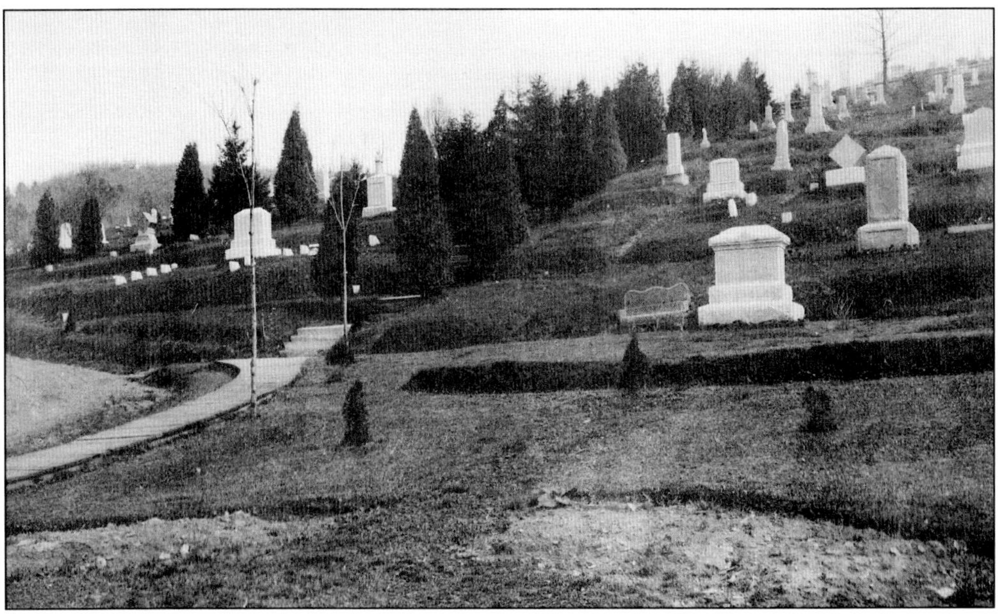

Oak Hill Cemetery, 1898. One of the largest cemeteries in Bradford, it was begun as a business venture in the early 1880s by P.L. Webster, an enterprising surveyor, entrepreneur, landowner, and not coincidentally, undertaker. It was incorporated in December 1883. When the old Bradford Cemetery (currently Hanley Park) was abandoned in the early 1900s, over three hundred graves were relocated to Oak Hill Cemetery.

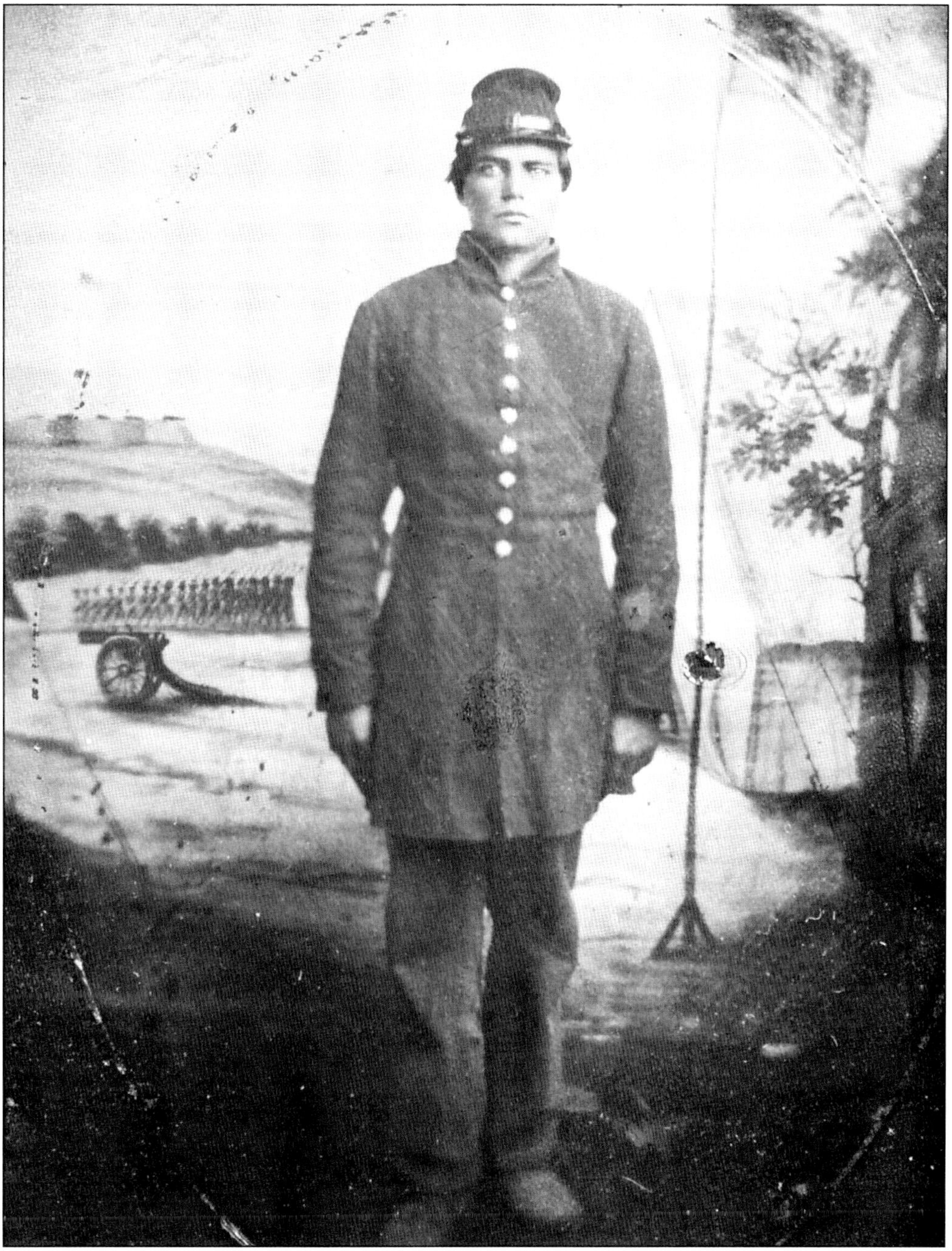

Eighteen-year-old Harlow Pike, 1861. One of the last surviving Civil War veterans in Bradford, he fought in more than forty battles including Chancellorsville, the Battle of the Wilderness, Yorktown, and Gettysburg. He was wounded first at the Battle of Kettle Run in 1862 and again at Wapping Height in 1863, when he was shot through the back of the neck. Born in Bradford in 1844, a son of Barnabas Pike, one of the first settlers in the area, Harlow Pike died on April 3, 1935, at the age of ninety-one.

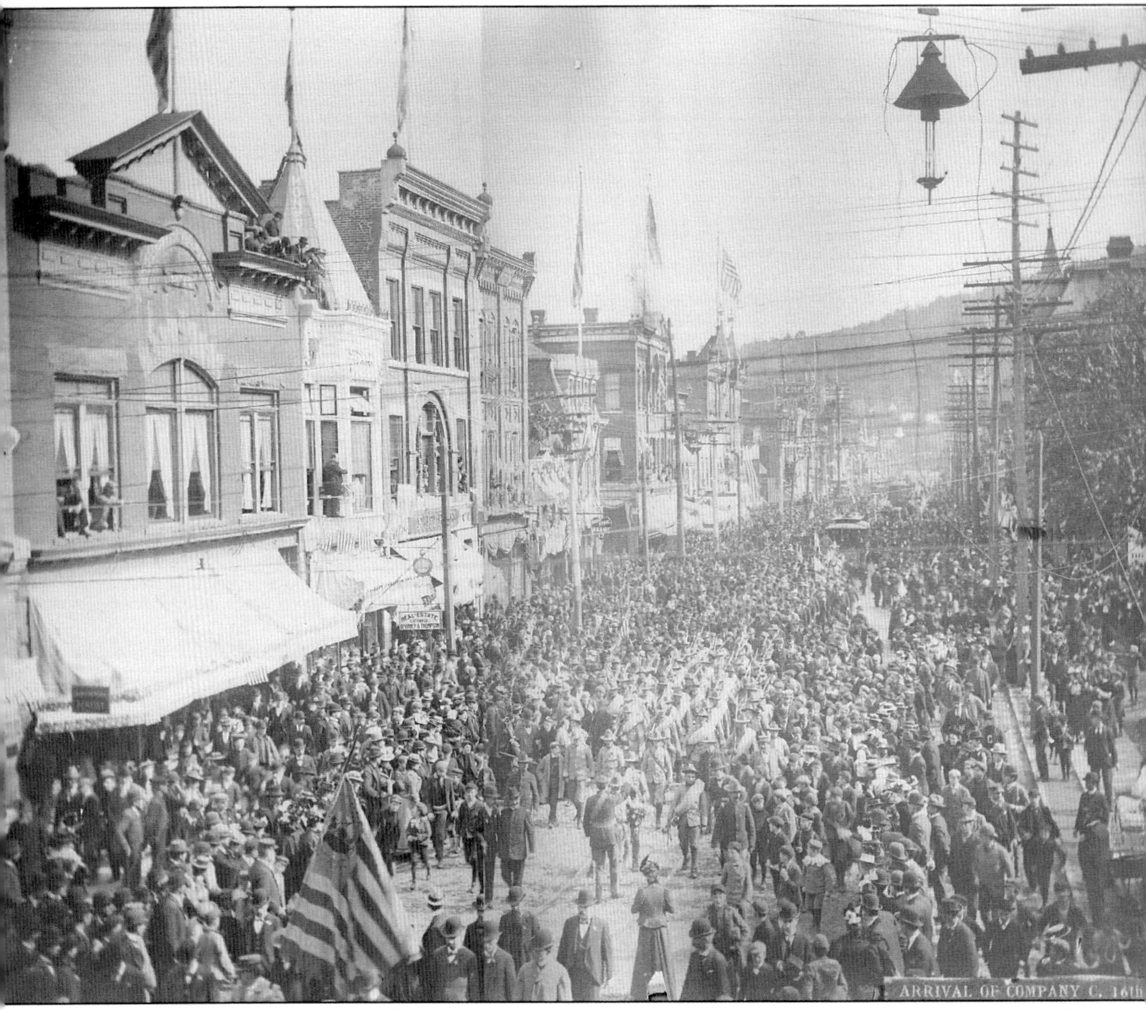

Company C returns to Bradford, October 19, 1898. Thousands turned out to greet the returning veterans of the Spanish-American War. Although their war service had been brief, it stirred the patriotism of Bradfordians. Of the 180 men that enlisted, only four men died. One, Charles Ward, son of former Mayor Loyal Ward, died en route home, and was buried at sea.

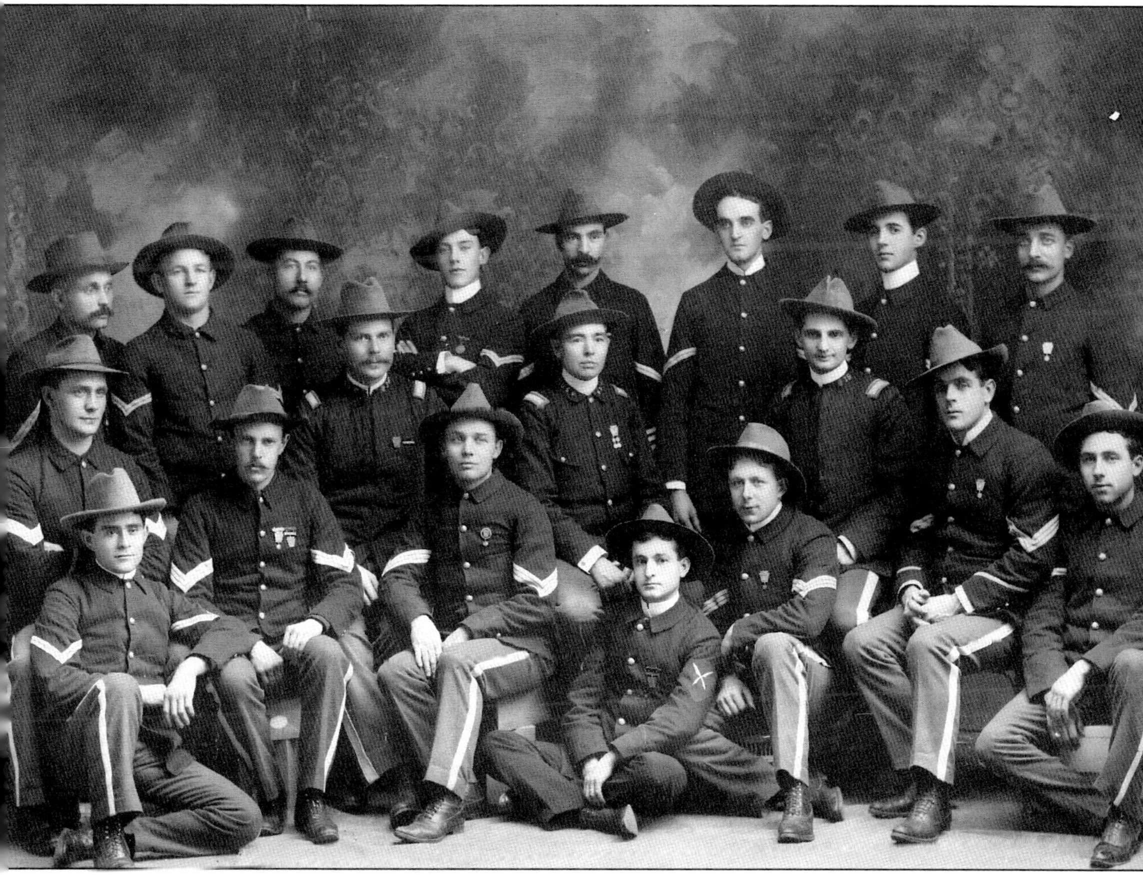

Commissioned and non-commissioned officers of Company C. Sent in August to Puerto Rico, they returned to Bradford with only four men lost. A monument in Veteran's Square, the metal of which is from the USS *Maine*, honors all those who fought in the Spanish-American War.

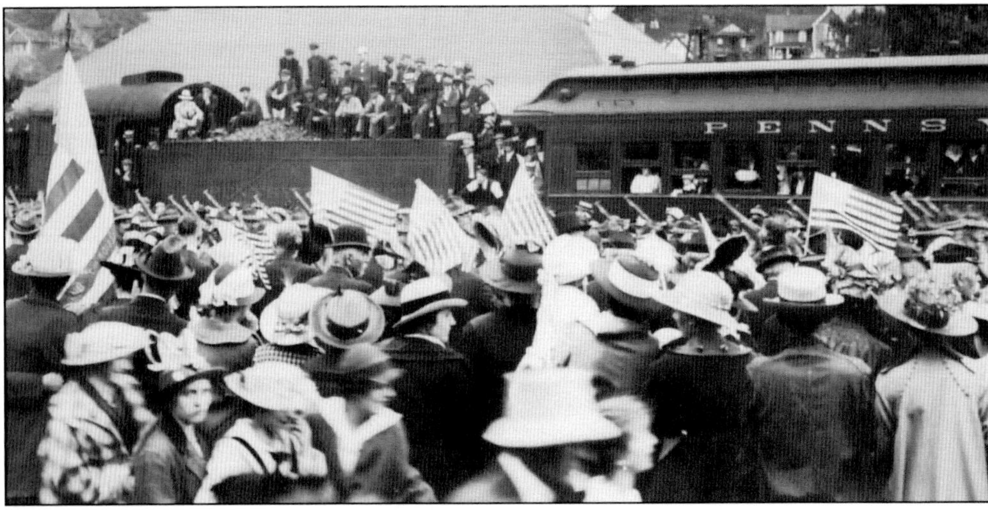

World War I soldiers return to Bradford, May 7, 1919. An estimated twenty thousand Bradfordians—"living masses of cheering, whistling, horn blowing humanity" wrote the *Bradford Era*—turned out to welcome "the boys back home" down at the B.R. & P. train station at North Kendall Avenue. Of the over 360 casualties from McKean County during World War I, nearly one-fourth were from Bradford.

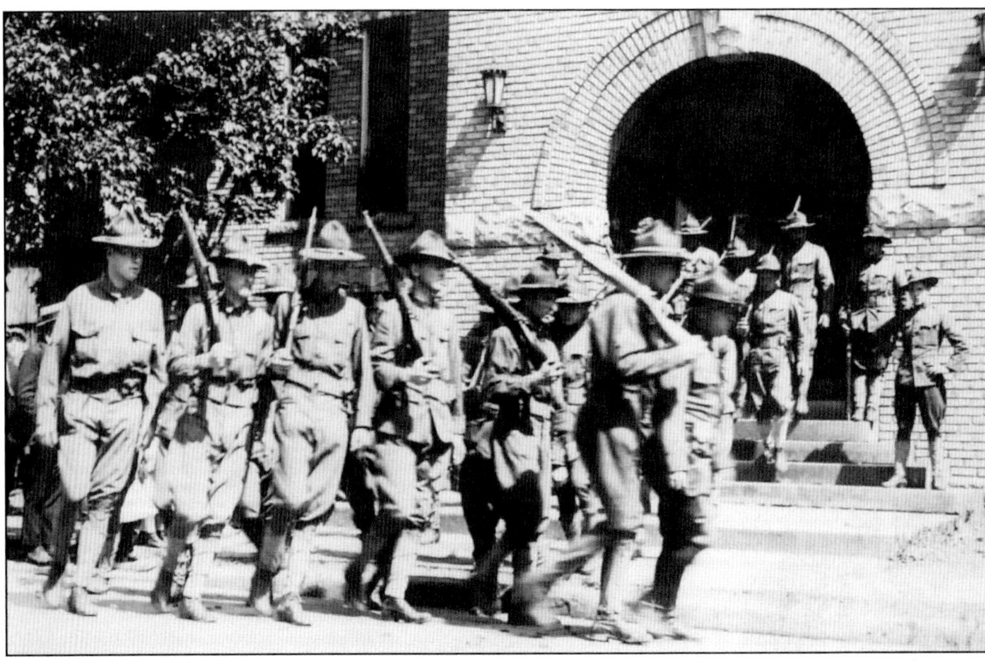

The boys come home. World War I soldiers pass by the armory on Barbour Street during a celebration parade on May 7, 1919.

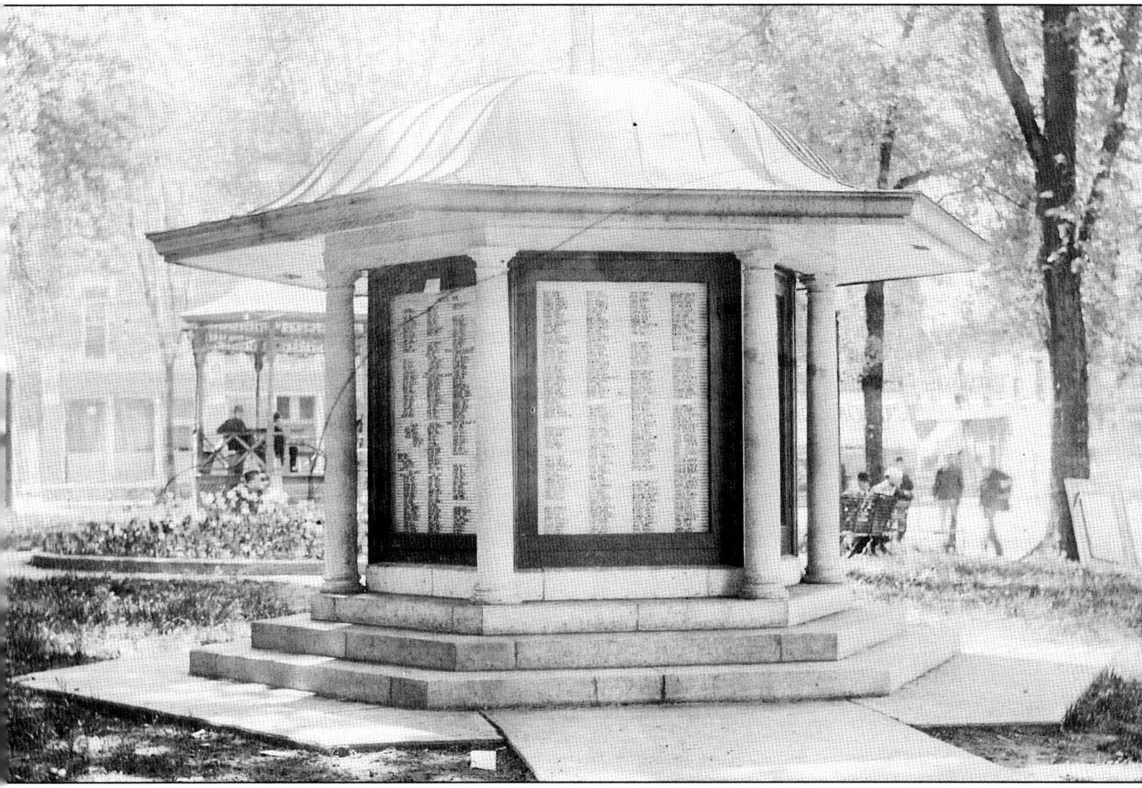

The World War I Monument in the square, *c.* 1920s. Amid "cheers for the living and tears for the dead," the men of the 112th Infantry, 28th "Iron" Division, returned to Bradford. A monument was unveiled on May 14, 1919, in honor of all the soldiers, sailors, marines, and nurses that had fought in "the Great War." Constructed to endure for all time, its hexagonal shape was uniquely suited to showcase the soldiers' names. Officer's names were placed on the western face, toward the St. James' Hotel; the other five sides contained the names of privates. All were covered with glass, and the monument was lit with electric lights at night. Today, the monument is still standing in the square, but the names have been removed.

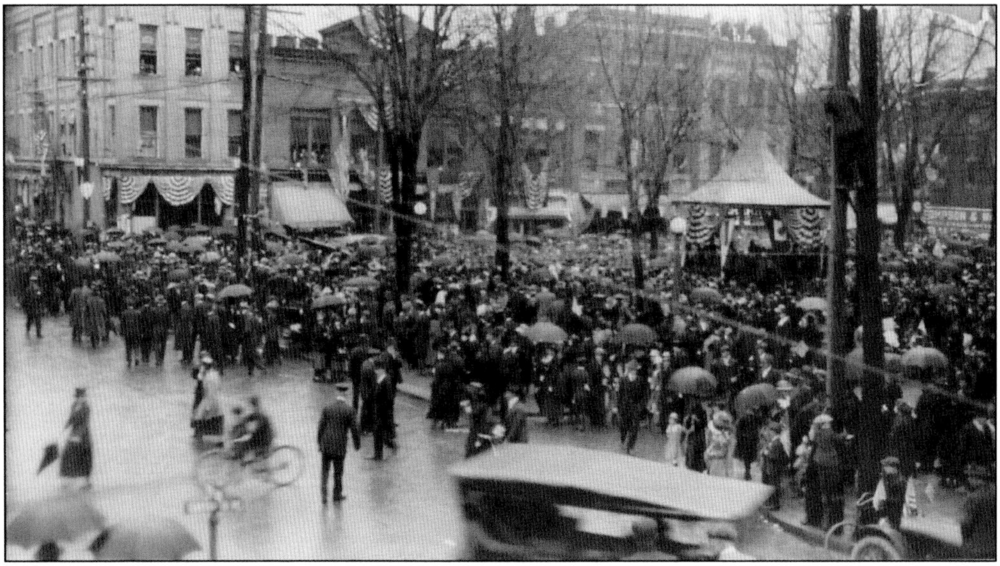

The first anniversary of Armistice Day, November 11, 1919. The cold rainy morning barely dampened the spirits of over one thousand Bradfordians in the square as veterans from past wars paraded up Main Street. Men stood on rooftops, and more than one boy climbed a telegraph pole to get a better view.

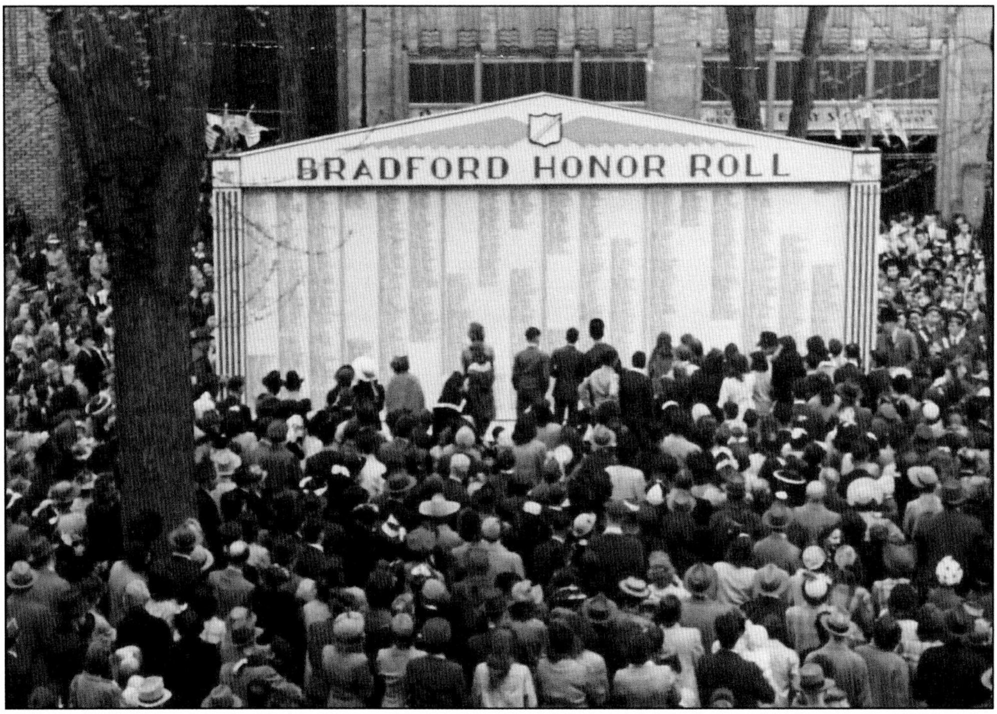

The World War II Honor Roll. Erected in the square and dedicated on May 16, 1943, this monument honored nearly three thousand Bradfordians serving in World War II. The honor roll was the gift of the Exchange Club, who raised the funds from local businesses, organizations, and private individuals. It remained standing until March 10, 1954, when it was removed due to its deteriorating condition.

Six

Industry and Business

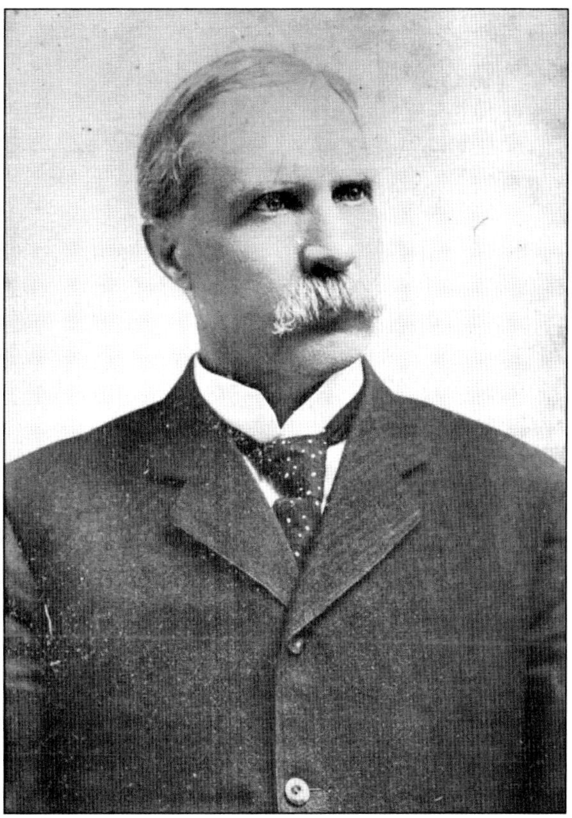

A Lewis Emery for Governor poster, 1906. Independent oil producer, Pennsylvania state representative, entrepreneur, and businessman, Emery was the champion of the oil boom in Bradford. Besides his many business interests in producing, refining, and transporting facilities, he also owned a manufacturing company, hardware store, wheat farm, gold mine, rubber plantation, and the only oxalic acid plant in the United States at the outbreak of World War I. Always active in politics, he ran for governor of Pennsylvania in 1906 on the Lincoln Republican ticket, losing by 56,000 votes. He died on November 18, 1924, at the age of eighty-five.

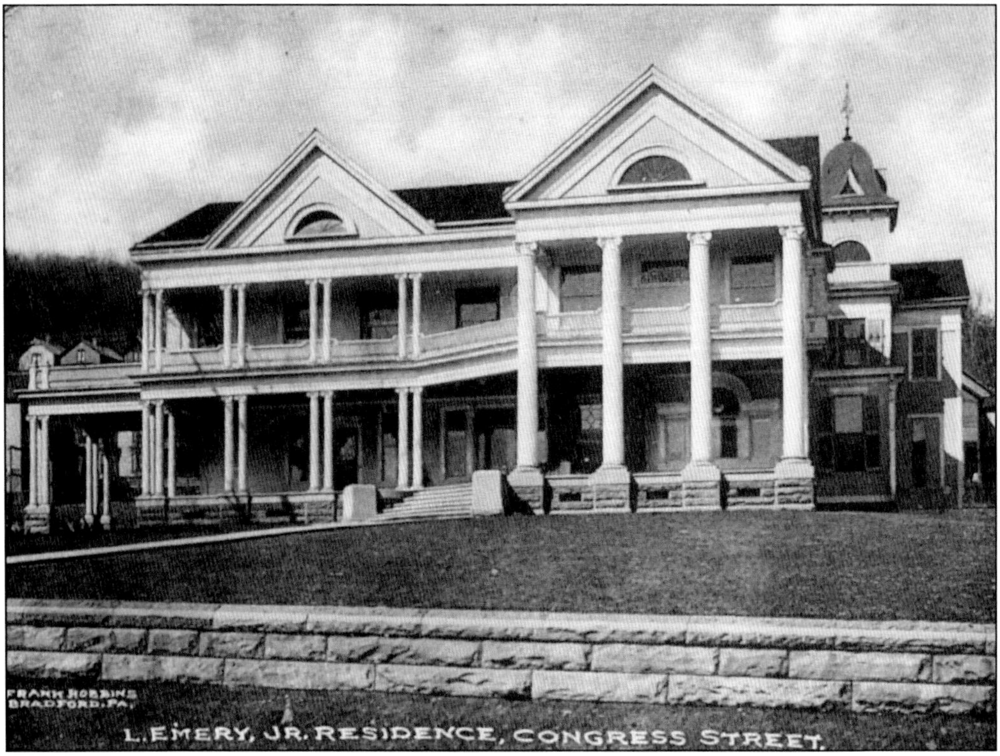

The Lewis Emery estate, Congress Street, 1906. Emery built this spacious mansion in 1890.

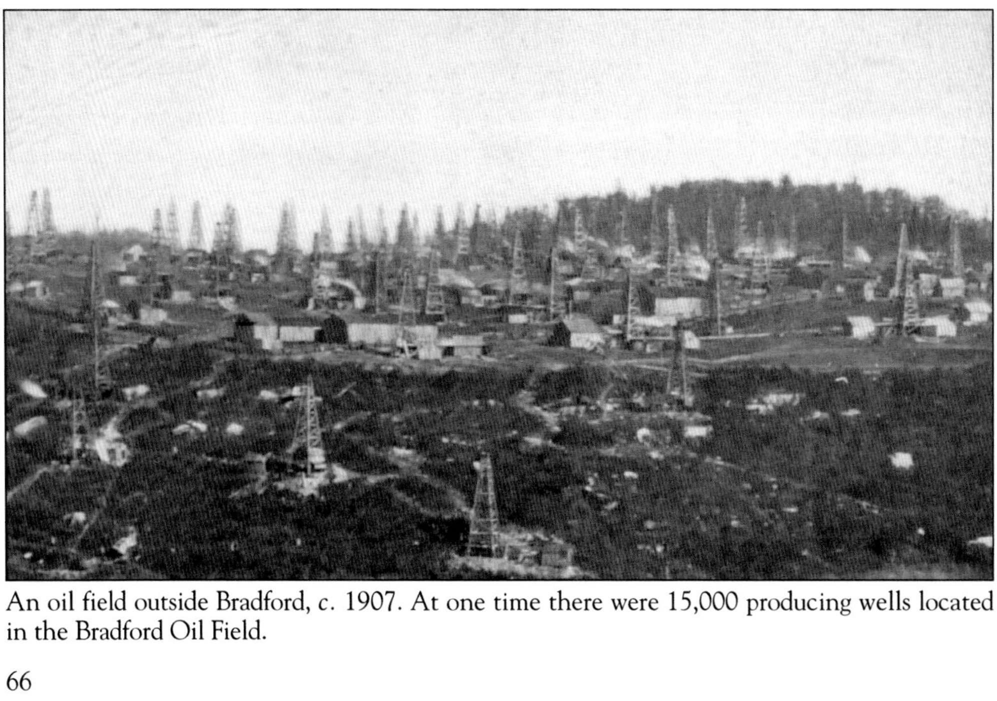

An oil field outside Bradford, *c.* 1907. At one time there were 15,000 producing wells located in the Bradford Oil Field.

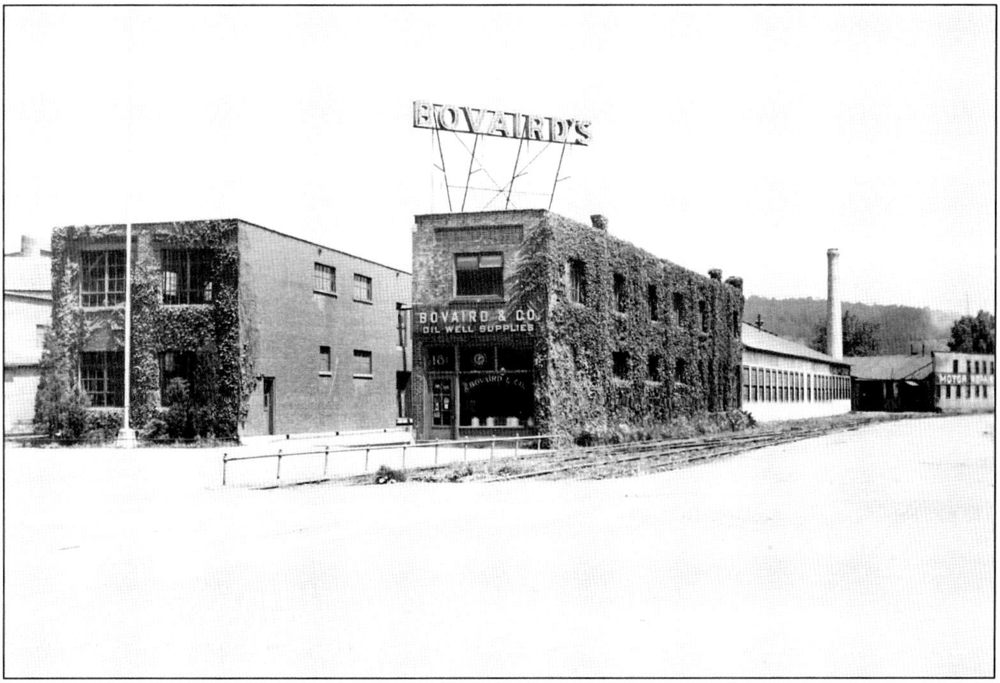

Bovairds & Company. Established in 1895, it supplied the necessary tools and equipment needed in the oil fields. This company is still in existence today.

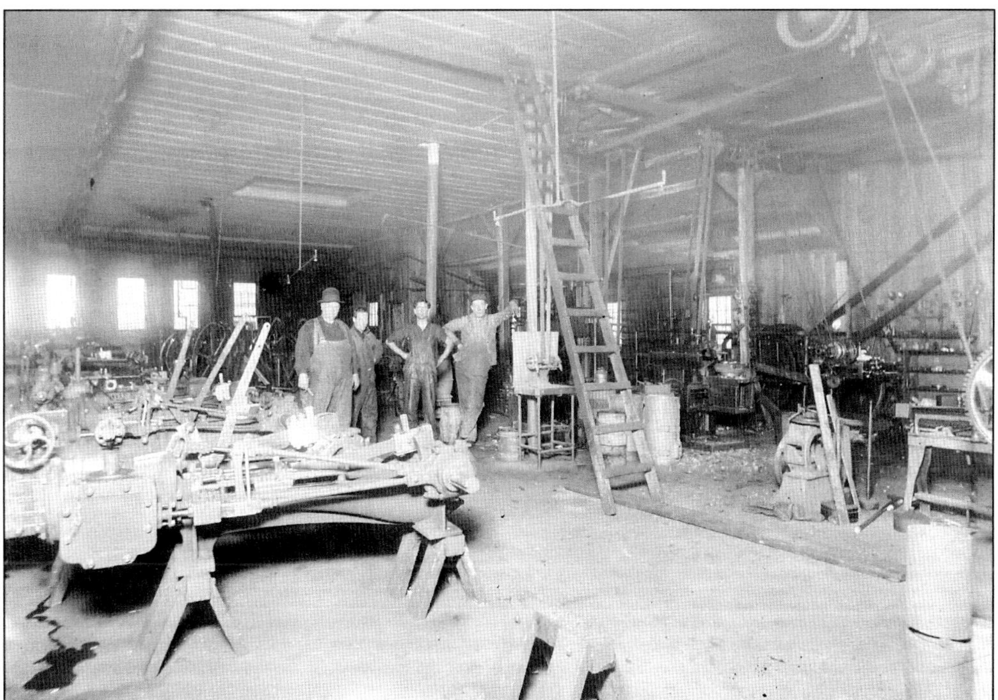

An interior view of the Bovaird & Seyfang Company, Davis Street, *c.* 1900.

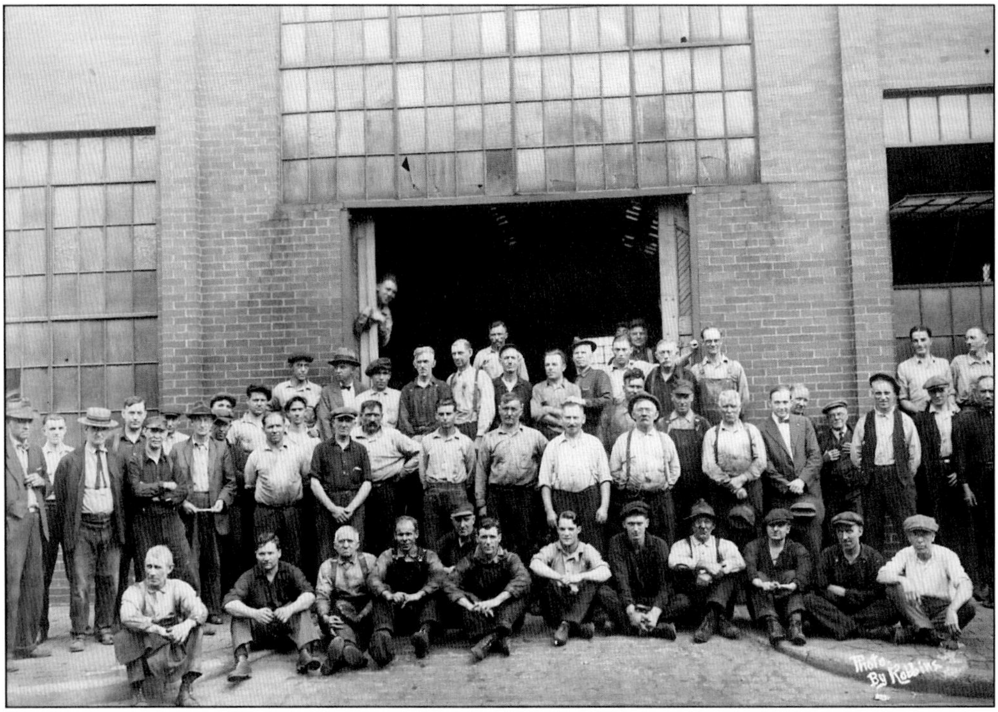

Employees of Bovaird & Seyfang, c. 1925.

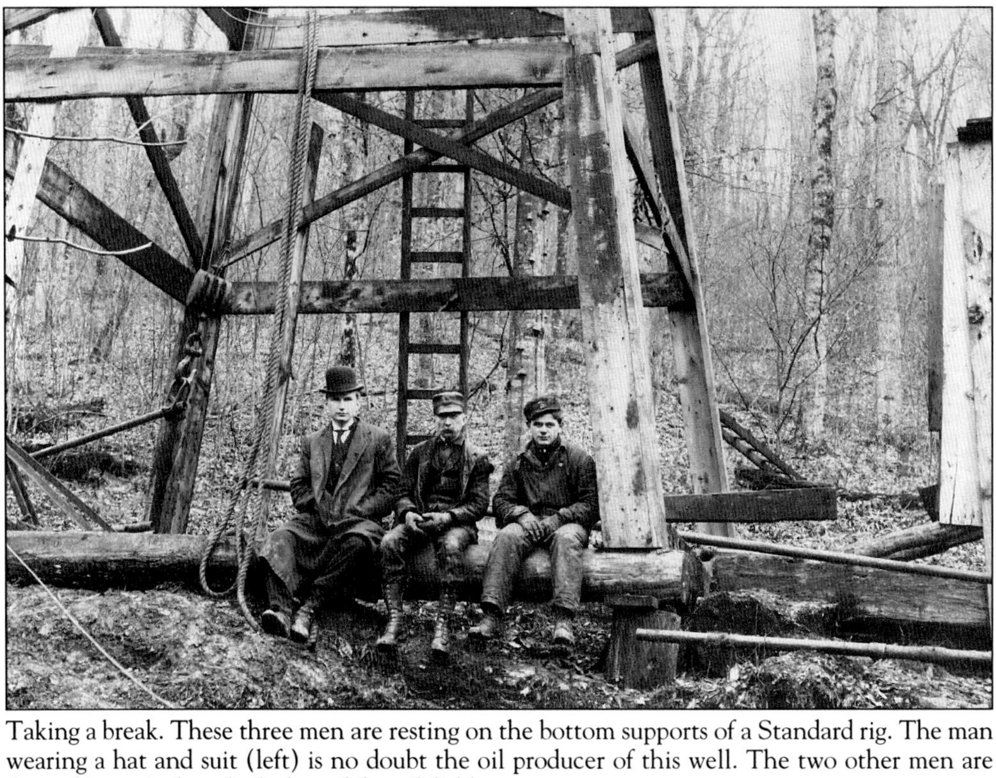

Taking a break. These three men are resting on the bottom supports of a Standard rig. The man wearing a hat and suit (left) is no doubt the oil producer of this well. The two other men are dressed in typical work clothes of the oil field.

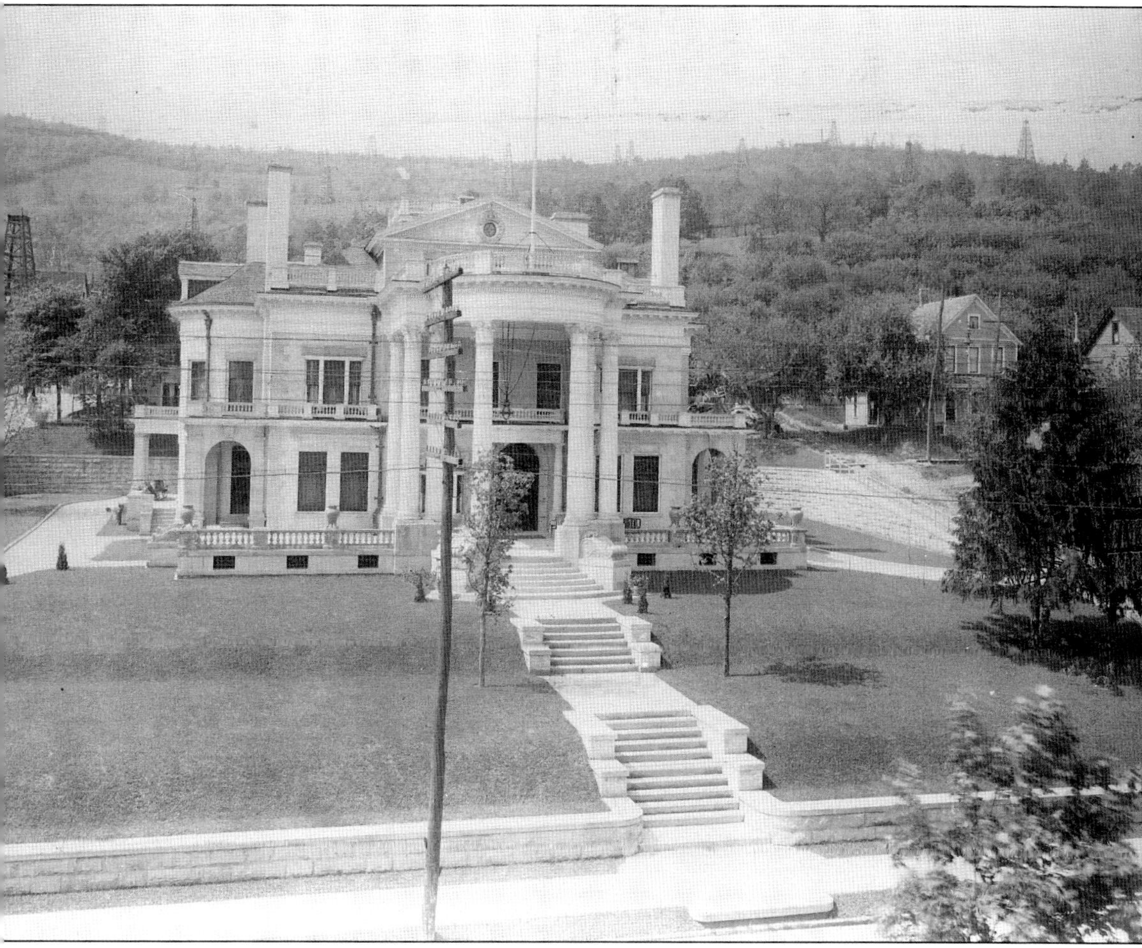

The Dresser mansion, 1905. Built by Solomon R. Dresser in 1903 and patterned after the Michigan Pavilion (which he had visited at the Pan American exposition in Buffalo), it boasted impressive architecture and an exquisite interior design. Regretfully, Dresser would live for only four years after its construction. The Dresser mansion itself was destroyed by fire on February 28, 1986.

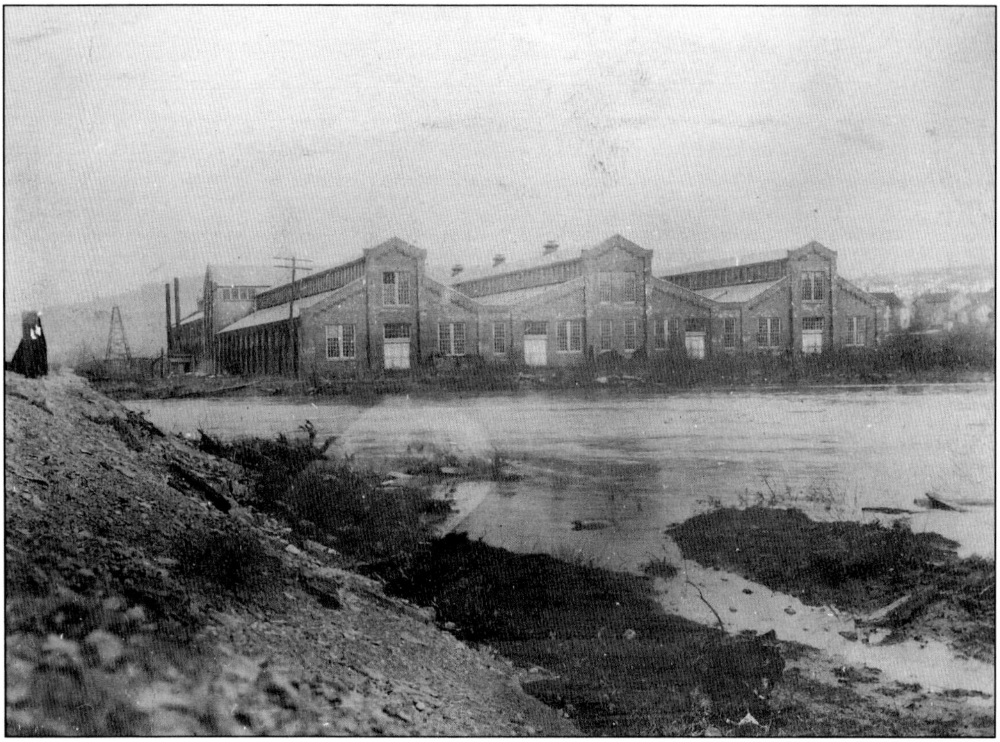

The Dresser Manufacturing Company. Organized in the 1880s by Solomon R. Dresser, it manufactured specialties for oil and gas wells and lines. Dresser's inventions for the oil industry gained him a fortune and made the company known worldwide.

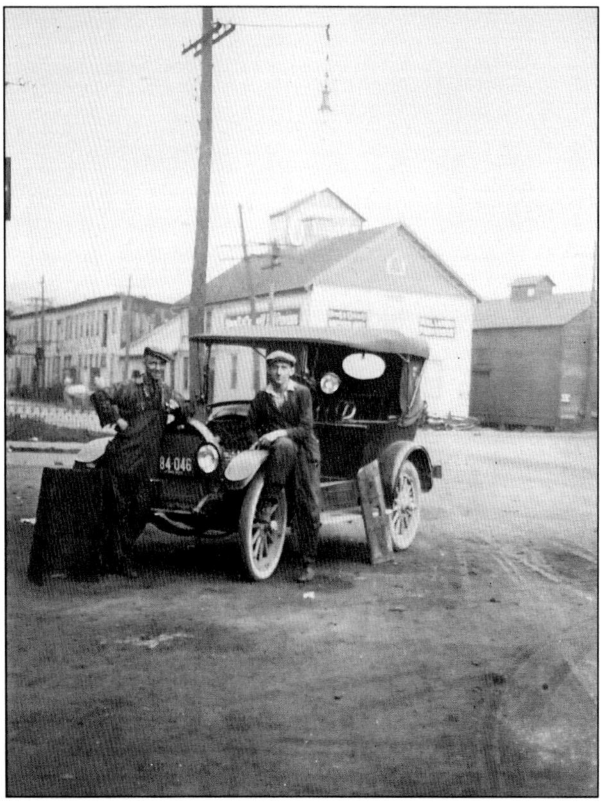

John Beatty and Allan Charles, employees of the Crescent Garage & Machine Shop, Webster Street, 1929. The long, low building in the rear is the Locke Machine shop. The building on the corner of Elm and Webster Streets (behind the automobile) is the Swift Packing house.

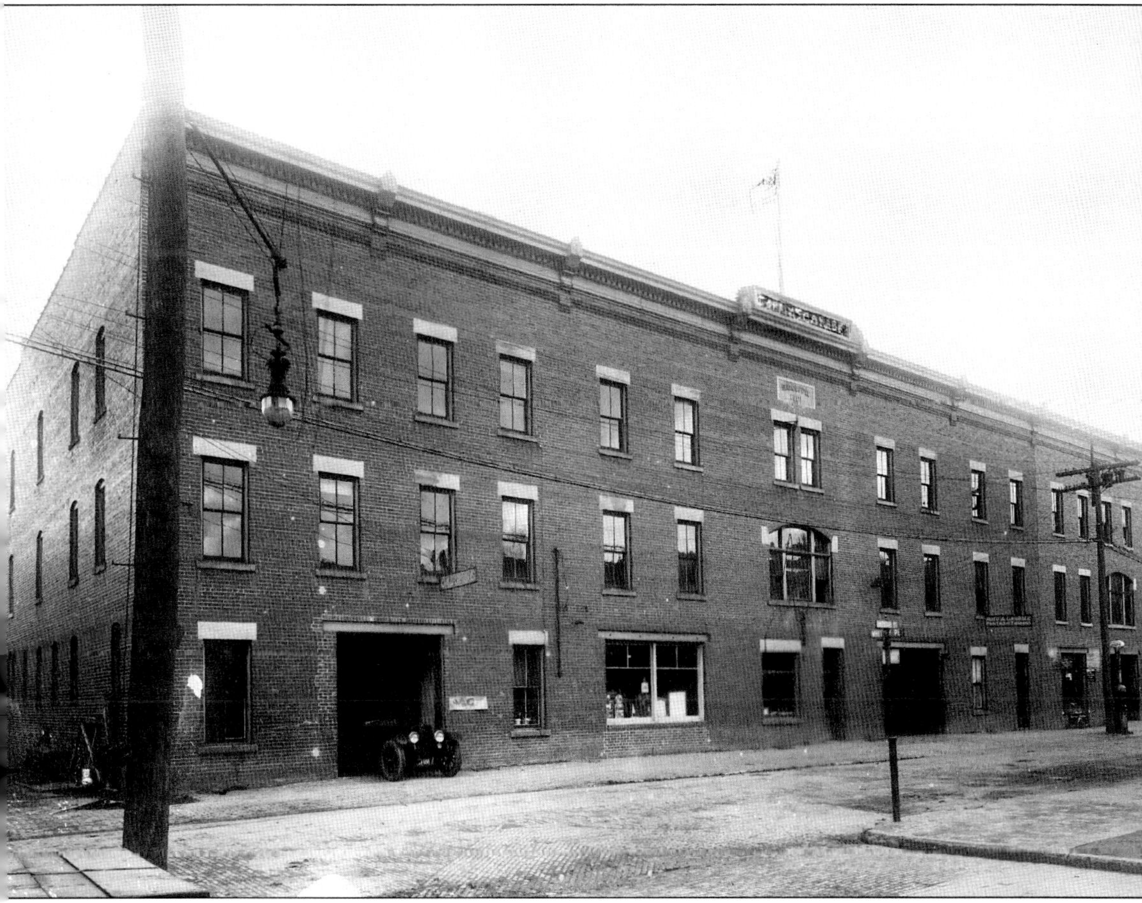

The Star Garage Company, formerly Coffin's Garage, *c.* 1910. A big, three-story building on Barbour Street, it burned in a disastrous fire on November 6, 1924. The garage was one of the largest in this part of Pennsylvania. The fire caused $350,000 in damage, and destroyed over two hundred cars. Exploding gasoline tanks throughout the building hampered the fire fighters; despite this, another one hundred cars, located on the ground floor, and horses kept in the building by the American Glycerin Company were saved. All the firemen in the city turned out, as well as over one thousand spectators. The *Bradford Era* called it "Bradford's Most Destructive Blaze in Years."

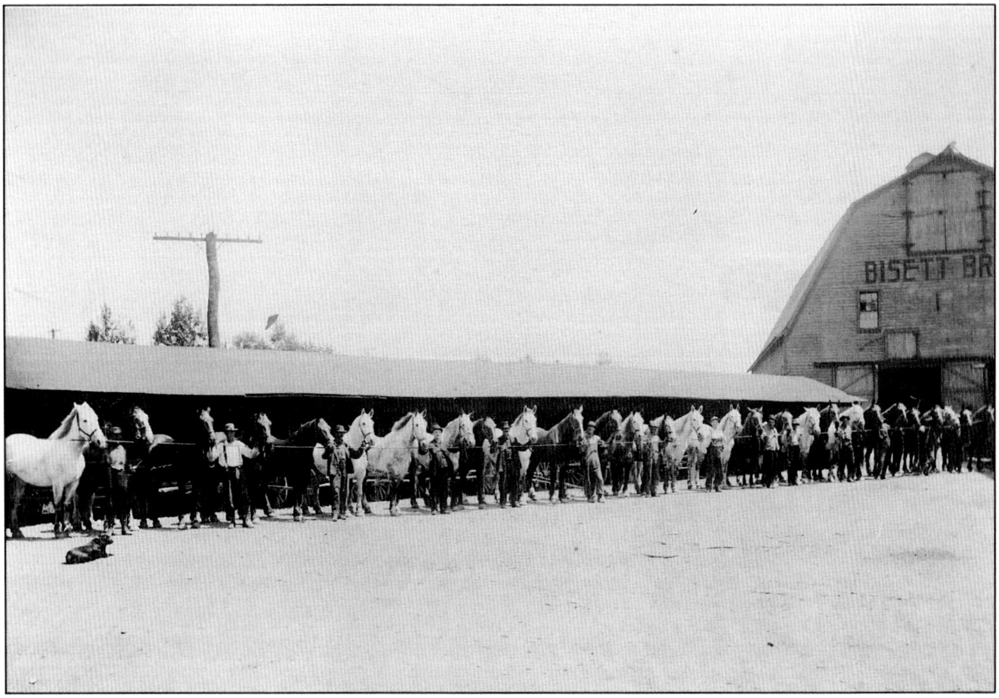

Bissett Brothers' horse teams, *c.* 1910. Their motto was "Ten Trucks and 20 Teams All Pulling for Bradford." These horse sheds and barn were located behind Bovaird & Co. along the creek.

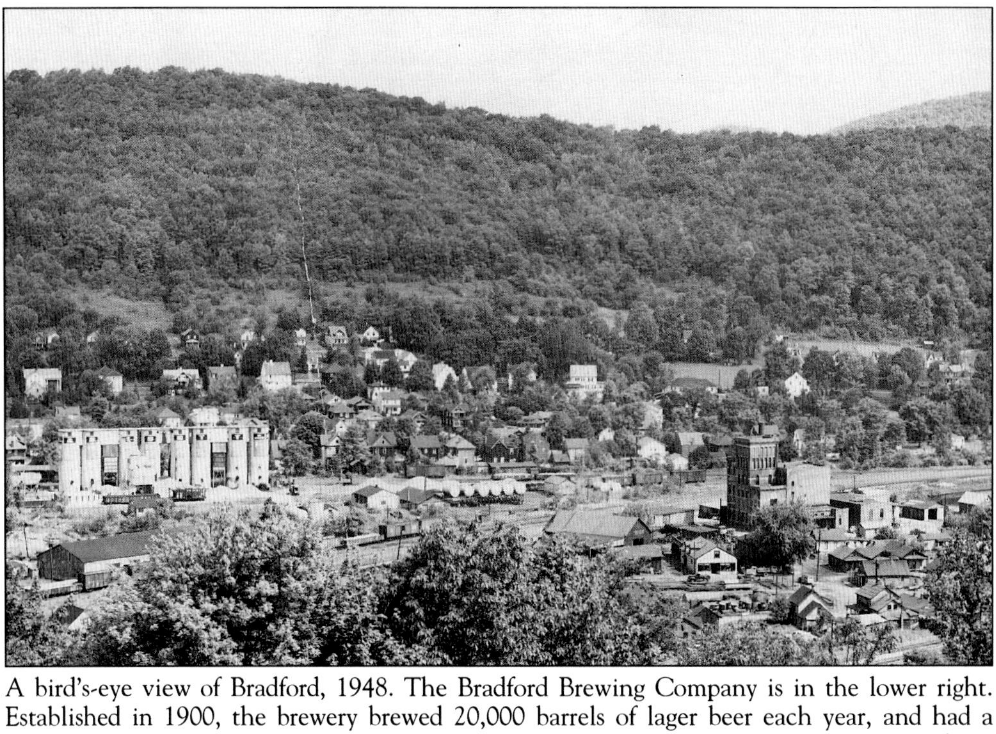

A bird's-eye view of Bradford, 1948. The Bradford Brewing Company is in the lower right. Established in 1900, the brewery brewed 20,000 barrels of lager beer each year, and had a storage capacity inside the plant of 5,000 barrels. The towers at left belong to Bissett Brothers, and contain sand, gravel, and cement.

The McCourt Label Cabinet Co. Building, *c.* 1940s. Incorporated one hundred years ago, the major stockholders were influential men of the day, including William Barnsdall Jr., T.N. Barnsdall II, Newton W. McCourt, George McAllister, Matthias Flaherty, and George Fagnan. Between 1909 and 1911 it moved its operations to this building, the site of the former Maple Grove Ice Company.

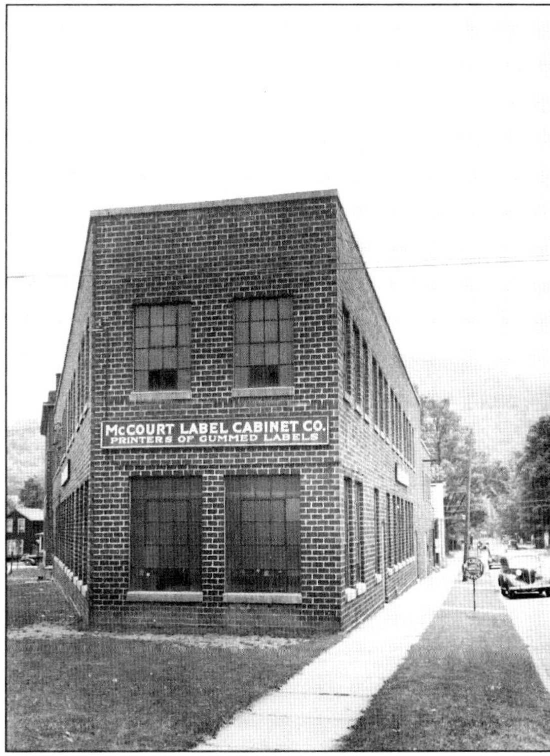

An interior view of the McCourt Label Cabinet Company, *c.* 1914. The company began in 1896, printing druggists labels. In 1904 it was issued a patent on a innovative druggist's cabinet that could store a wide variety of labels and simplified their selection. Here, employees pause in the midst of a busy printing run.

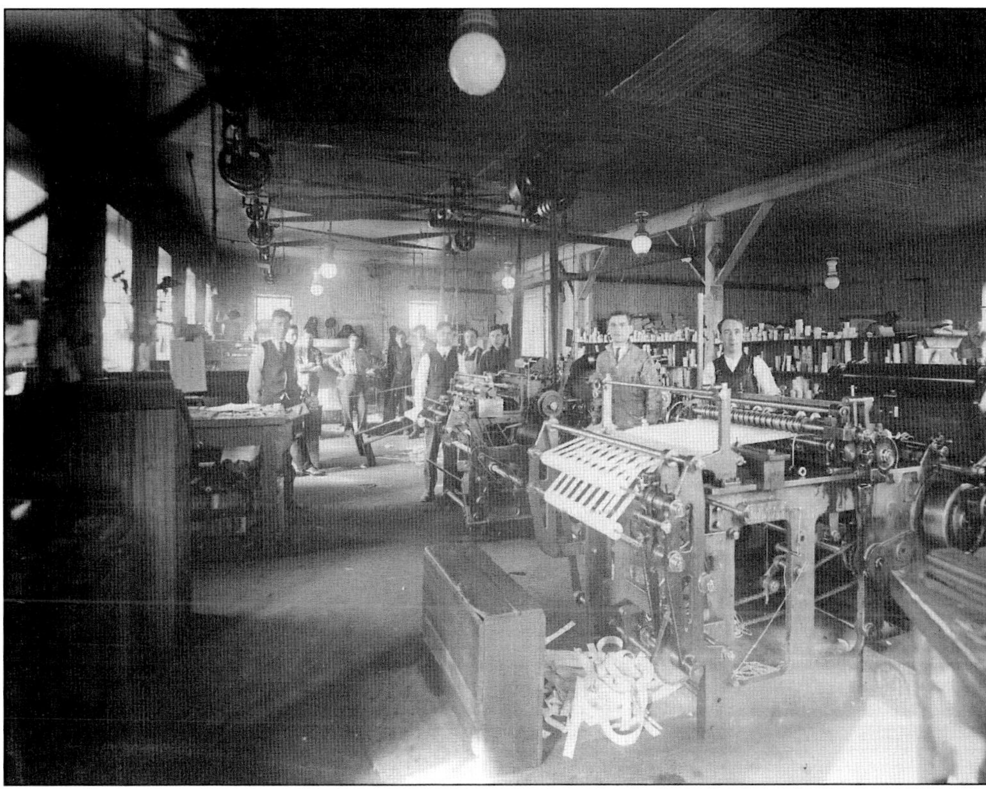

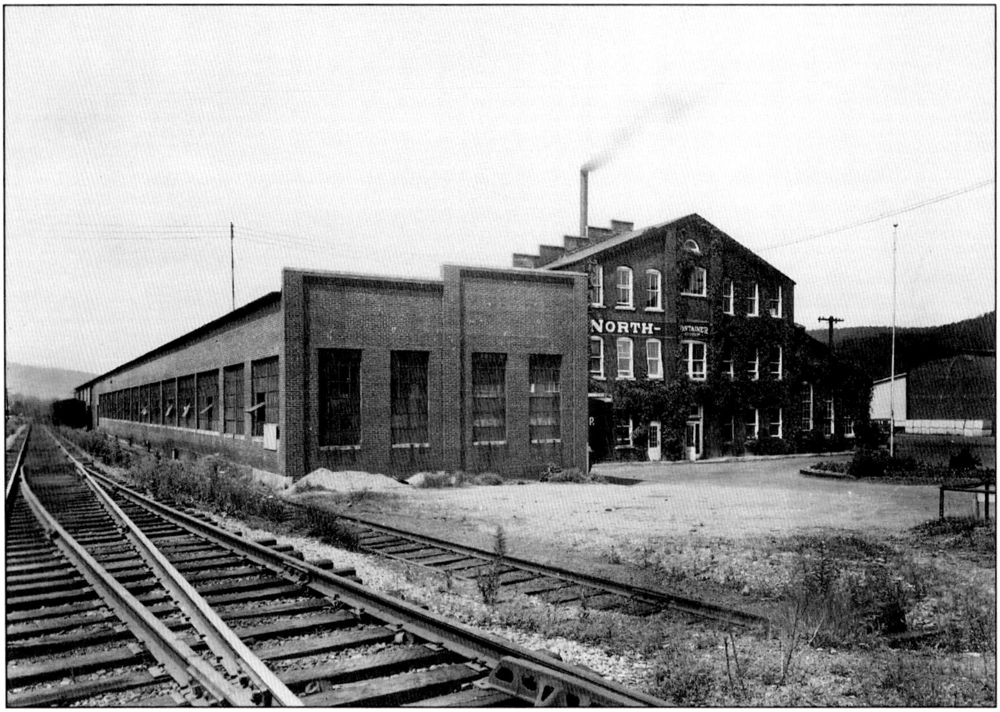

The Northeastern Container Corp., South Bradford, *c.* 1935. There has been a box factory operating in Bradford for over sixty years, albeit under different names. This brick building was originally built in 1897, and is now currently part of the Georgia Pacific manufacturing complex.

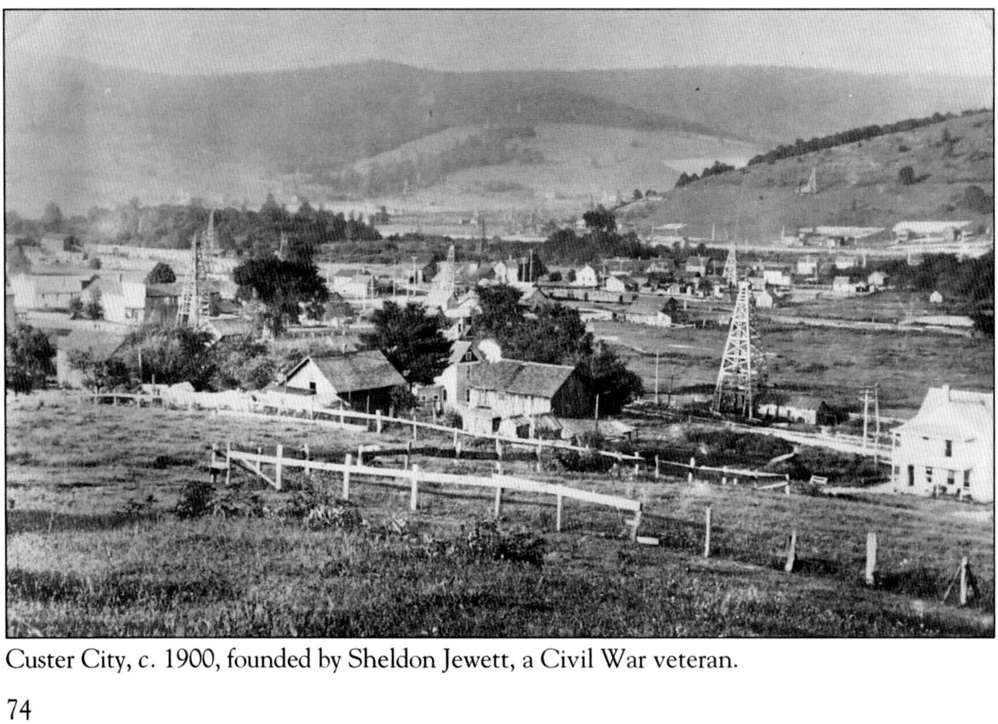

Custer City, *c.* 1900, founded by Sheldon Jewett, a Civil War veteran.

Telephone operators at the Bell Telephone Office on Corydon Street, *c*. 1910. Bradford has had telephone service since 1879.

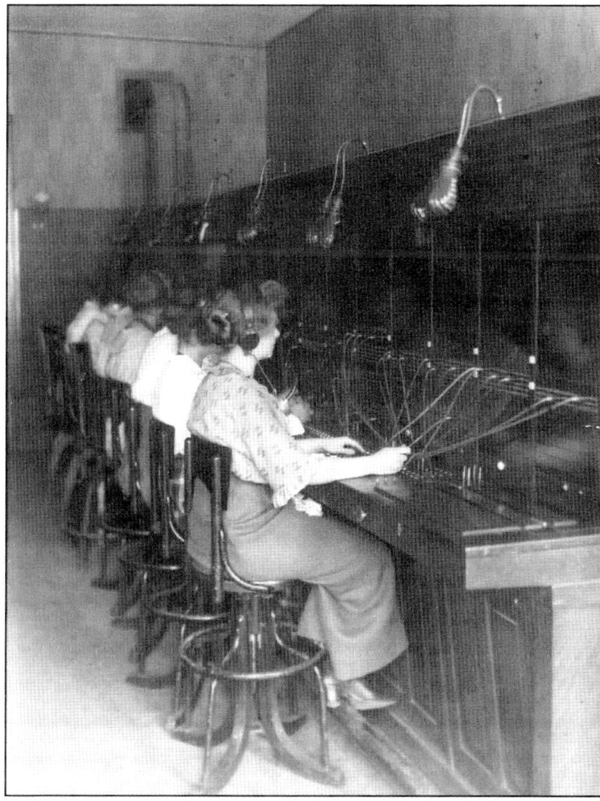

Office workers, 1914. Before the days of computers, fax machines, word processors, and copy machines, there existed the everyday method of office work. These men were busy with bookkeeping and accounts. The machines are adding machines.

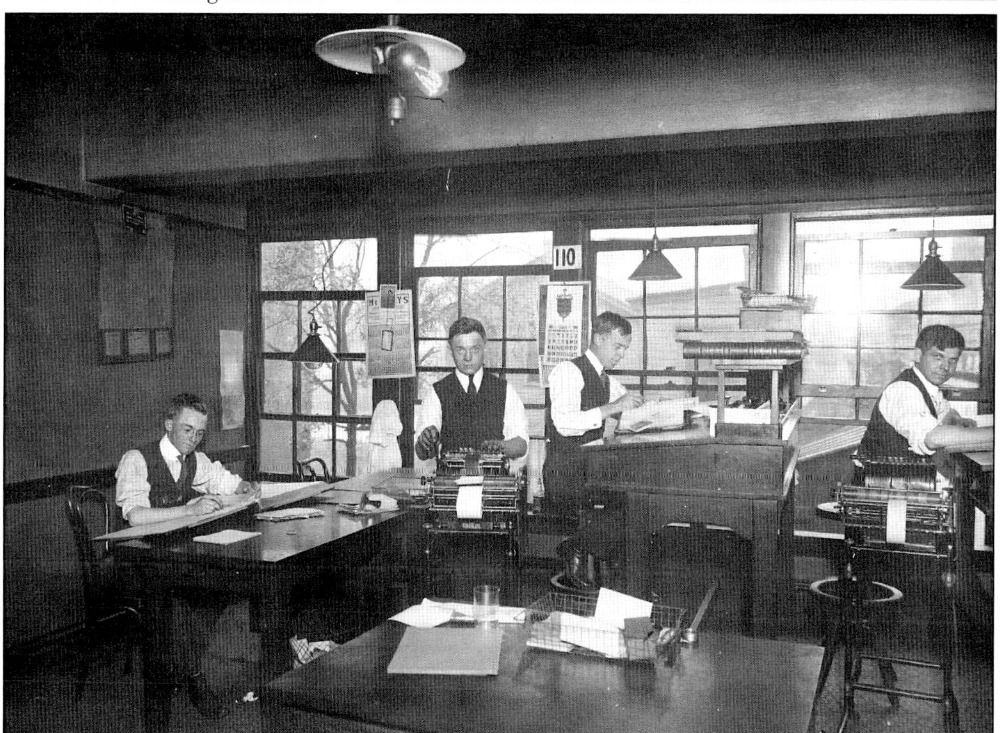

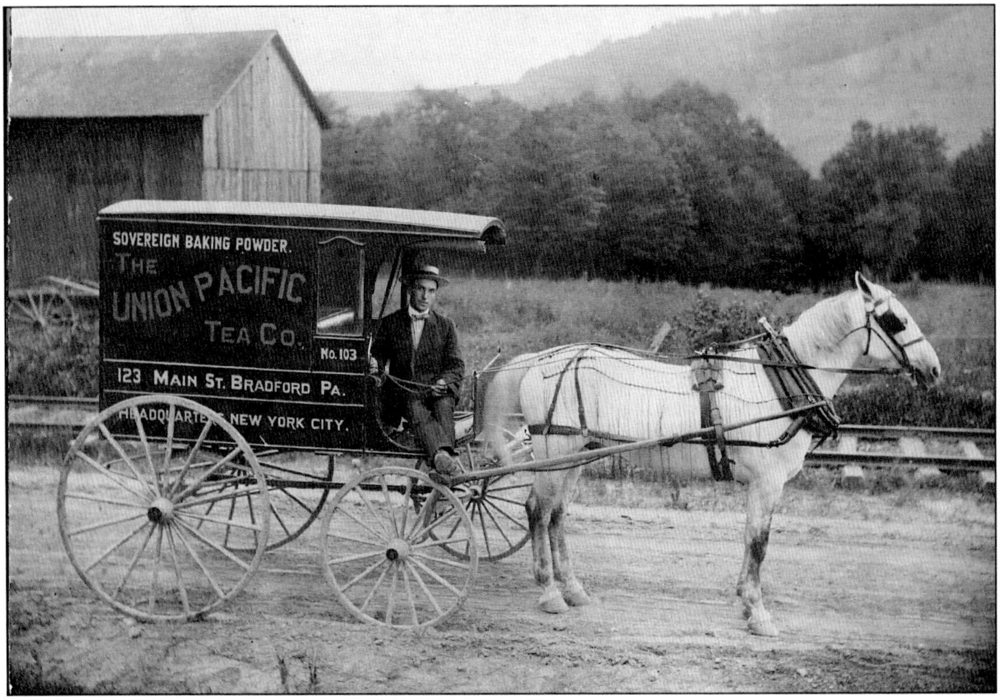

A Union Pacific Tea Company delivery wagon, 1900.

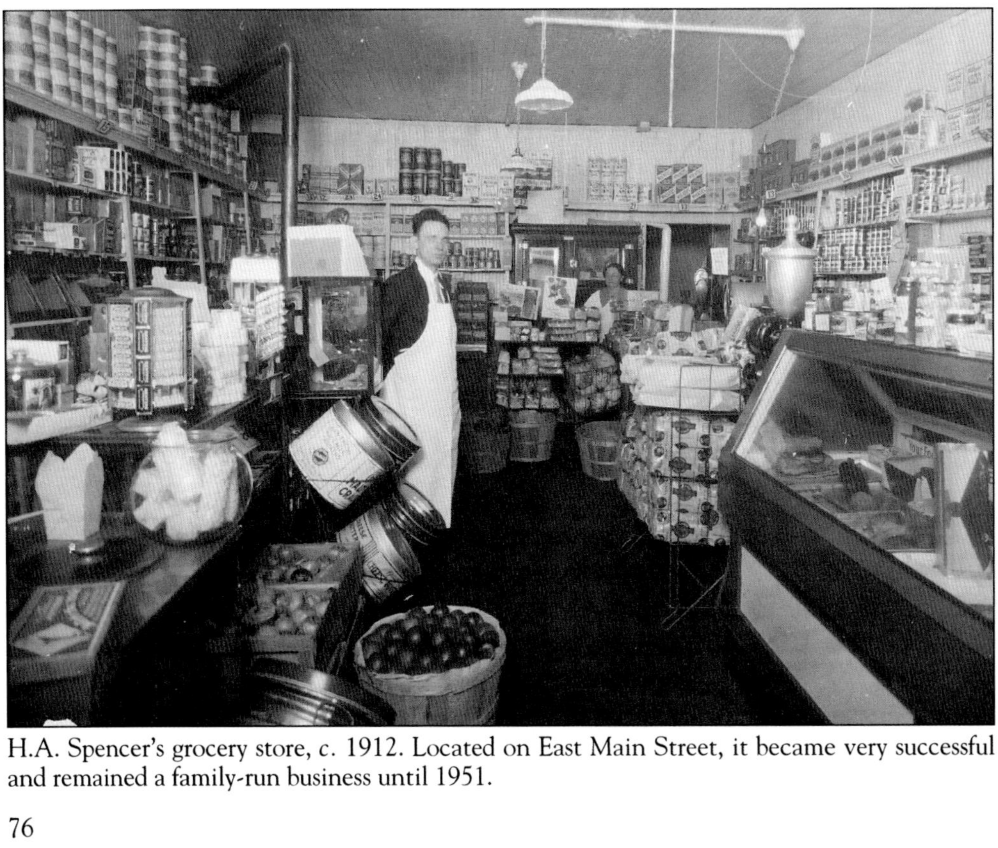

H.A. Spencer's grocery store, *c.* 1912. Located on East Main Street, it became very successful and remained a family-run business until 1951.

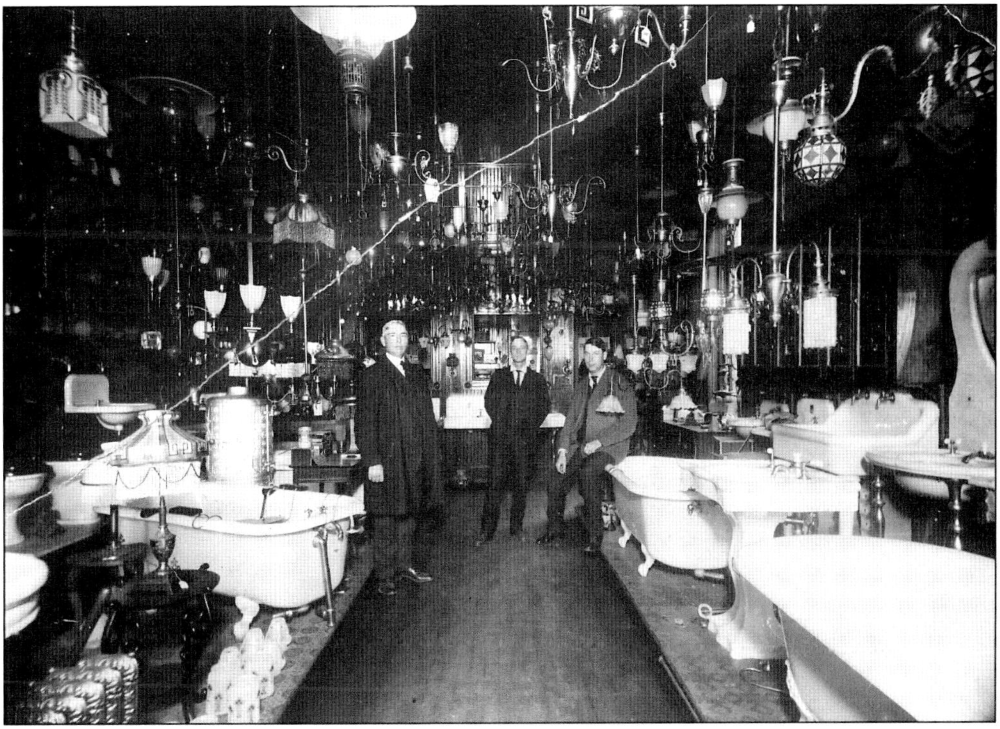

An interior view of A.D. Burns Plumbing Supply at 16 Main Street on the square, 1910. Men pictured are, from left to right, Andrew D. Burns, Edgar Rhone, and Oscar J. Peart. Burns served as captain of Bradford's Company C during the Spanish-American War in 1898.

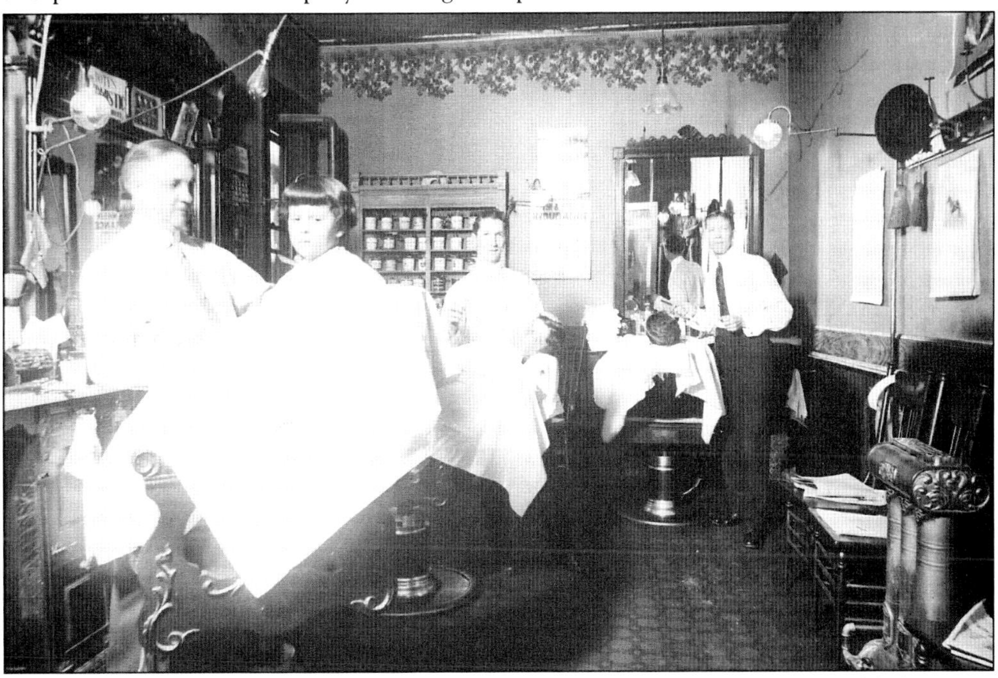

Shave and a haircut, two bits. Coke Newman, the barber in front cutting the child's hair, was the owner of this busy barber shop in 1913. Jim Lackey is the barber at the rear right.

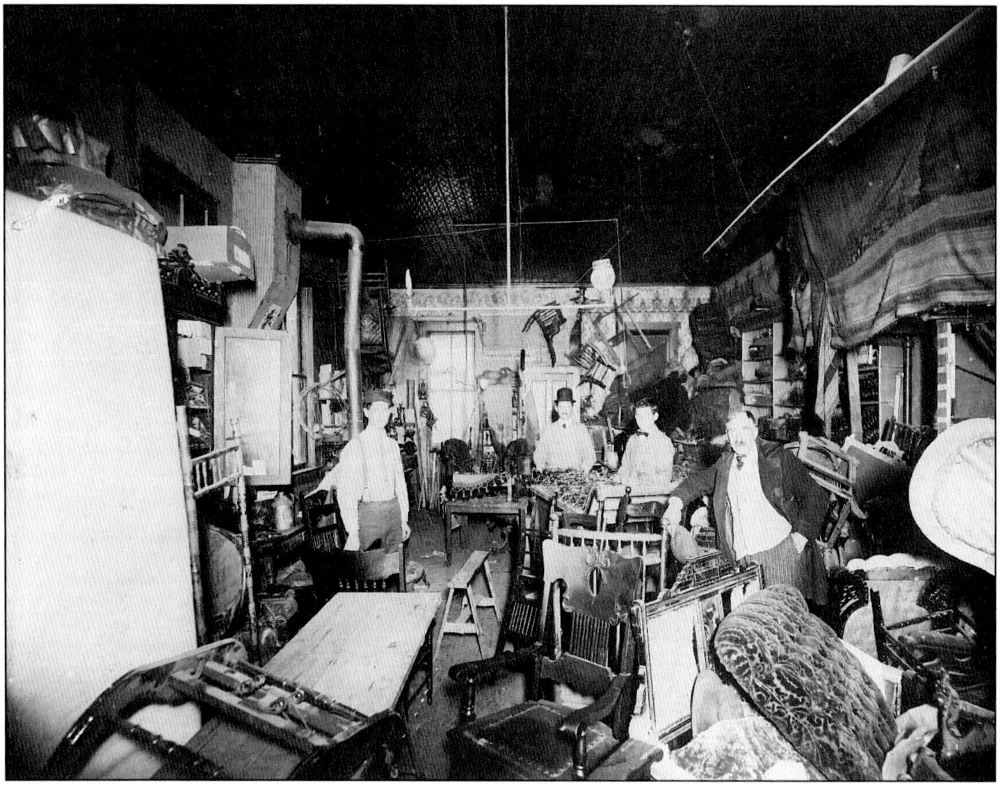

A second-hand store at the corner of Chambers and East Corydon Streets. Such junk stores provided a valuable source of used goods in the days before garage sales!

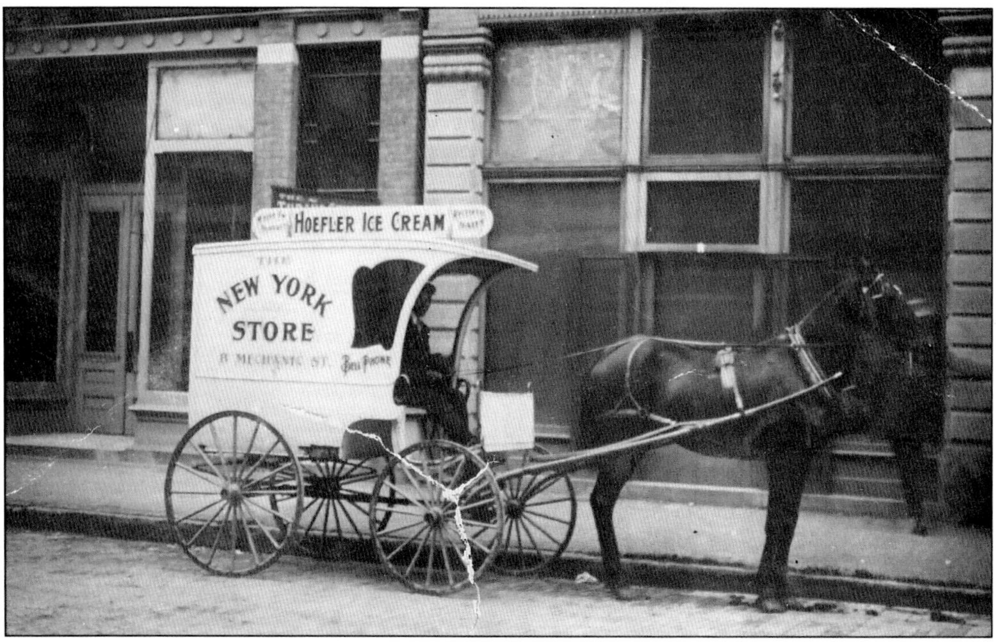

The New York Store delivery wagon, 1911. Owned by "Patsy" Tito, the confectionary store was located at 8 Mechanic Street.

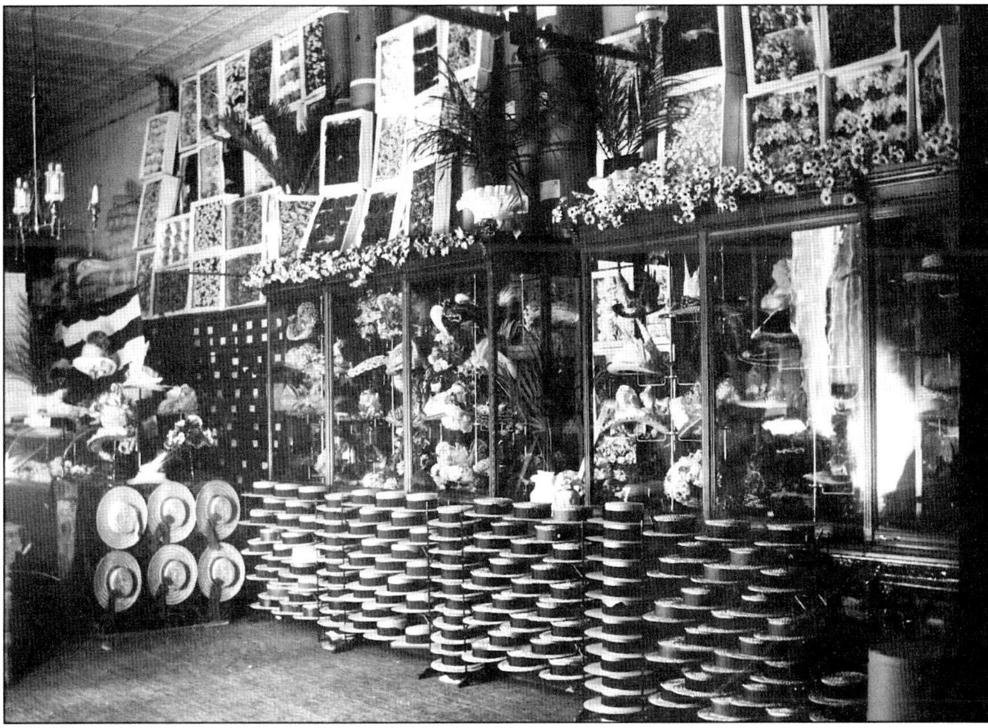

An interior view of R.B. Johnston's store, 51 Main Street. Hats of all types, including these stacks of "boaters" and ladies hats, made Johnston's store a popular shop.

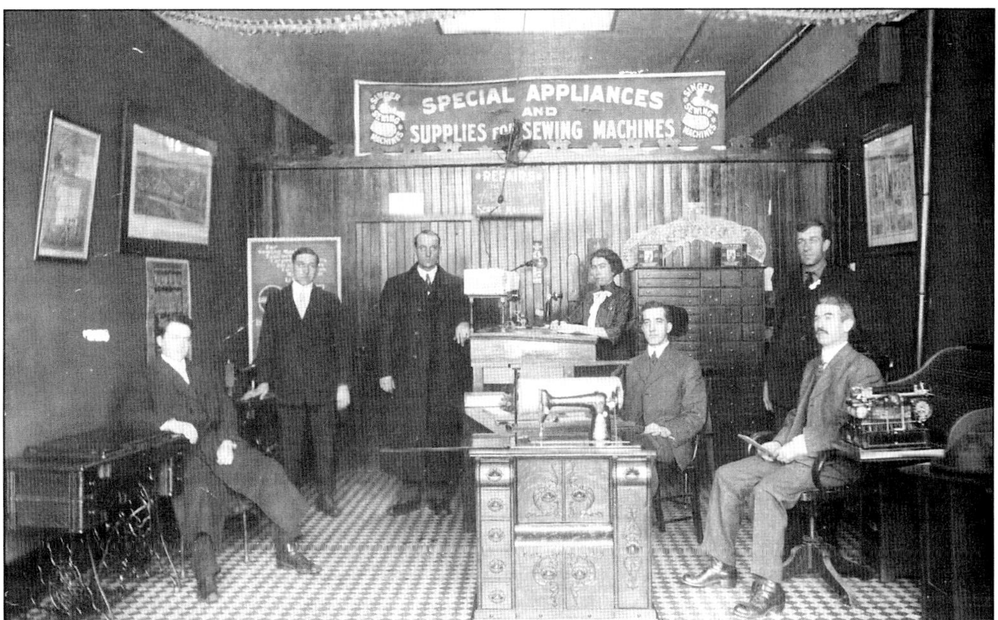

The Singer Sewing Machine Company, 1903. Located on Congress Street until 1913, it sold the latest innovations in sewing machines. Most women could sew, but with the increased popularity of mail-order catalogs such as Montgomery Ward, fewer clothes were being handmade.

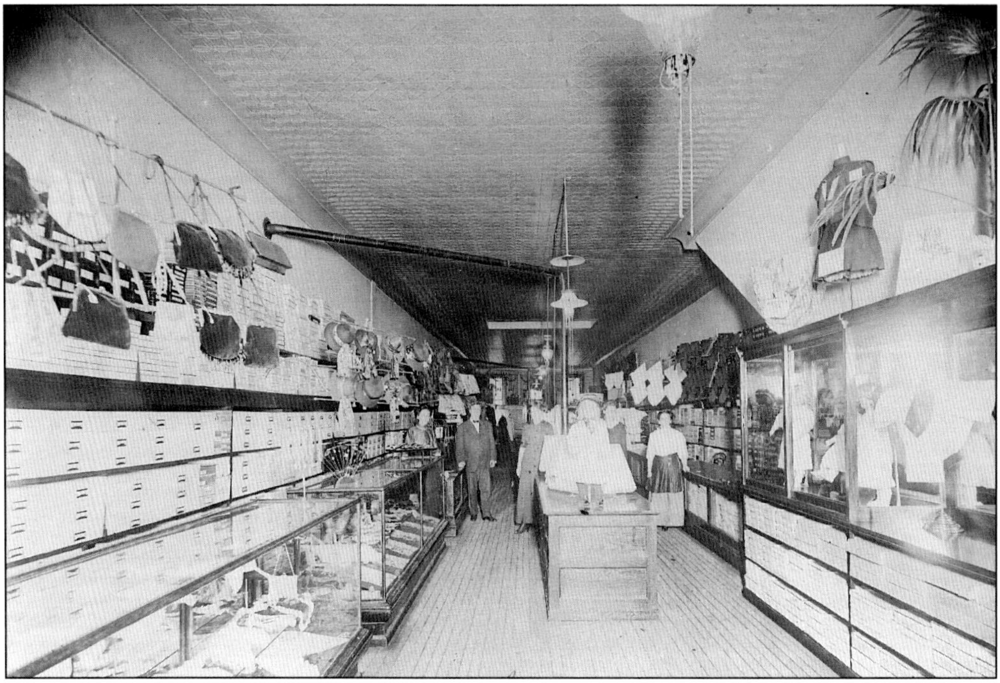

An interior view of Archie Cohan's Store, *c.* 1910.

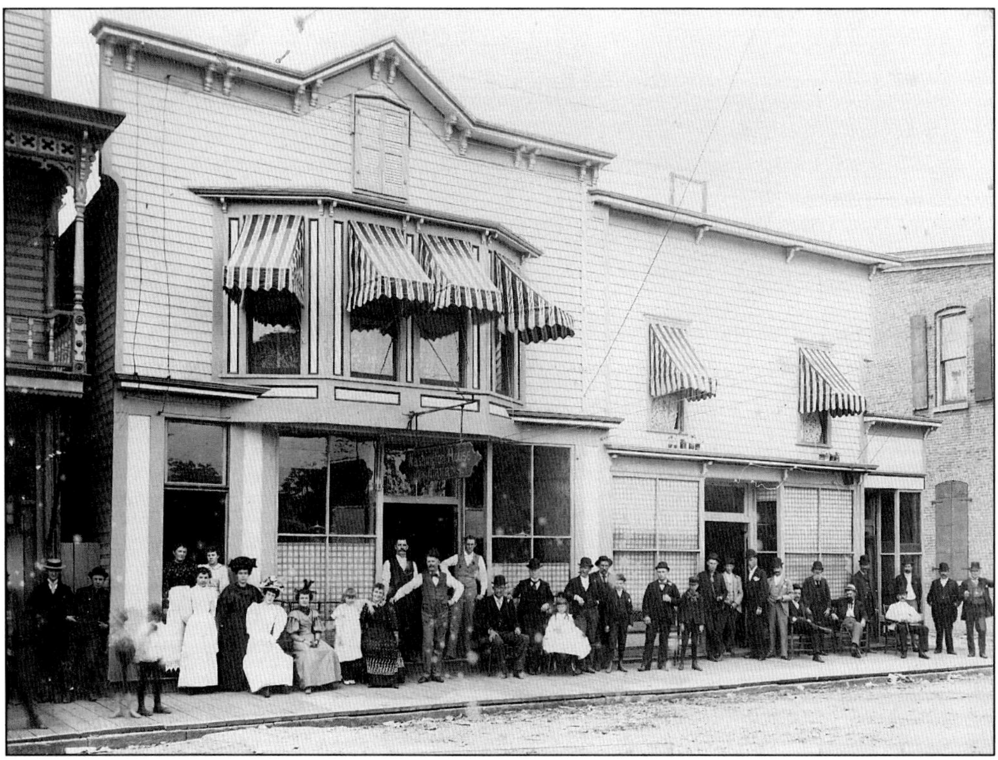

The Washington House, Webster Street. Its close proximity to the railroad stations made this a popular stop for weary travelers.

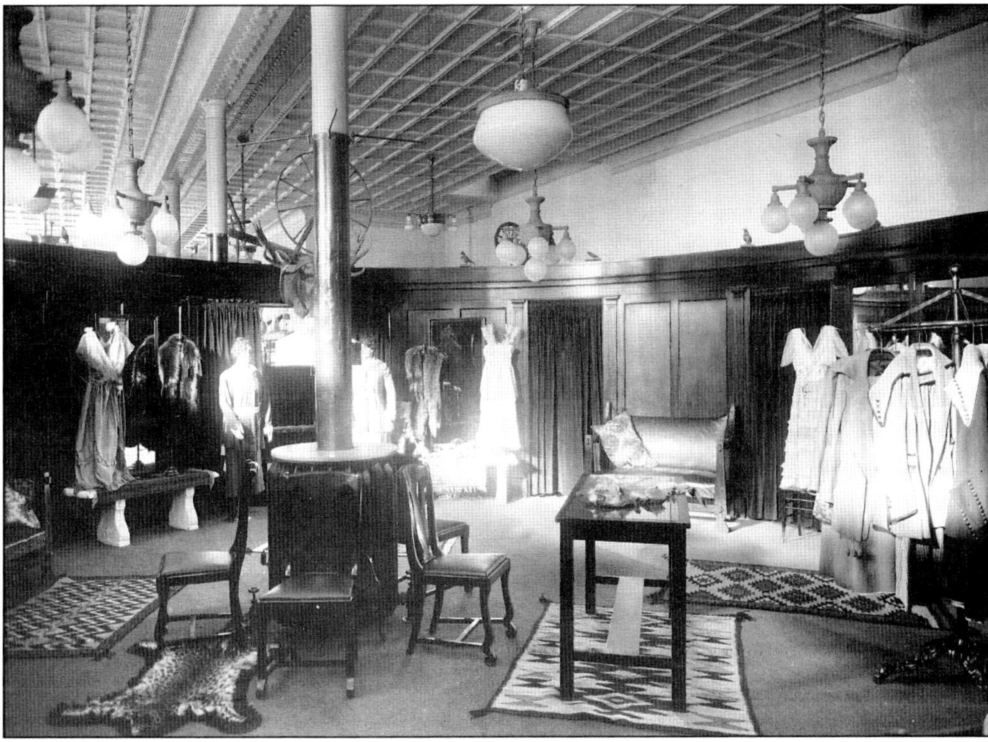

The interior of Auerhaim's Department Store, 1890. This building has been renovated and is currently the Forest Oil Building on Main Street.

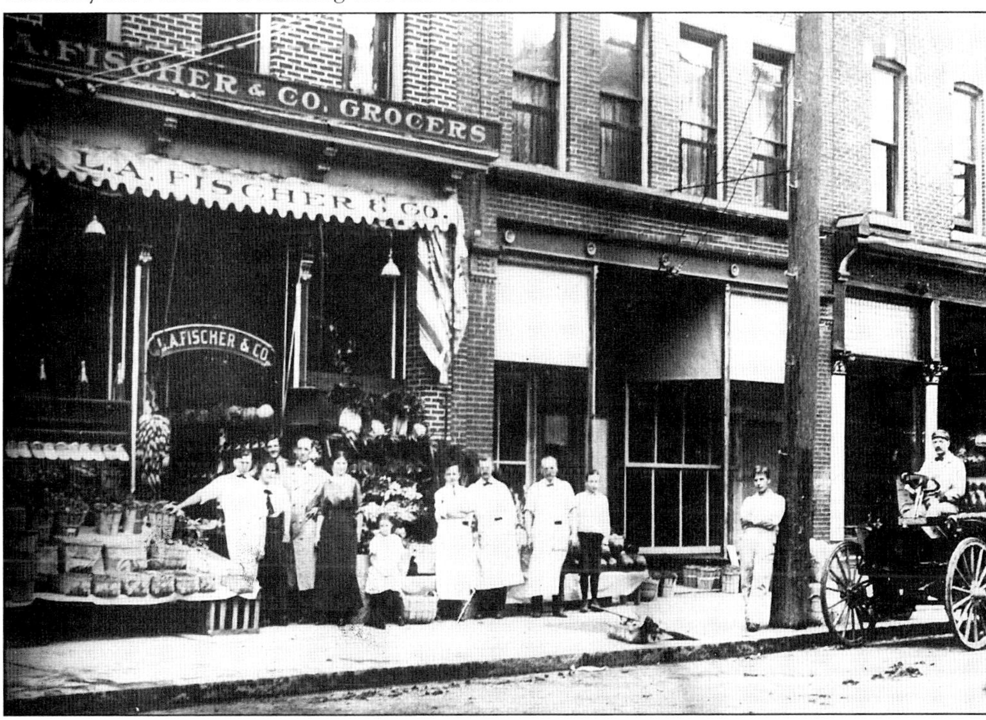

L.A. Fischer & Co., Grocers, 1910, at 106 Main Street.

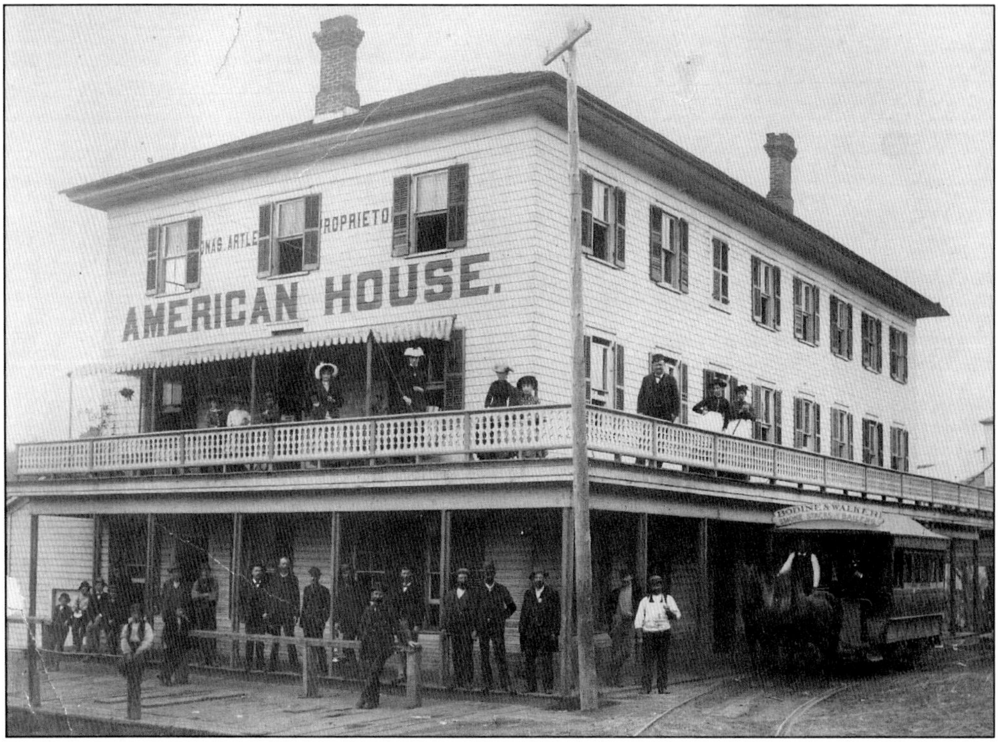

The American House, *c.* 1885. It was located on the corner of East Main Street and Kendall Avenue, an area then known as Tarport. Note the horse-drawn trolley to the right of the building. A well-known hotel and tavern, it was torn down in the early 1940s.

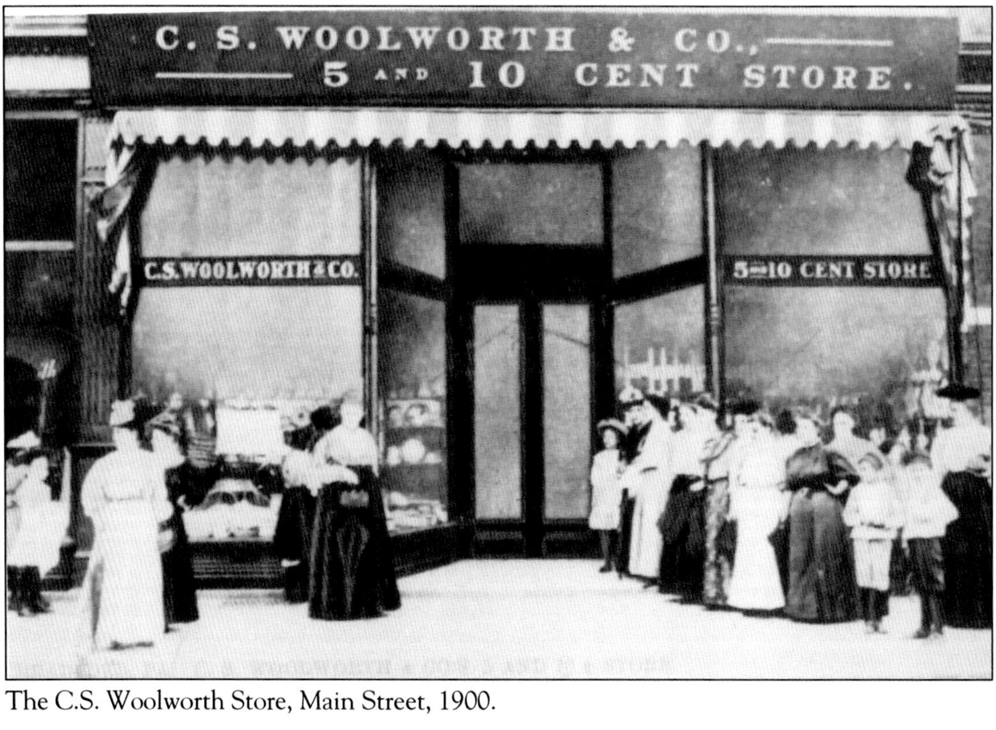

The C.S. Woolworth Store, Main Street, 1900.

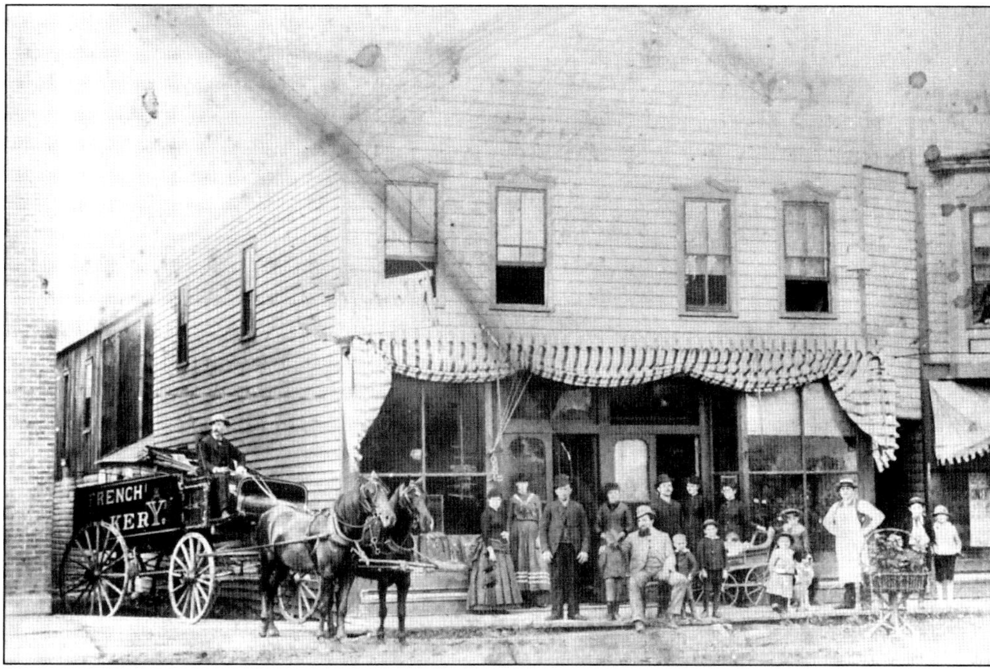

The Herbig Bakery, 45 East Corydon Street, 1900. Believed to be the oldest frame building in the city still in commercial use, it is currently the headquarters of the Bradford Landmark Society. It began as a French bakery in 1879. Sold by Celeste Gaul to Gustav Herbig in the 1890s, it remained in the Herbig family until the 1970s. At that time Virginia Loveland Miles, Herbig's granddaughter, donated the building to the Landmark Society. Gus Herbig is the man seated in front; the man at right with the white apron is Jacob Heckel, the butcher from next door.

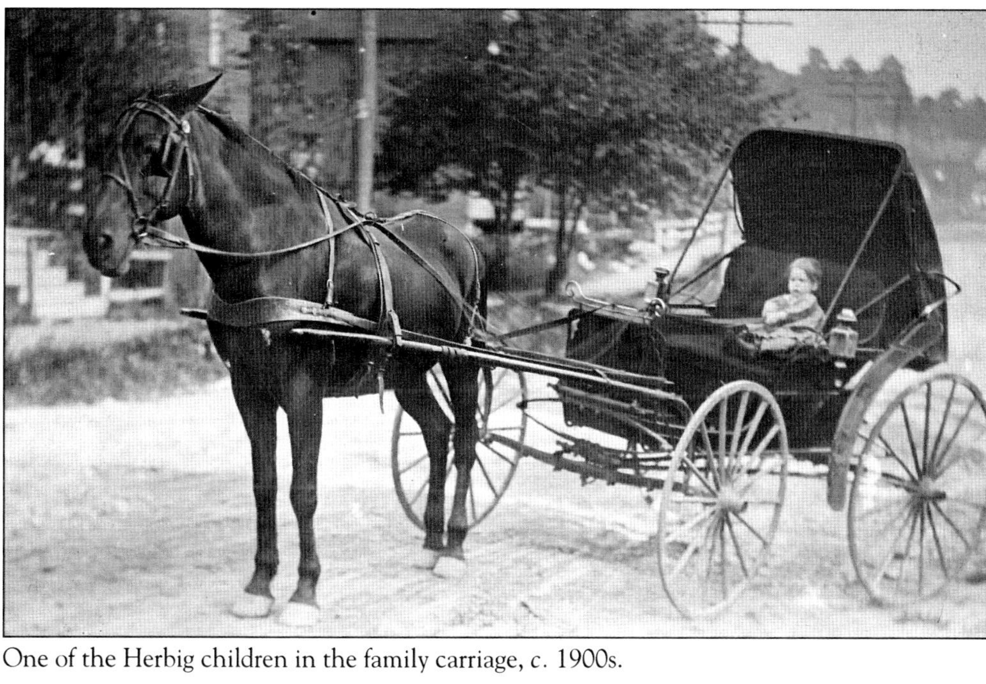

One of the Herbig children in the family carriage, c. 1900s.

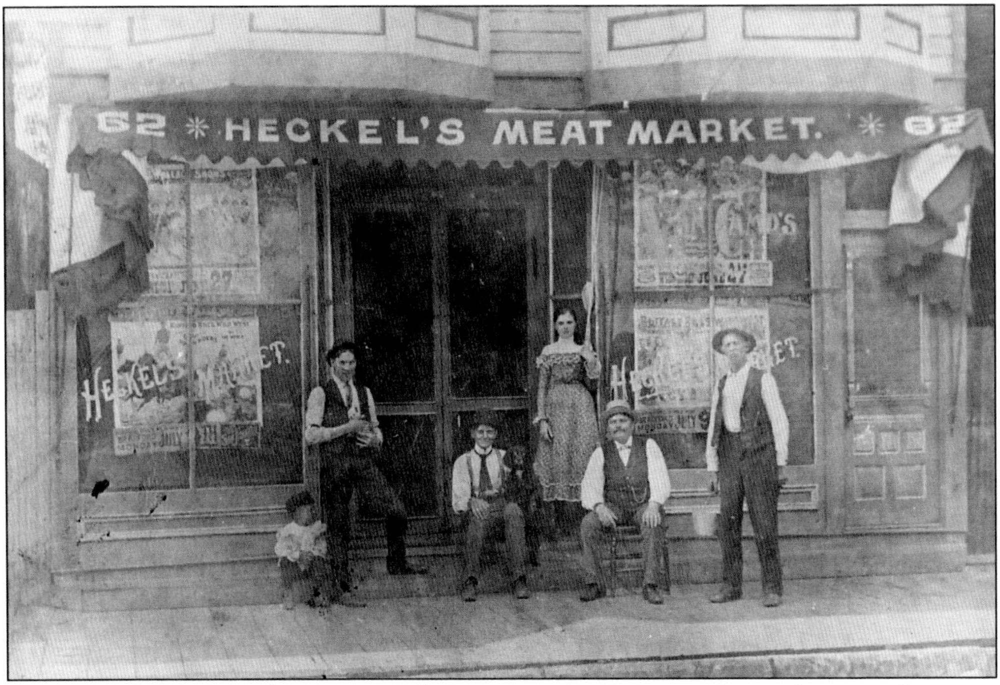

Jacob Heckel's Meat Market, East Corydon Street, 1900. Posters in the windows are advertising the arrival of Buffalo Bill's Wild West Show in Bradford that July.

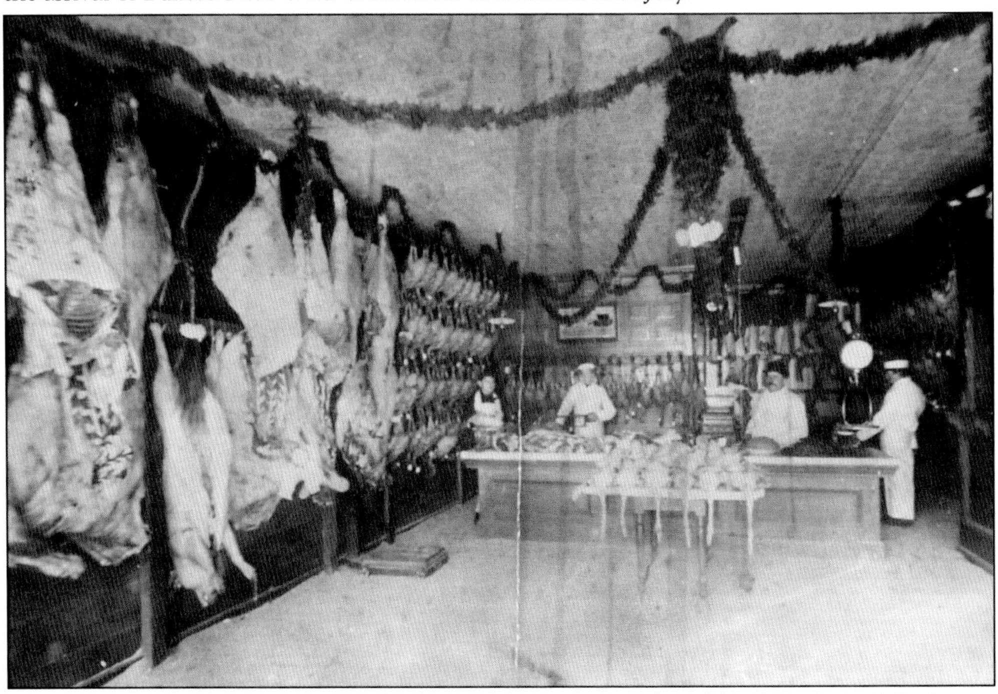

The interior of Heckel's Meat Market, *c.* 1904. Hanging sides of beef, pork, and fowl were common methods of displaying meat at this time. The large number of turkeys in the photograph and the decorations on the ceiling indicate that this picture was taken near the Christmas holidays.

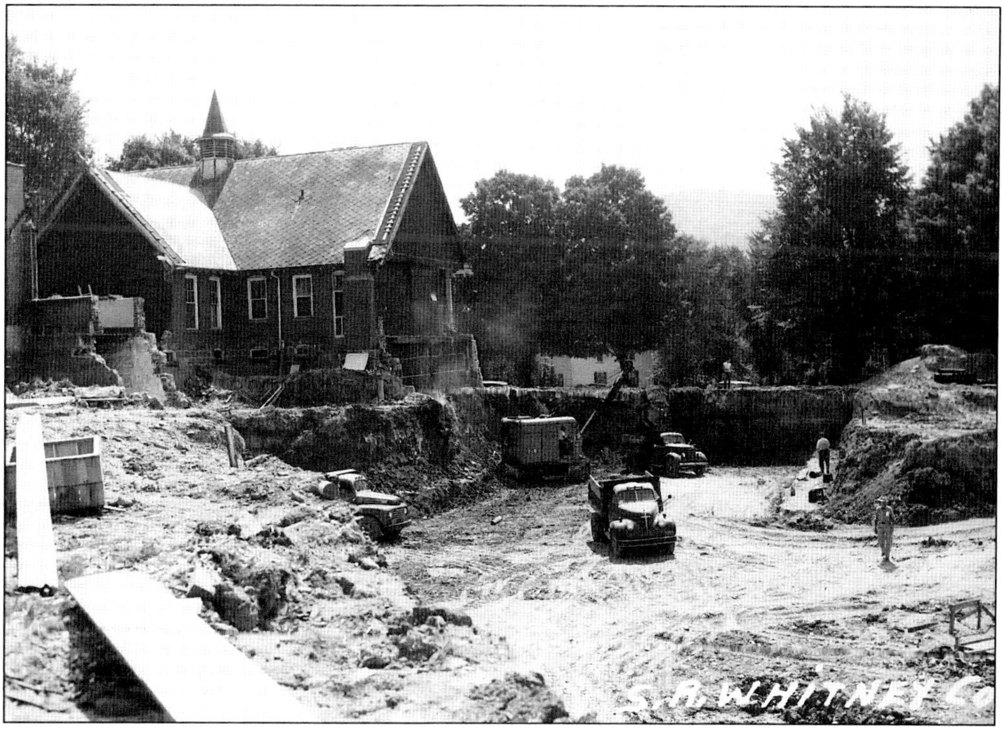

The S.R. Whitney Company, *c.* 1949, building the new hospital. The present hospital was the first aluminum-sided hospital in the world.

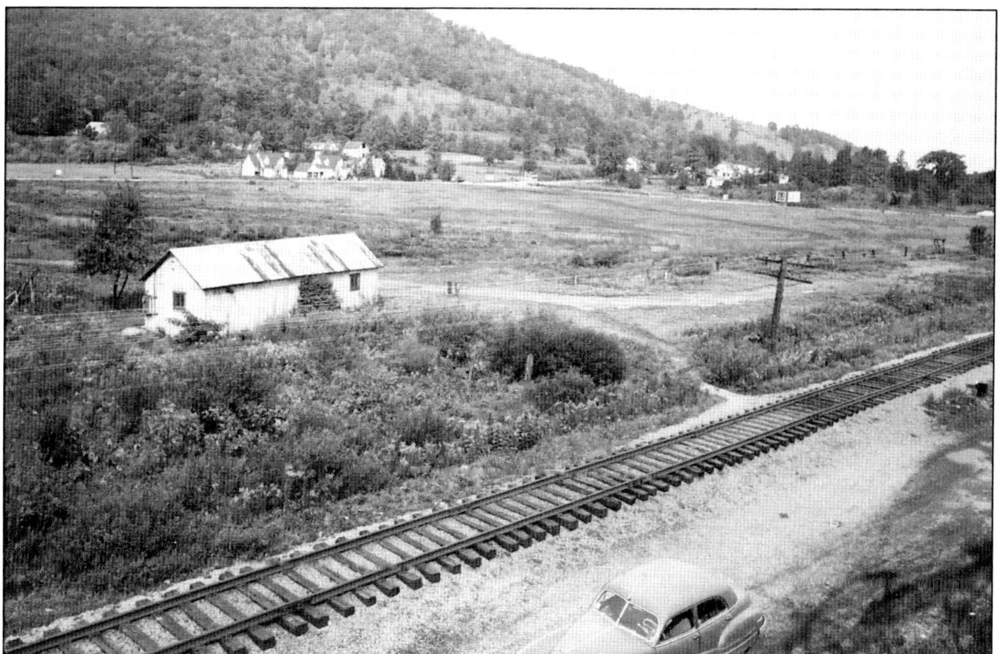

The intersection of Bolivar Drive and Seaward Avenue, *c.* 1935. The site of many family reunions, carnivals, and picnics, this large field is now the location of the KOA Speer plant and has been extensively built up. Homes on both streets can be can be seen in the background.

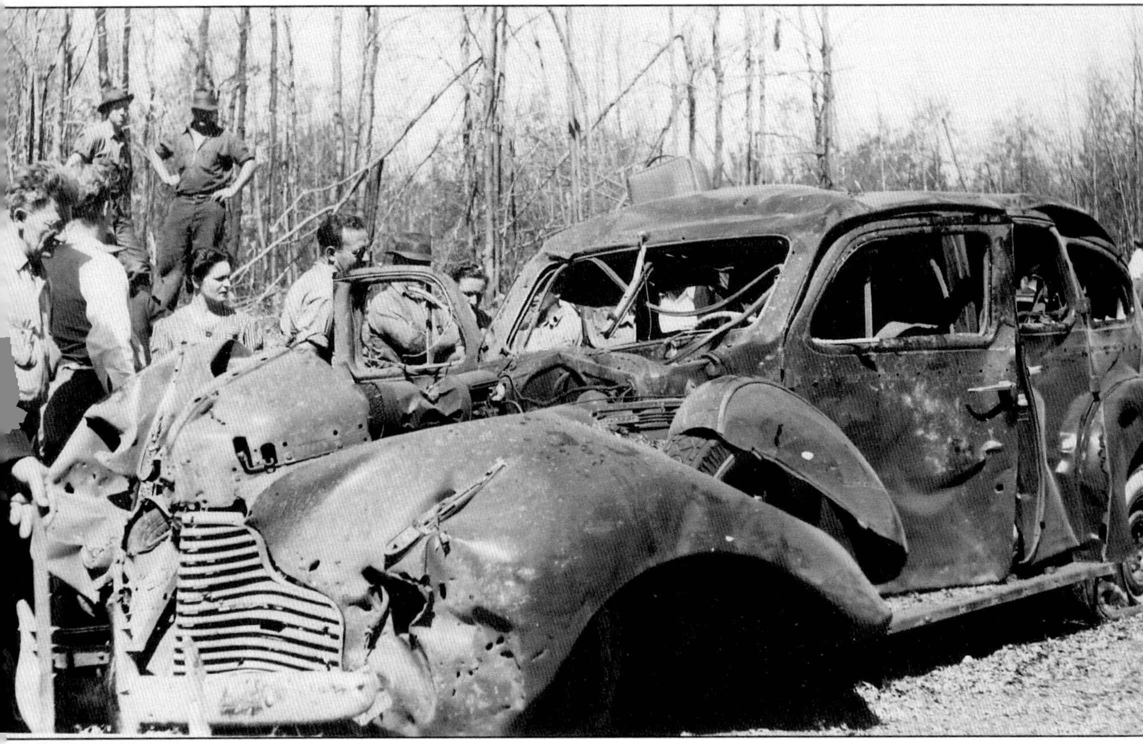

A nitroglycerin explosion. Over 500 quarts of explosives being transported by an American Glycerin truck exploded on September 19, 1941, at 10:30 am on the road near Marshburg. Killed in the accident were John Gloss, age twenty-four, driver of the truck (the *Bradford Era* reported that both truck and driver were "blown to bits") and Clifford Martin, age forty-six, an oil company executive. Witnesses reported that Martin, and another man, Clarence Streeter, were directly behind the nitro truck when they attempted to pass. At that instant the explosion occurred. The Streeter automobile was shattered and thrown 50 yards from the scene. The explosion ripped a hole 18 feet wide, 10 feet long, and 4 feet deep in the asphalt and leveled trees for 100 yards along the highway on either side. Remarkably, Streeter himself was not killed, but did suffer the loss of one of his eyes.

Seven

People and Pleasant Pastimes

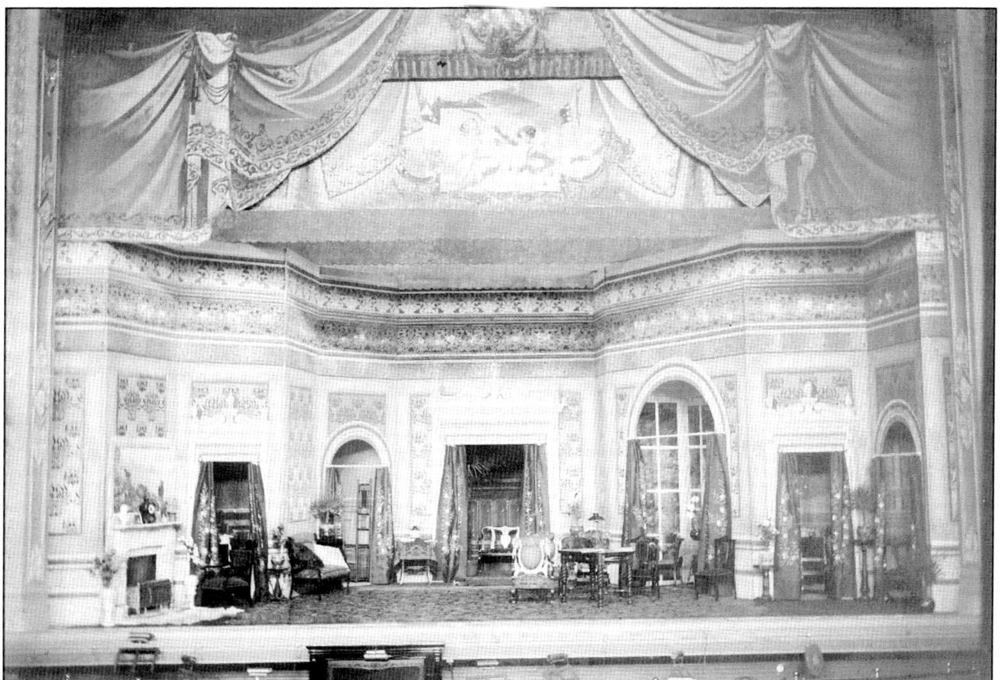

The interior of the Bradford Theater, later Shea's. Opening night on December 23, 1901, saw the best of Bradford society enjoying *The Prince of Pilsen*. During its existence, a wide variety of famous entertainers played here, including Boris Karloff, Lillian Russell, John Phillip Sousa, and others. In the 1930s and '40s the big bands often played "The Shea's" and popular movies were shown nightly. But time took its toll, and on May 30, 1956, the Shea's closed its door forever, and the building was torn down to make a parking lot. It is still fondly remembered by most Bradfordians.

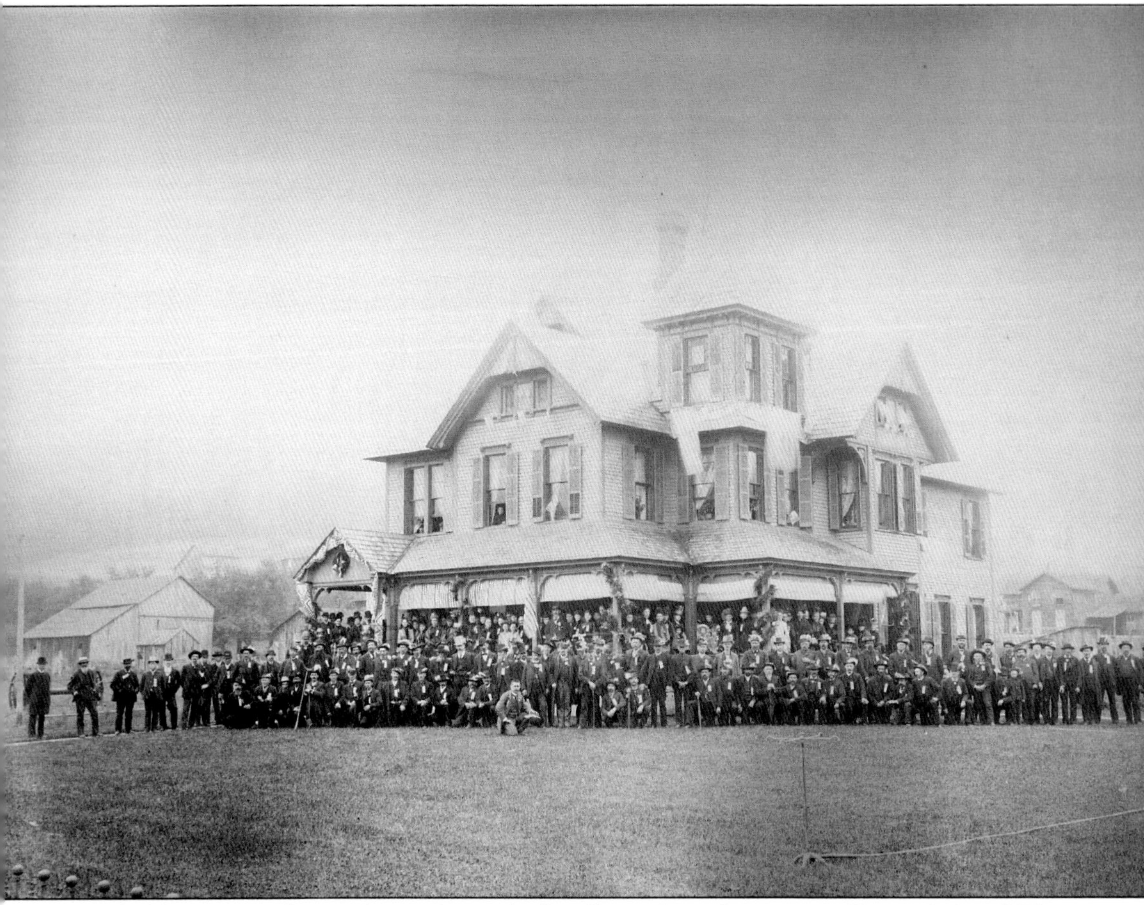

Sheldon Jewett's home, Custer City, which still stands on the corner of Route 219 and Warren Road. Jewett was an important landowner in Custer City, and at one time owned over 140 buildings in the borough. A Civil War veteran who had been in Andersonville during the war, Jewett hosted the second Bucktail Reunion on September 25, 1888, at this house.

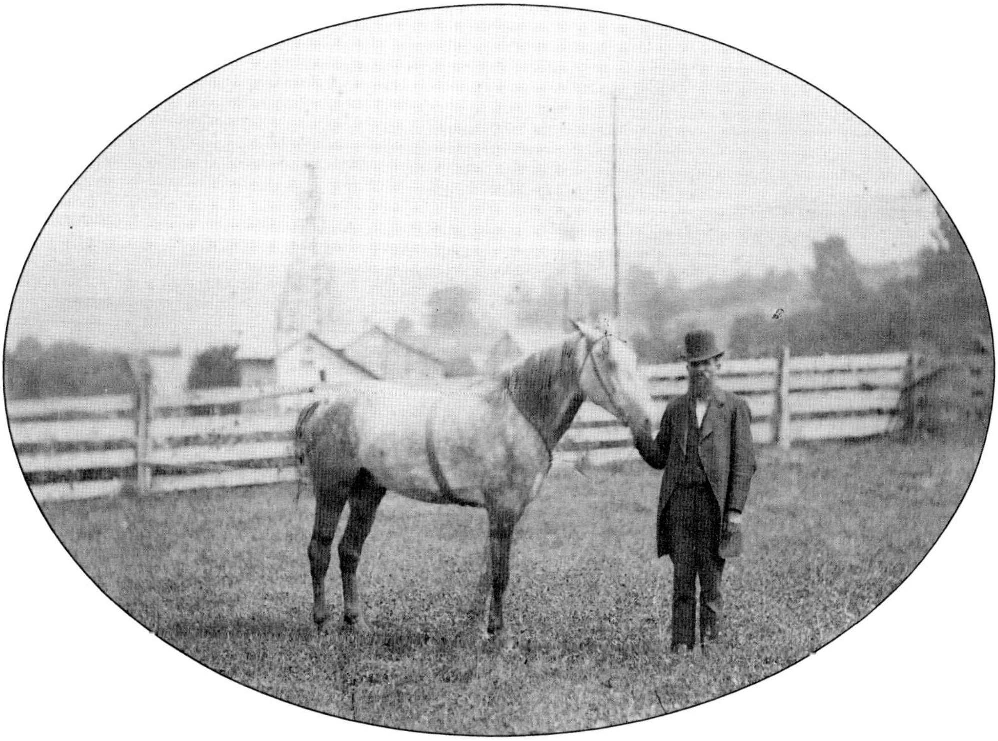

Benjamin Jewett, *c.* 1880. The father of Sheldon Jewett (who founded Custer City), Benjamin came to the Bradford area in 1836 from Vermont. He is shown here on one of his son's farms.

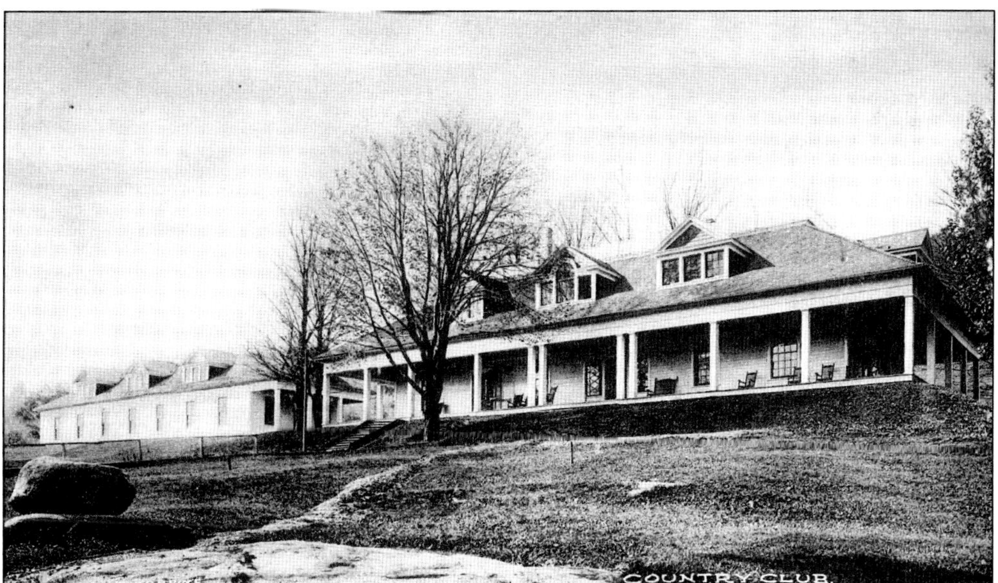

The Bradford Country Club. The club was organized in the early 1900s, and the streetcar line conveniently went right past. In 1932, the North Penn Country Club was organized here, becoming the forerunner of the PennHills Country Club. Today it is the Satterwhite home on South Avenue.

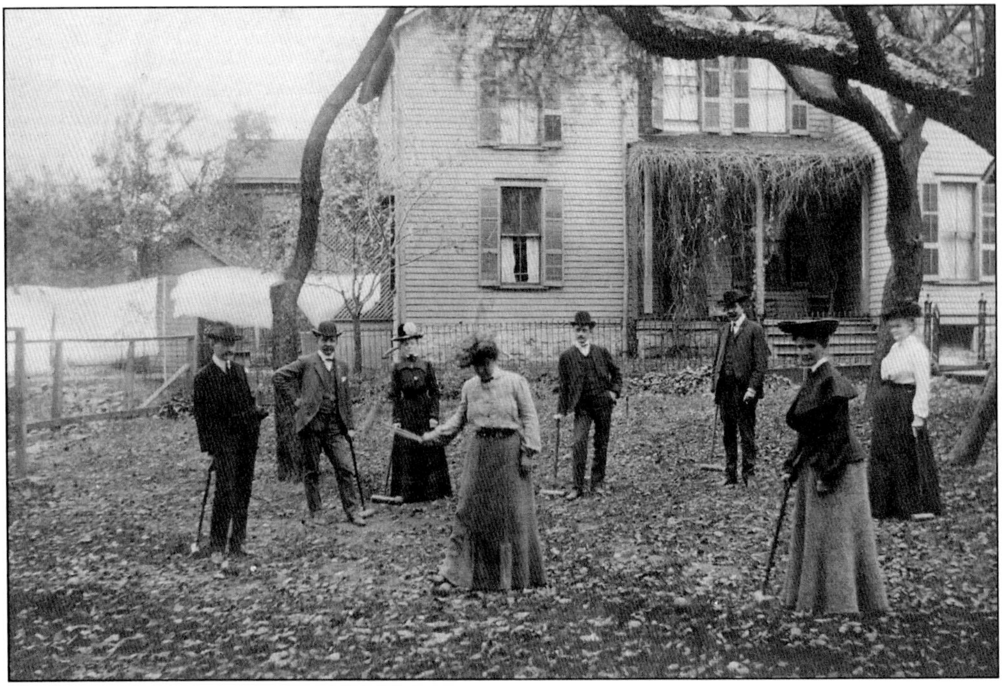

A pleasant game of croquet, a delightful diversion in any time period.

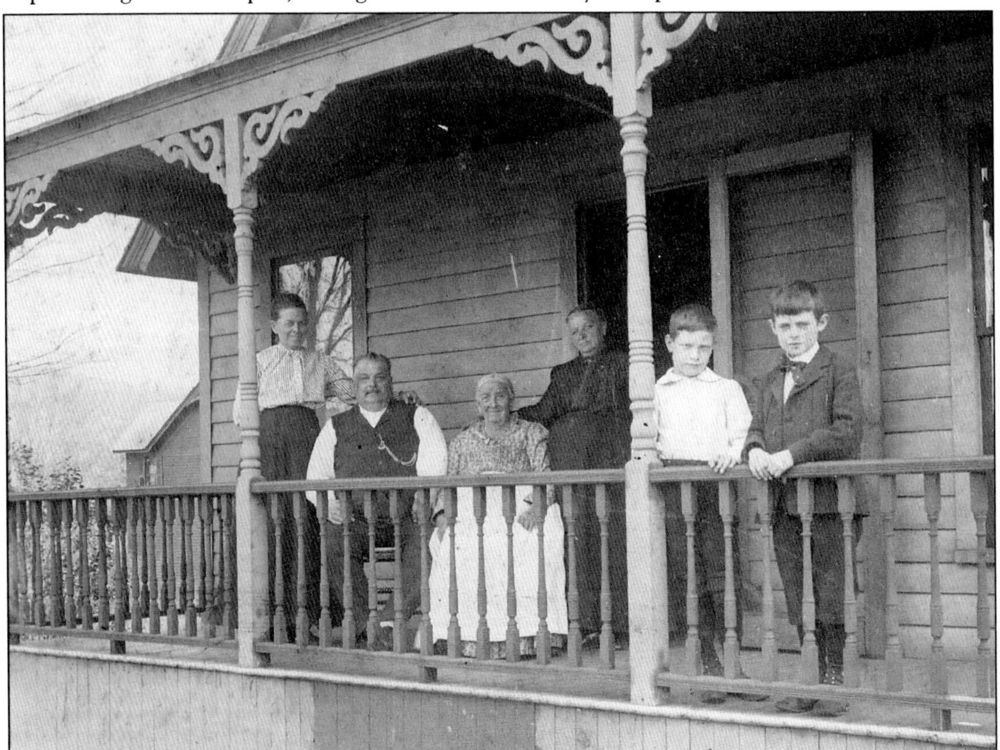

George Sackarnd and family, 1909. Sackarnd, a bartender at the Oil City House (which burned in 1930), and his family relax on the porch of their home at 15 Lincoln Avenue.

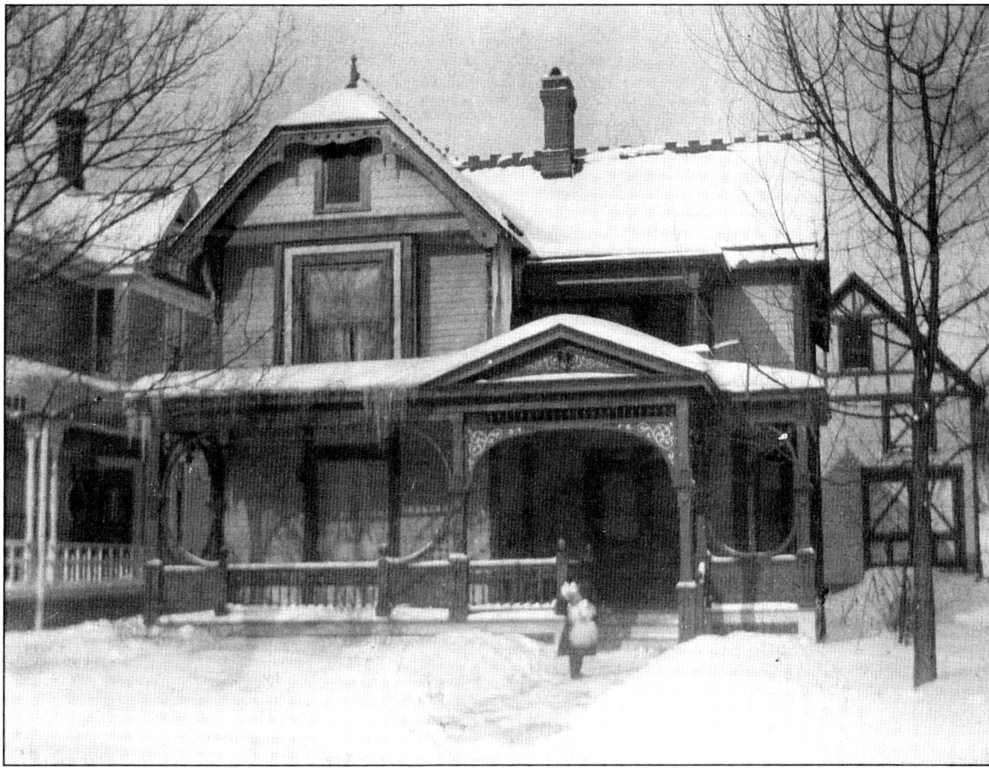

William Hyde's house, 1900, at 373 East Main Street. This home is still standing.

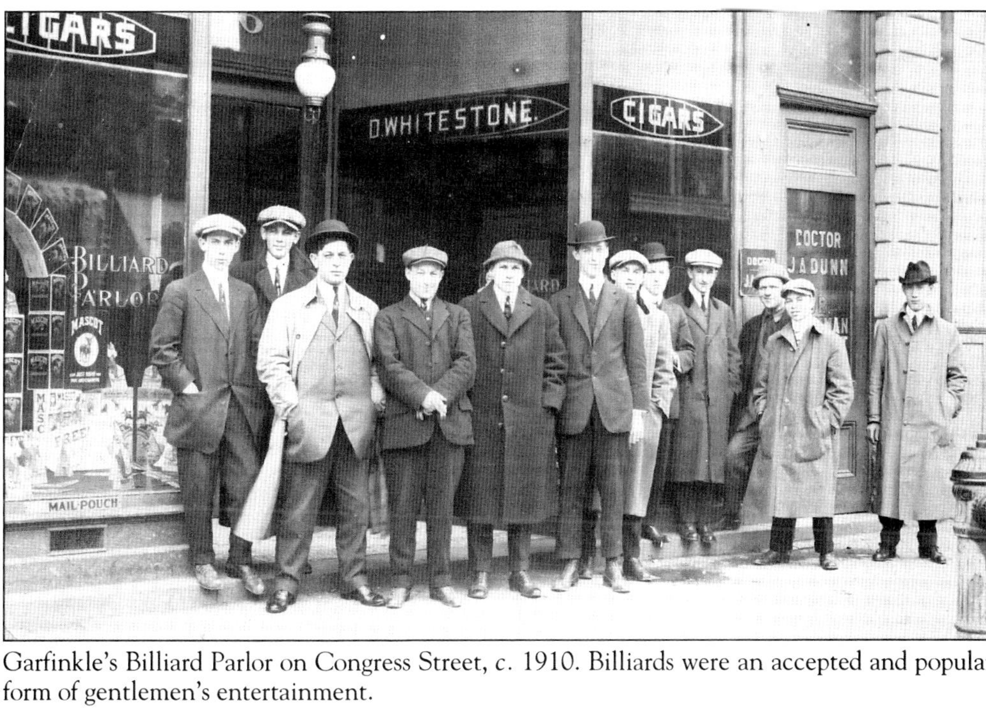

Garfinkle's Billiard Parlor on Congress Street, *c.* 1910. Billiards were an accepted and popular form of gentlemen's entertainment.

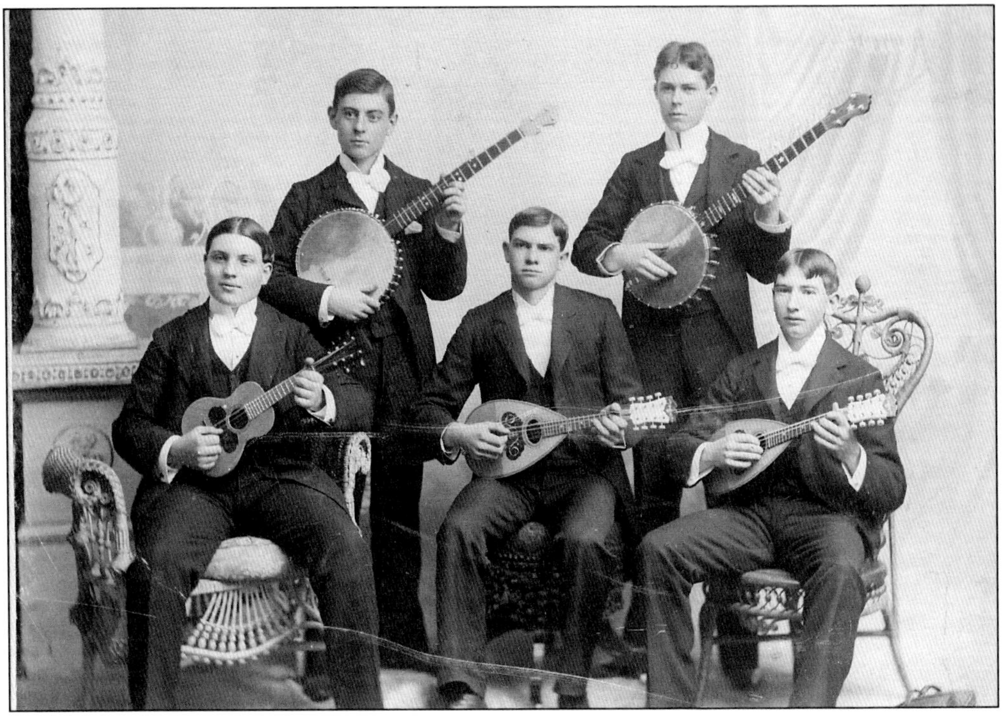

The Bradford Mandolin Club, 1900. Dr. Jake Heckel is seated in the center. Such social clubs were popular forms of entertainment in Bradford.

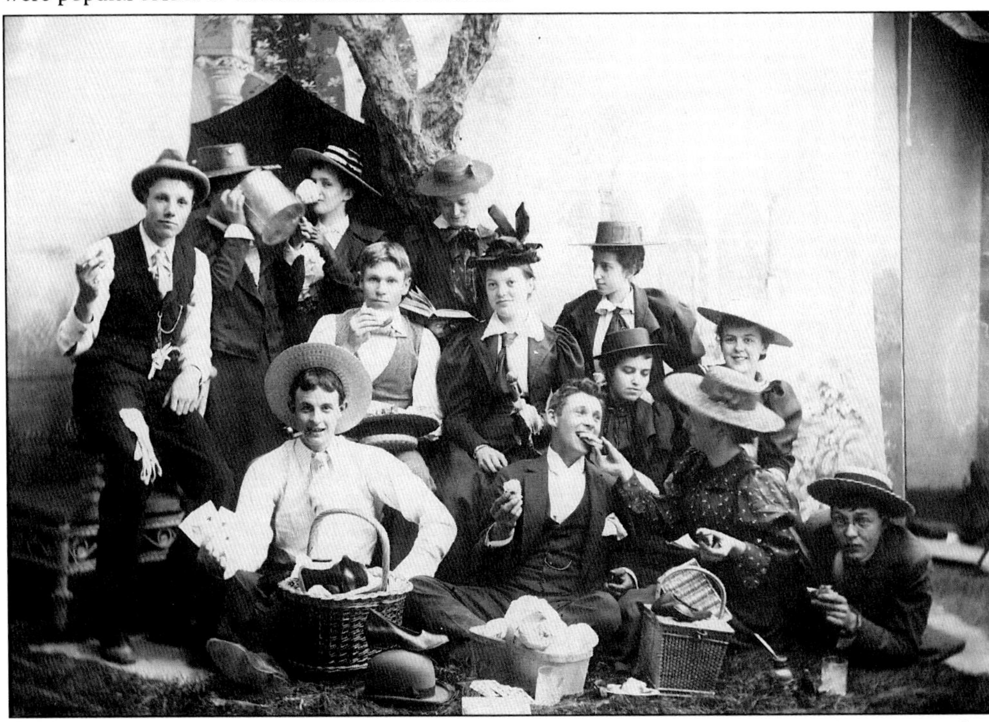

One of Bradford's first theatrical groups, the Home Talent players, 1890. This group often performed popular plays to the delight of audiences.

Ward Weaver, 1907. Like all boys, young Ward would probably rather be outside riding this wooden bicycle, and not posing for a photograph. His knickers, high button shoes, and knit stockings were normal attire for children of that era. W.E. Dettler, photographer, was one of many professionals in Bradford at the turn of the century.

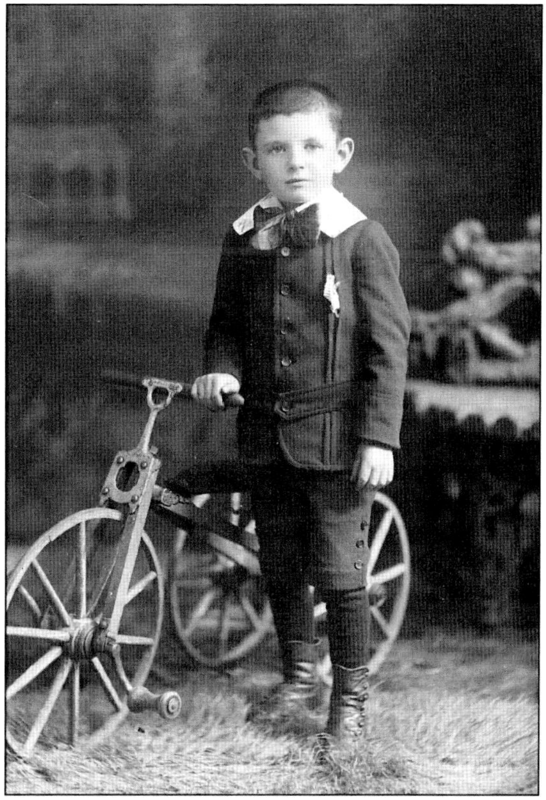

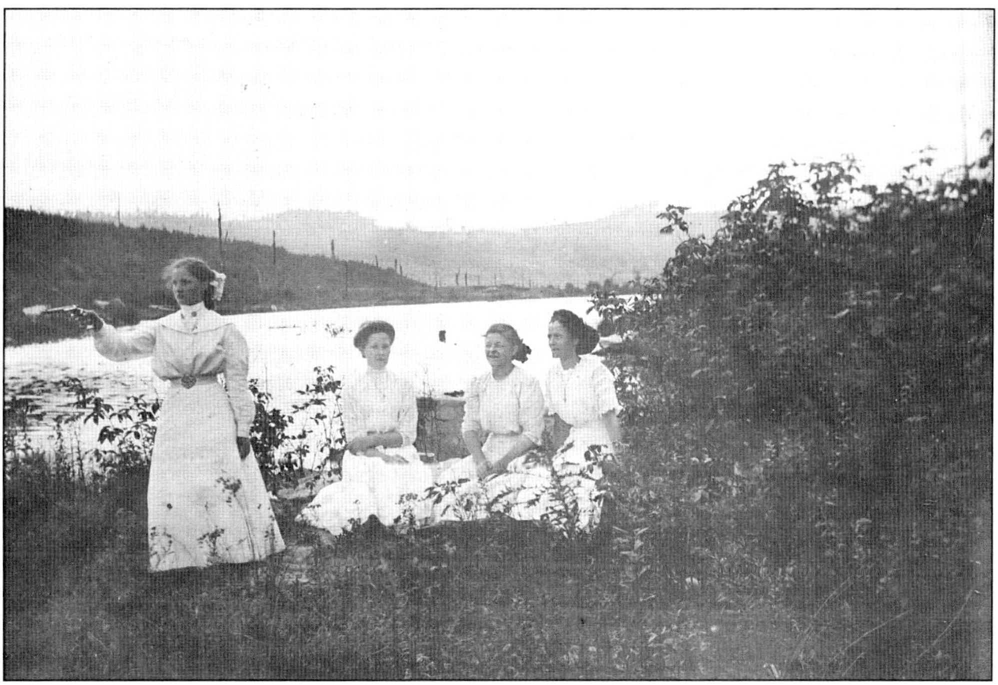

A Sunday picnic, c. 1900. These four women enjoy a pleasant afternoon of conversation, and apparently, target practice.

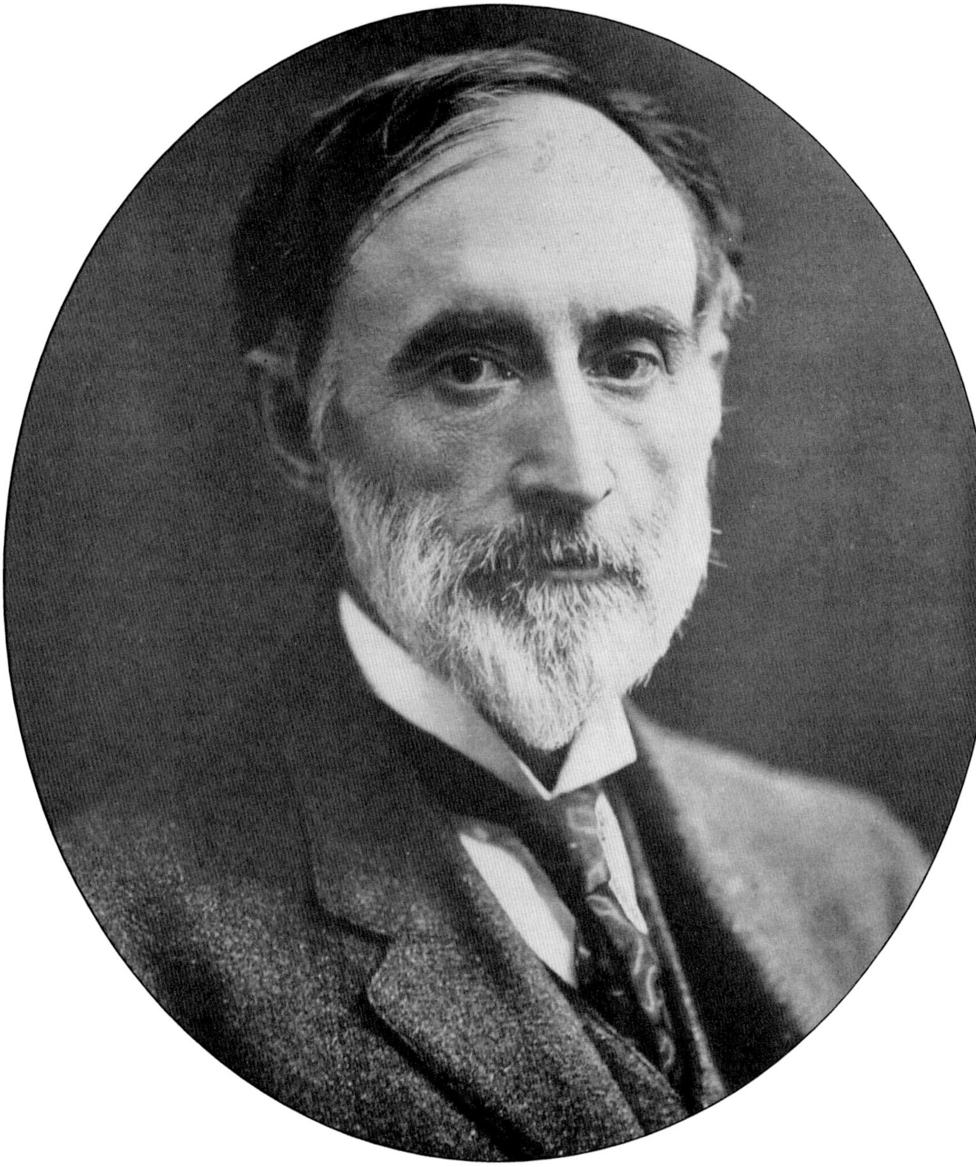

Rufus B. Stone (1847–1929). One of Bradford's most distinguished citizens, Stone was president of the Bradford Bar Association, the Carnegie Public Library, the Bradford Hospital, the McKean County Historical Society, the Commonwealth Humane Society, and author of *McKean, the Governor's County*. He founded *The Evening Star* newspaper in 1879 and for many years resided in "Arkwood," his estate near Rock City.

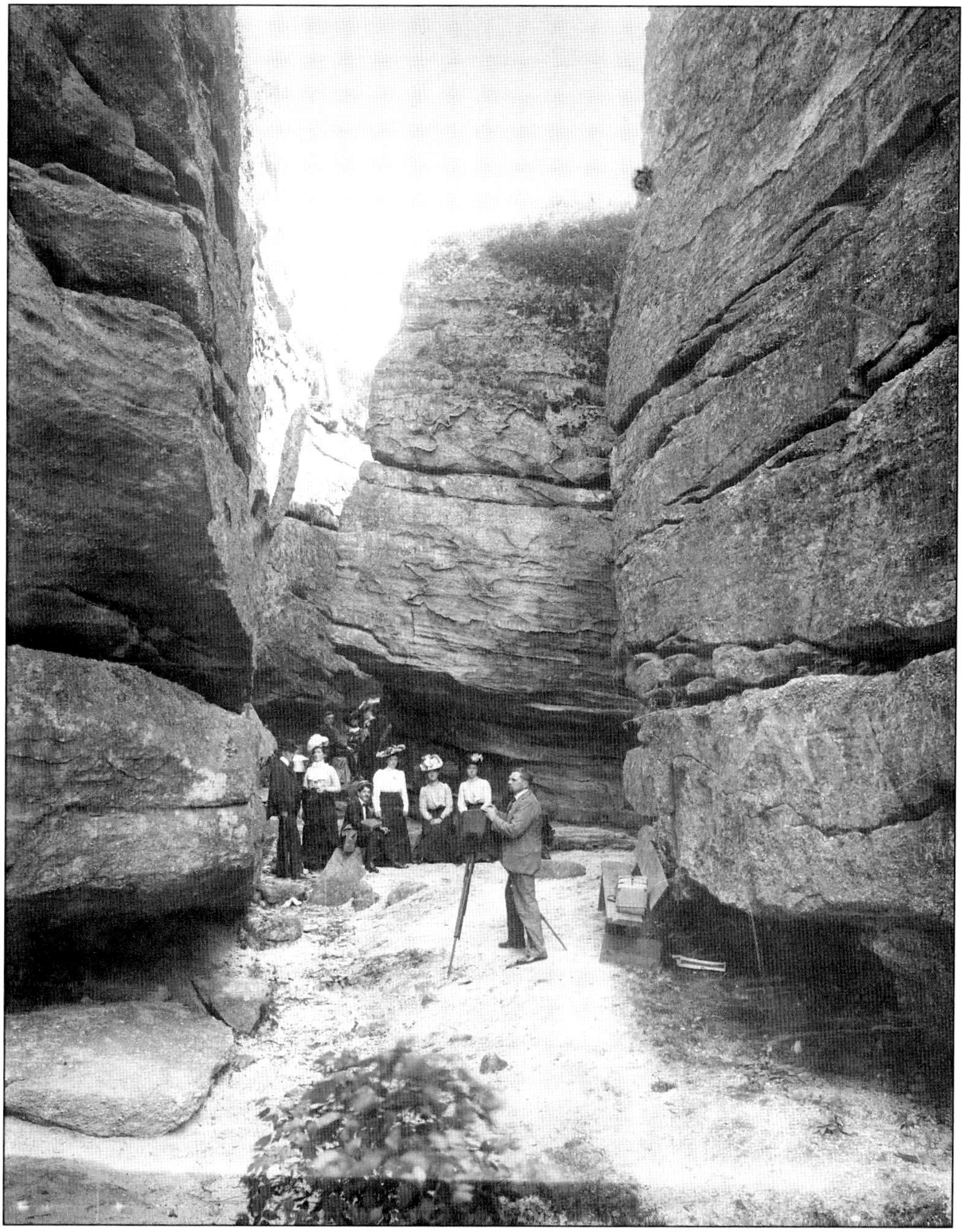

Rock City, c. 1900. Sightseeing at these huge rock formations just outside the city has been popular for over one hundred years, as has the custom of writing one's initials or name on the rock surface. Such graffiti is still visible today, dating back to the 1880s. Here, an elegantly dressed group is getting ready to have their photograph taken near the entrance to the rocks.

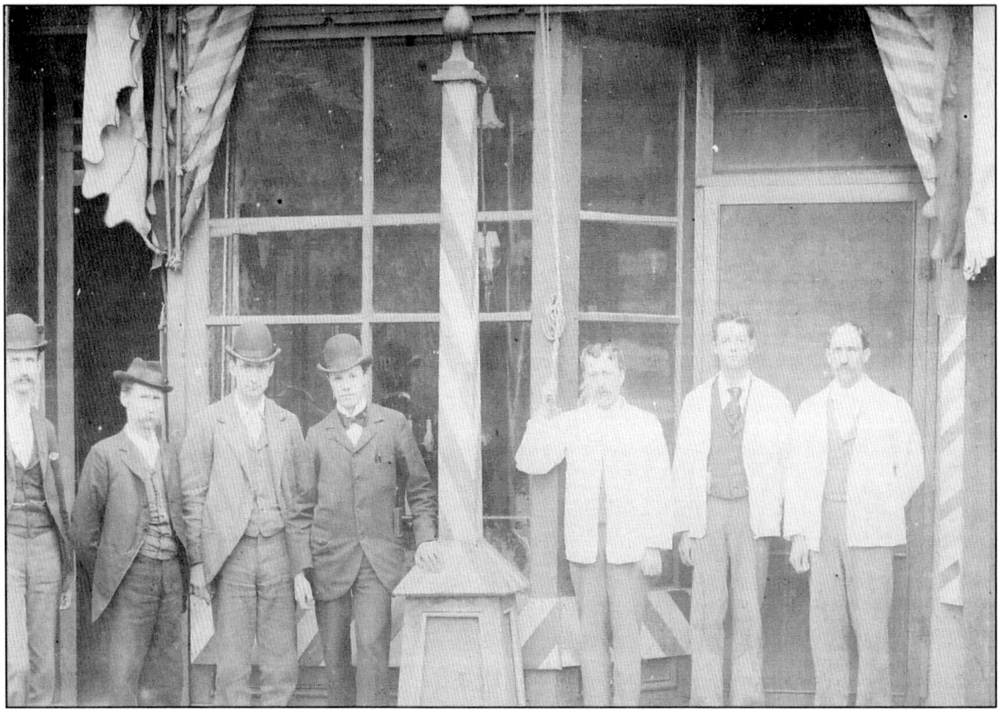

The barbershop at 101 Main Street in 1895. From left to right are Alex B. Hill, Edward Delaney, Dave Snakard, Harry Schonblom, and barbers Joe Lishman, Bob Williams, and Charles H. Denninger. Denninger served as mayor of Bradford from 1924 to 1927.

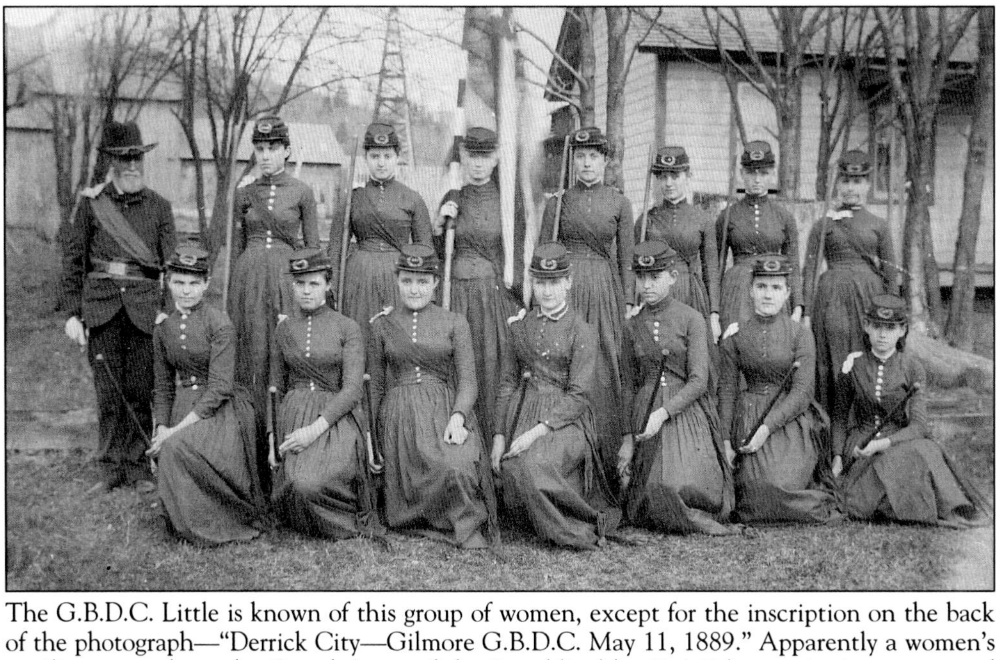

The G.B.D.C. Little is known of this group of women, except for the inscription on the back of the photograph—"Derrick City—Gilmore G.B.D.C. May 11, 1889." Apparently a women's auxiliary to perhaps the Grand Army of the Republic (the G.A.R.) organization, no record has been found to explain their name, the date, or why they are dressed as soldiers with broomstick guns.

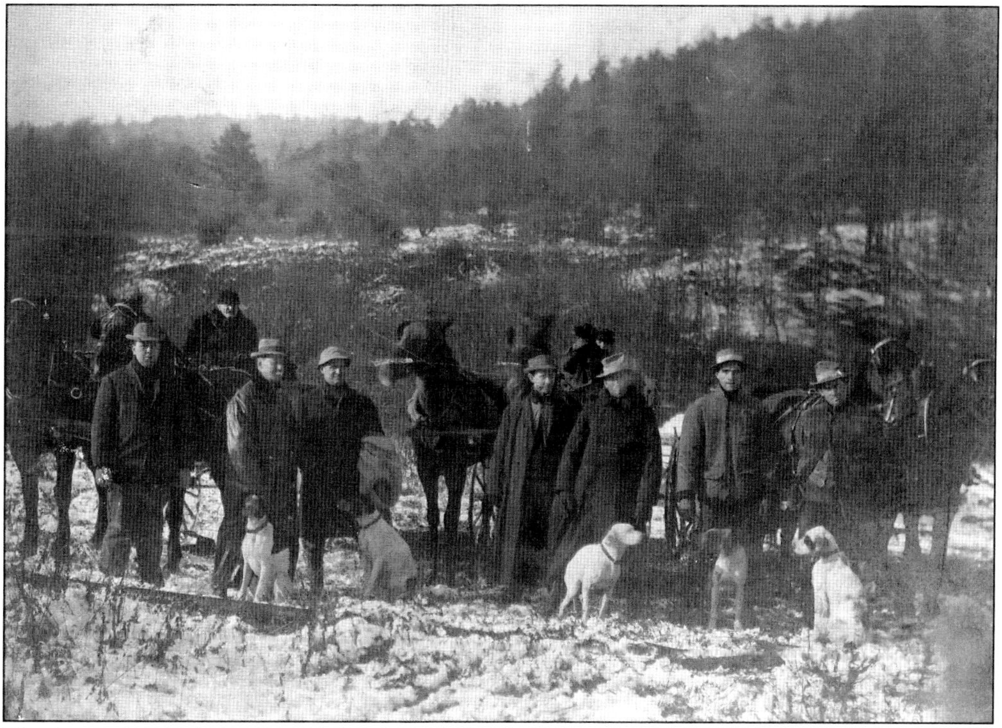

The Sugar Run Fish & Gun Club "training the dogs," December 3, 1908. Standing, from left to right, are Art Thompson, Thomas Kennedy, Sam Kennedy, Charles Hurley, Barry Griffith, Bob Bradley, and Frank Forester.

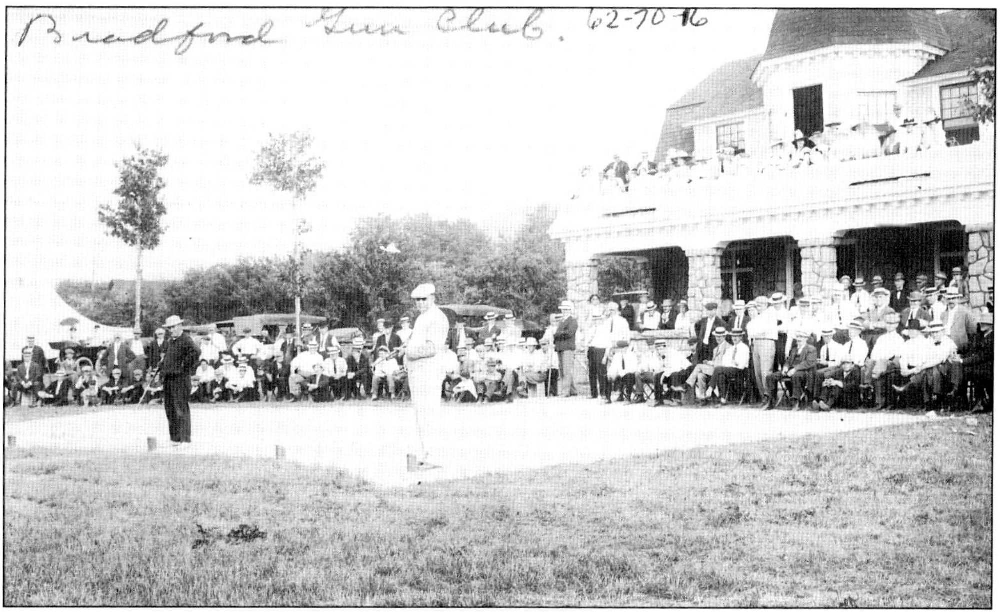

The Bradford Gun Club, c. 1905. A popular recreational spot, and renowned for its clay pigeon shoots, the gun club was located where the Bradford Mall now stands. Many influential men were members and international shooting matches were held yearly. It was demolished in 1968 to construct the mall.

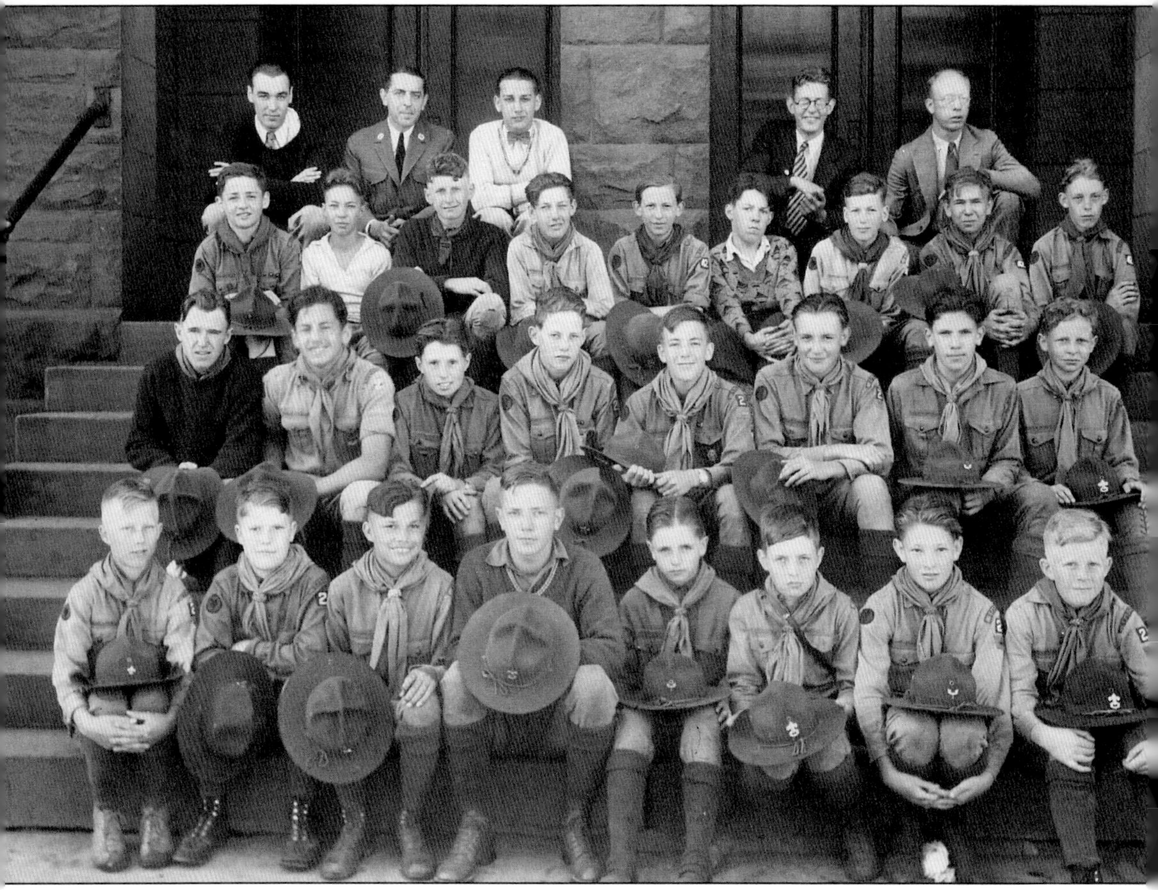

Boy Scout troops, June 19, 1930, at the regional jamboree at Natural Bridge, Virginia. Troop 2, from the First Presbyterian Church, is shown here. From left to right are as follows: (front row) Jim McCutcheon, Henry Beck, Clarence Ledden, Oscar Benton, Charles Grow, Tom Cornan, Bill Frizzell, and Dan Gibson; (second row) Herb Brandon, Murray Garber, George Jackson, Duane Dennis, Dick Johnson, Dick Hermes, Al Grow, and Chuck Collins; (third row) all unidentified boys, from the Hill Memorial Church, Troop 42; (back row) Harold German (from Smethport), Jack Keller (Scout executive), Wardloe Wilcox, Bob Knapp (Troop 2 scoutmaster), and the Troop 42 leader (name unknown).

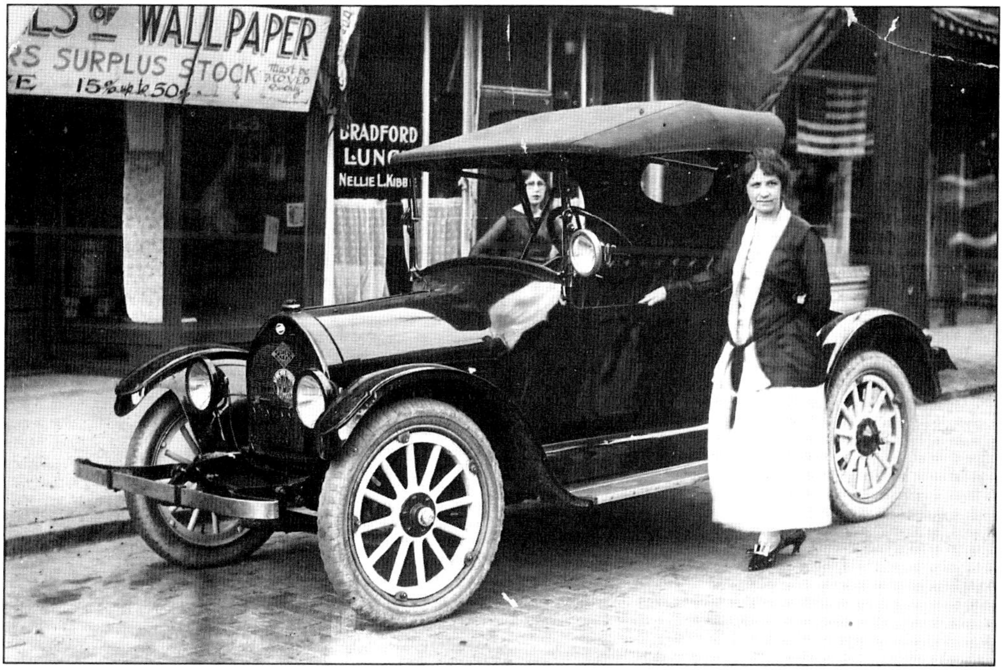

Nellie Kibbie, 1925. She is standing in front of the Bradford Lunch, which she owned, at 125 Main Street.

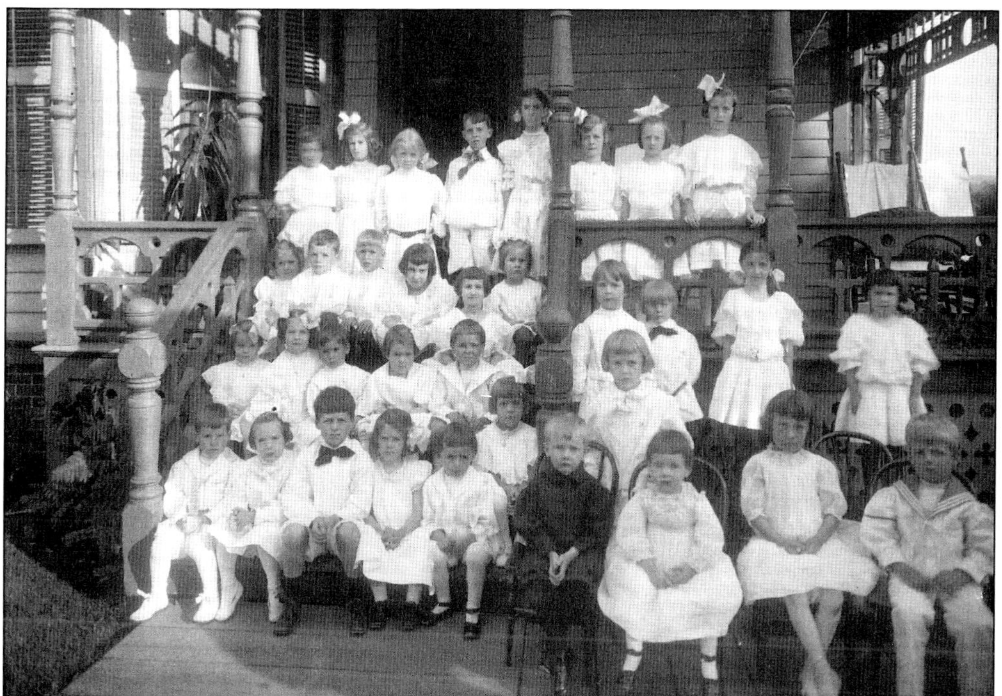

A children's birthday party at the William Burdick house on Jackson Avenue, 1905. The little boy at lower left is D. Harvey Phillips. This residence is currently known as the Mountain Laurel Inn.

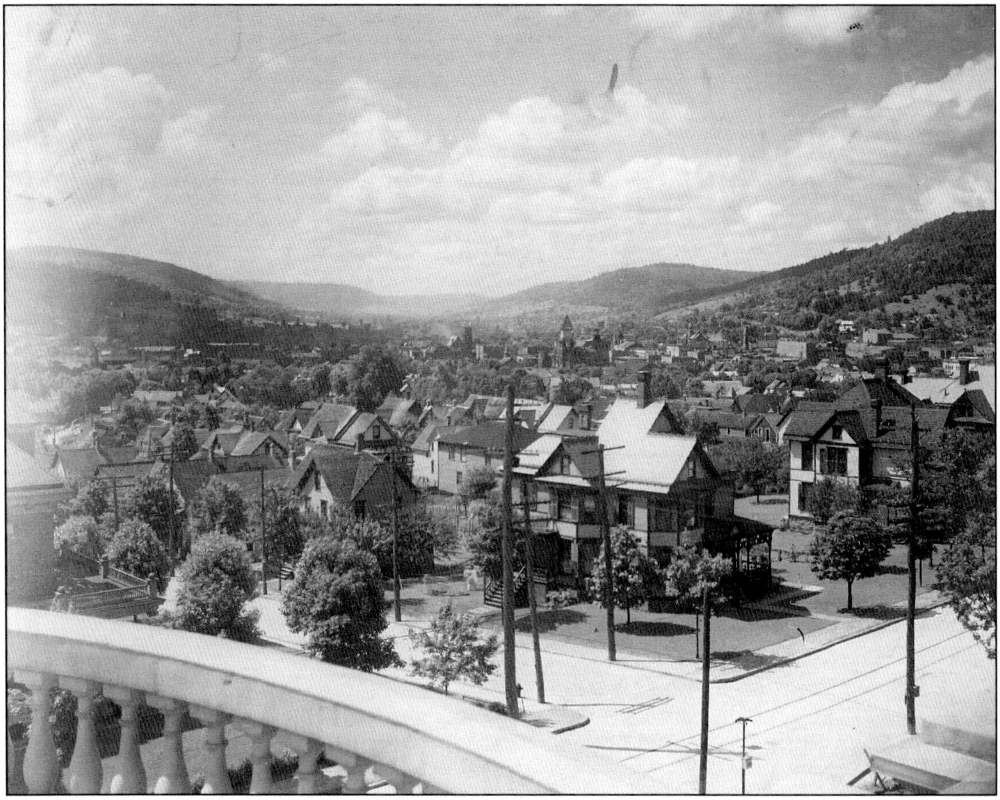

William E. Burdick's home, Jackson Avenue, 1913. Large, comfortable homes were commonplace in Bradford at the turn of the century. The photograph was taken from the porch roof of the Dresser mansion across the street.

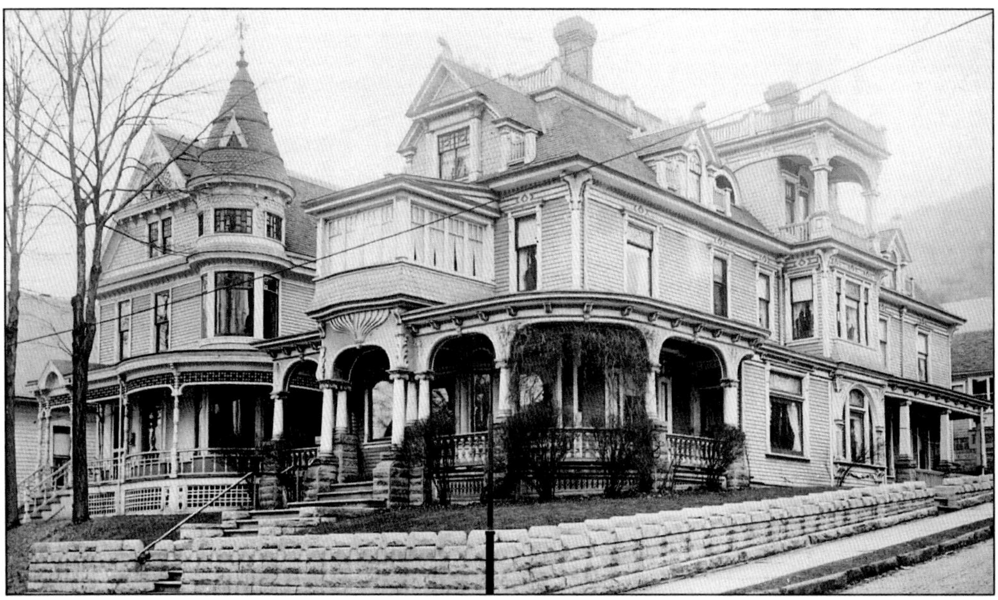

The Lewis E. Mallory estate, Congress Street.

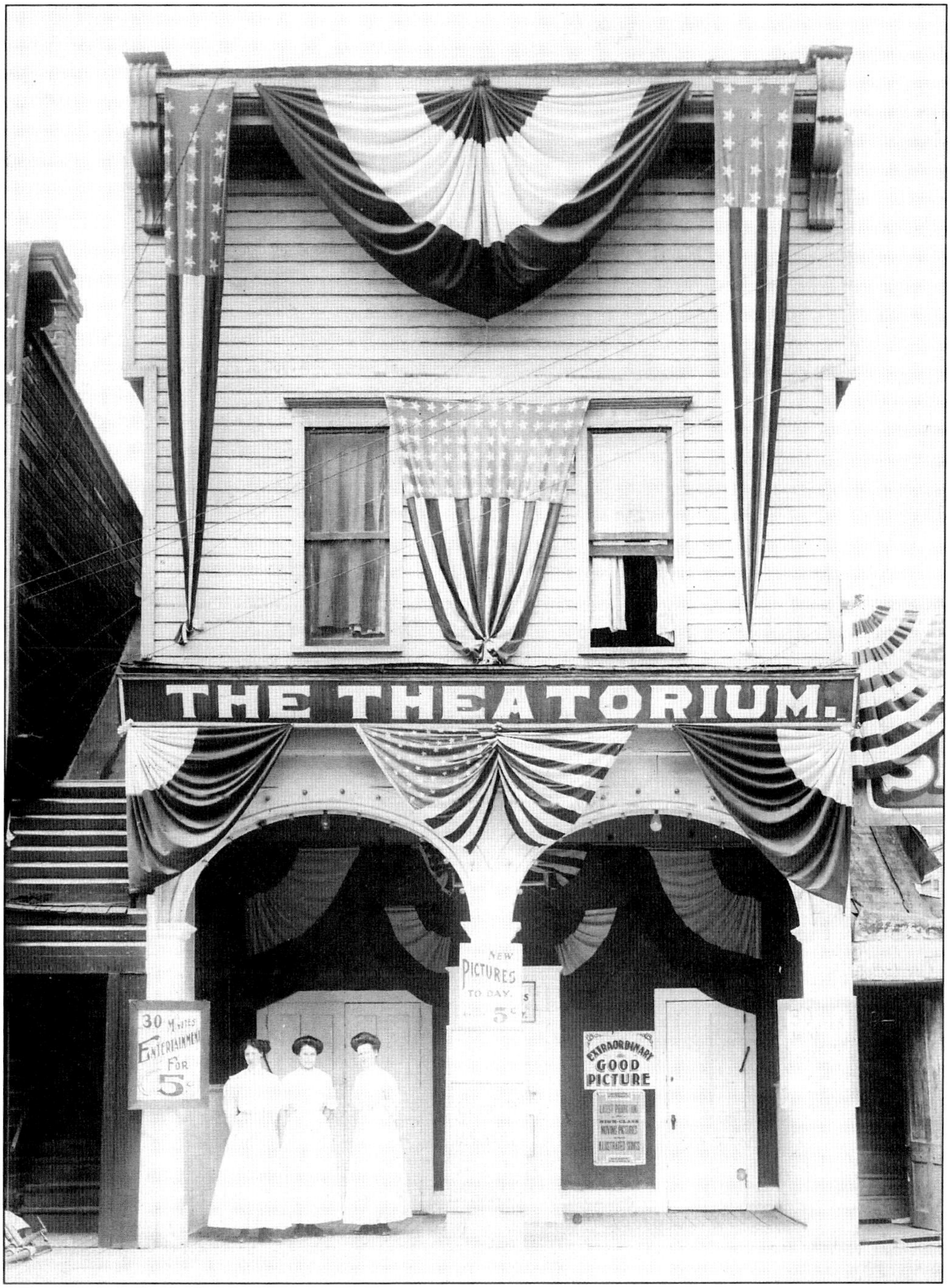

The Theatorium, 1909. Only in existence for a short time, this theater promised "moving pictures with illustrated songs." A forerunner of the Grand Theater, the Theatorium showed *A Soldier of the US Army in the Philippines* on this day. From left to right are Myrtle Langworth, Maxine Walker, and Bess Karns.

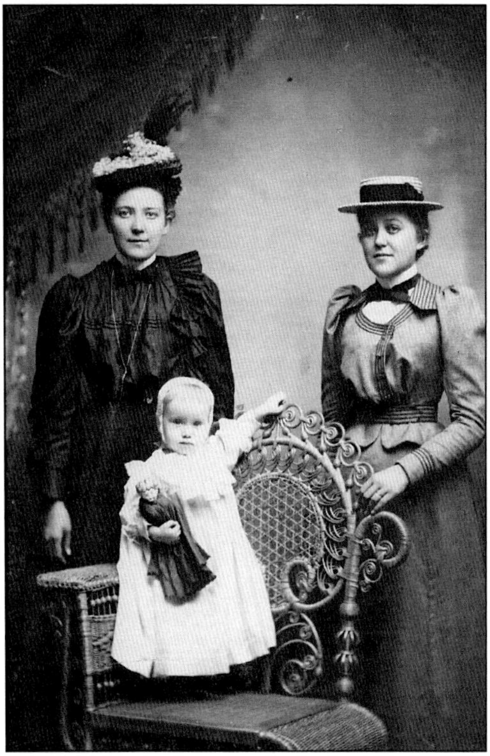

Fashion, 1898. These well-dressed women and small child are wearing the latest "turn-of-the-century" fashions. Having studio portraits done by one of Bradford's many photographers was a popular pastime.

Dr. Jake Heckel, dentist, and an unknown woman patient, early 1900s. Dr. Heckel's office was located on the second floor of the Schonblom Building at the corner of Main and Kennedy Streets.

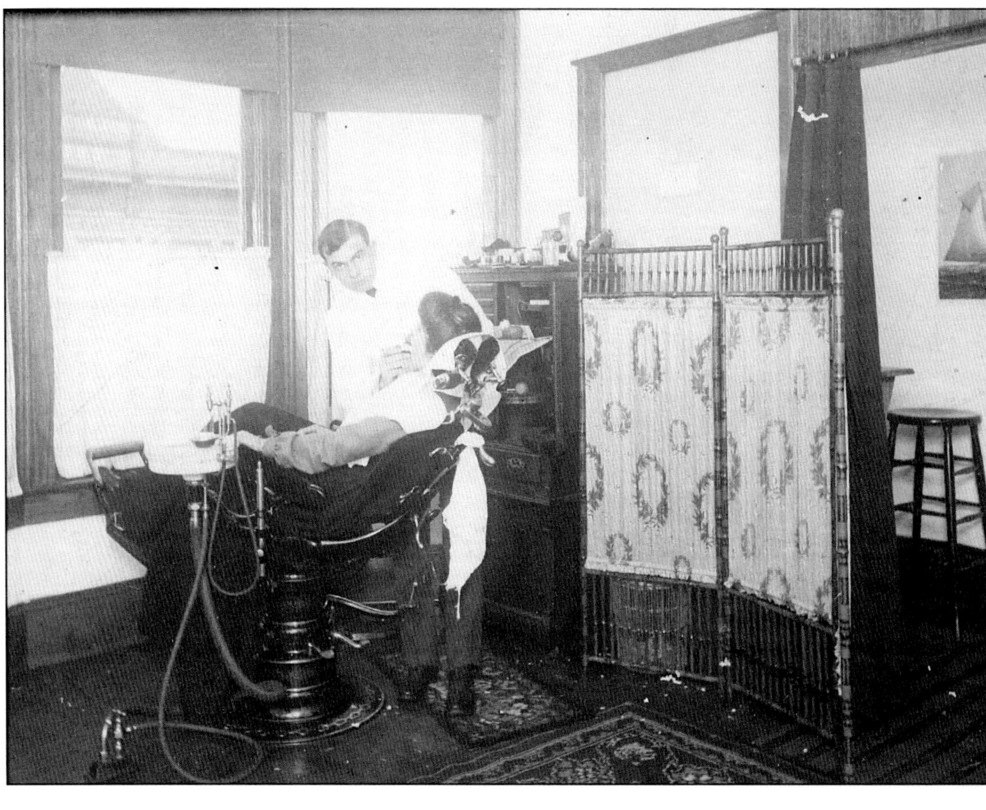

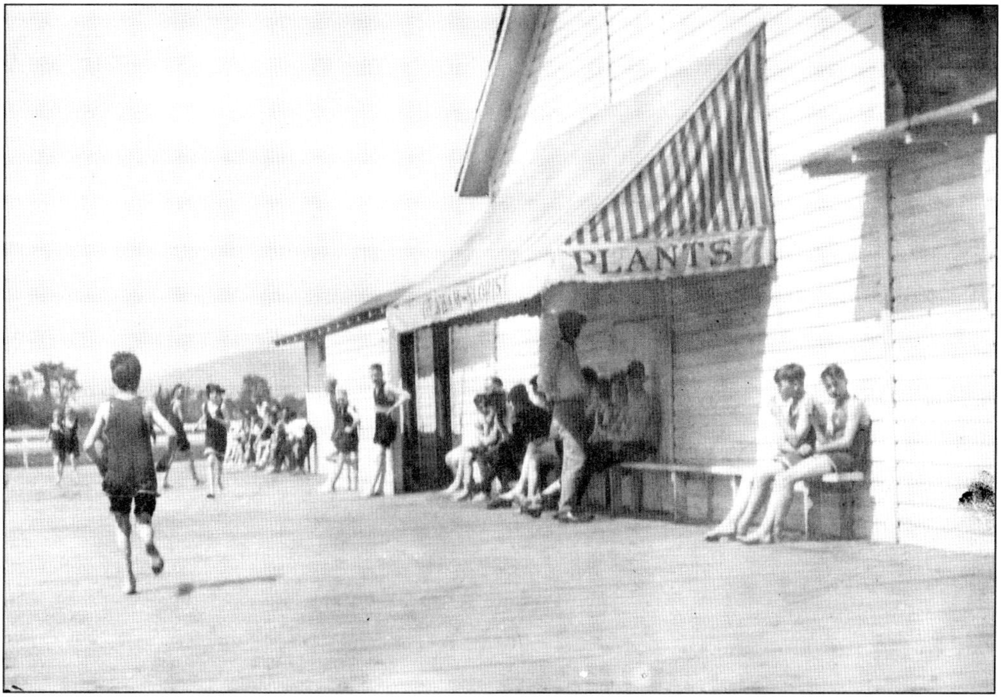

The Park Lake Swimming Pool, c. 1920, located off Seaward Avenue near the old Graham florist shop. Closed by 1931, this location is now under the Route 219 expressway.

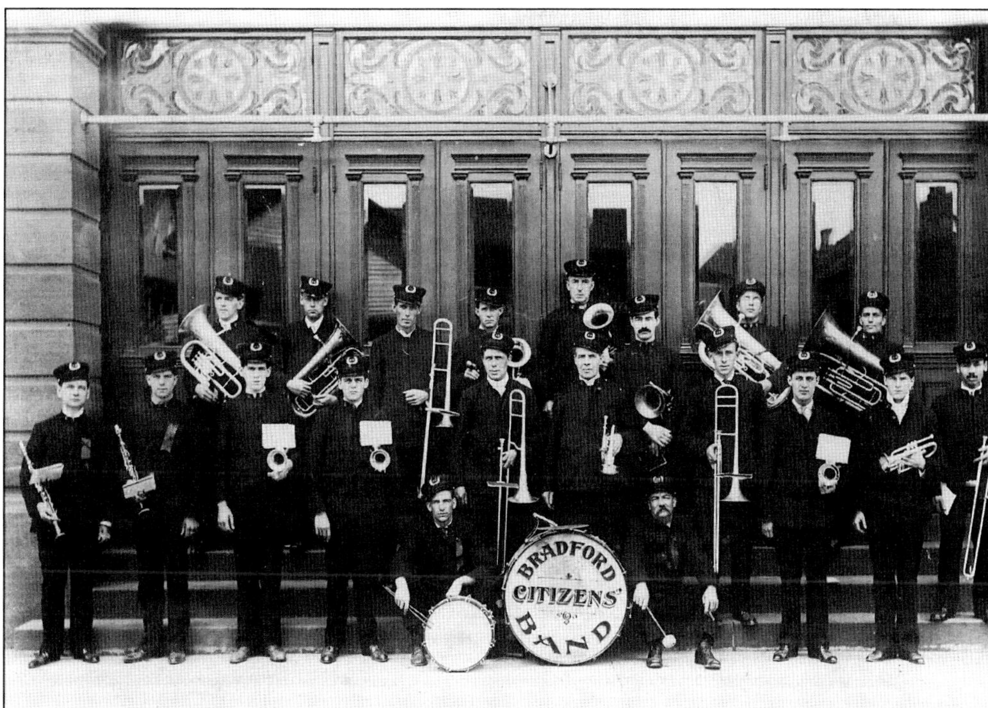

The Citizens' Band, c. 1915, in front of the entrance to the Bradford Theater (later the Shea's).

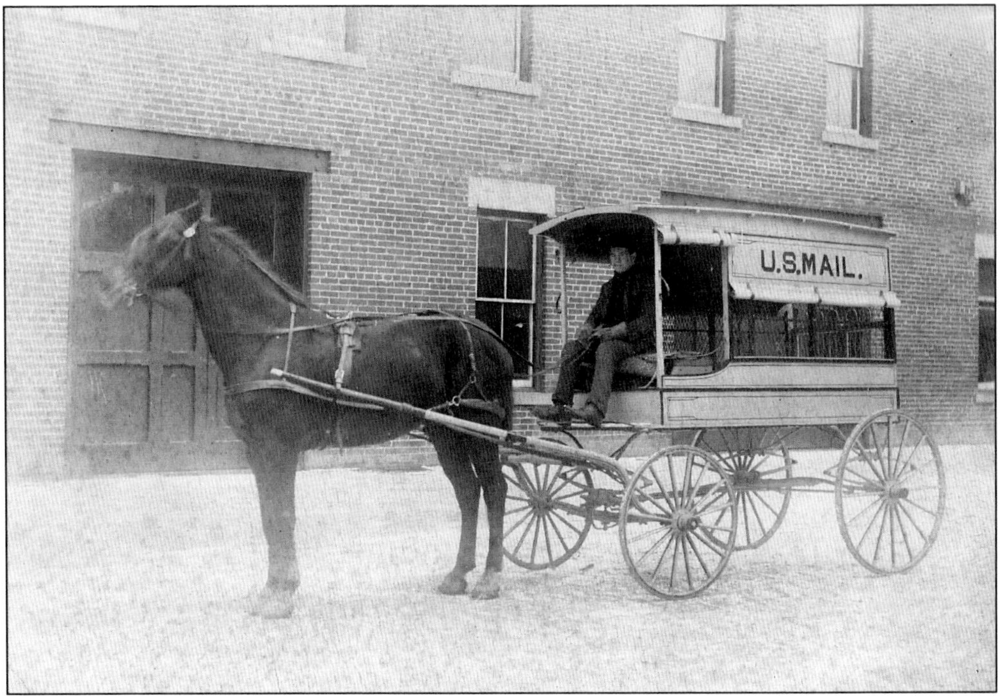

A parcel post delivery wagon, 1913. Upon completion of the new federal post office building on Corydon Street in 1913, package delivery was instituted.

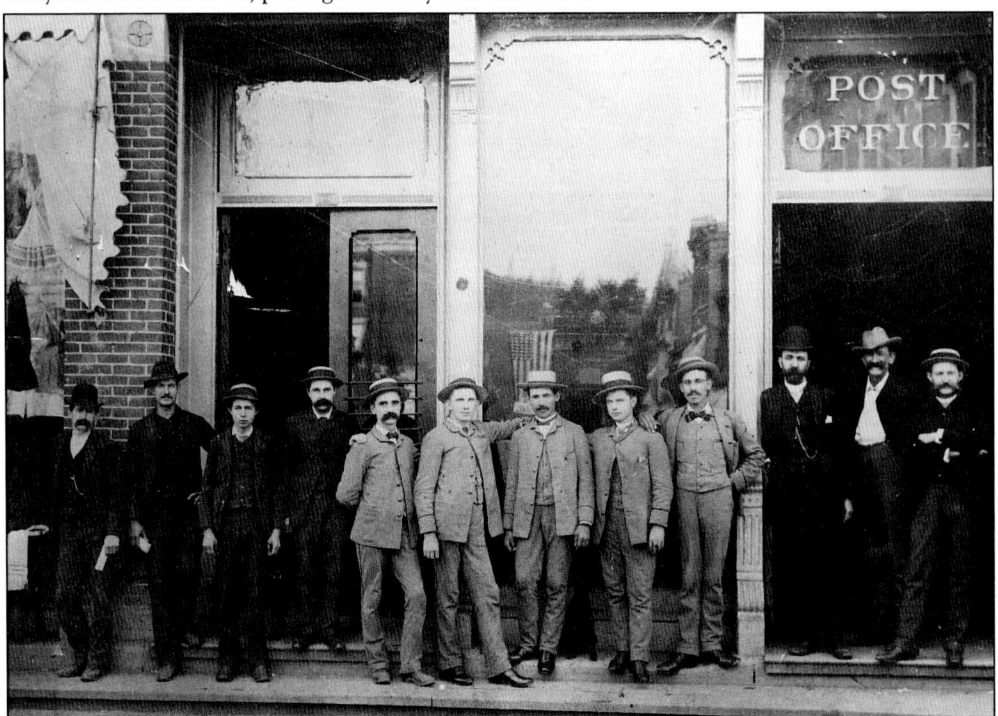

The Bradford Post Office, 1911. Located in the first Odd Fellows Building on the square, postal facilities were moved to Corydon Street in 1913 when the new federal post office was built.

Eight

Churches and Schools

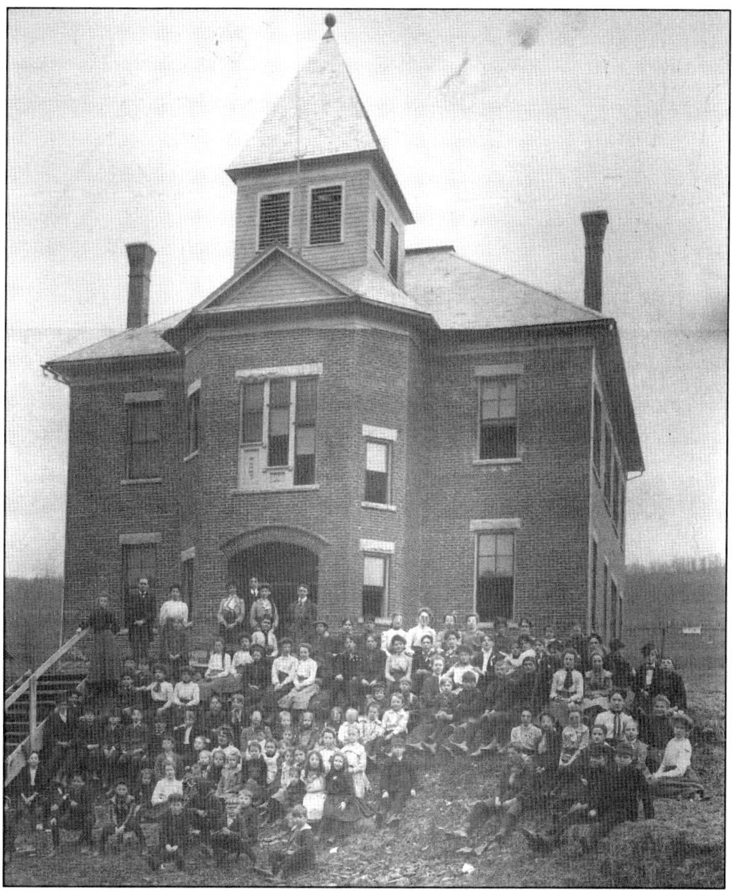

The Derrick City School. Due to high winds and a lack of fire-fighting equipment in the Derrick City area, a fire on March 6, 1920, completely destroyed the building. The present-day school in Derrick City is built on the site.

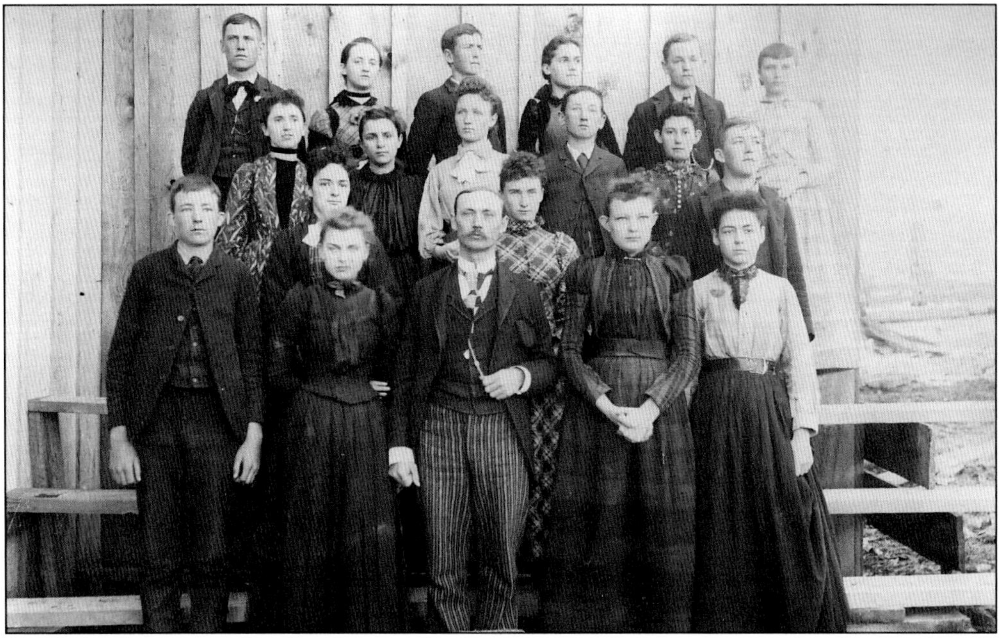

Gillmore High School, April 24, 1891. Once located just down the road from Derrick City, Gillmore no longer exists.

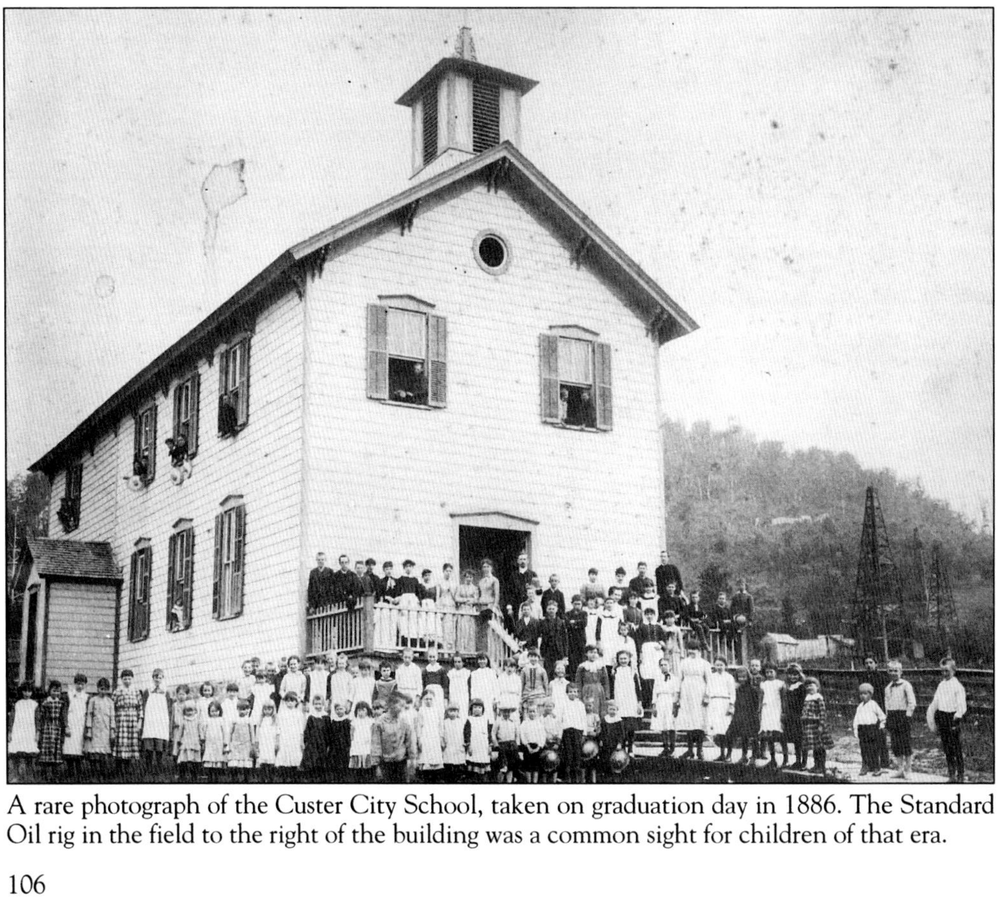

A rare photograph of the Custer City School, taken on graduation day in 1886. The Standard Oil rig in the field to the right of the building was a common sight for children of that era.

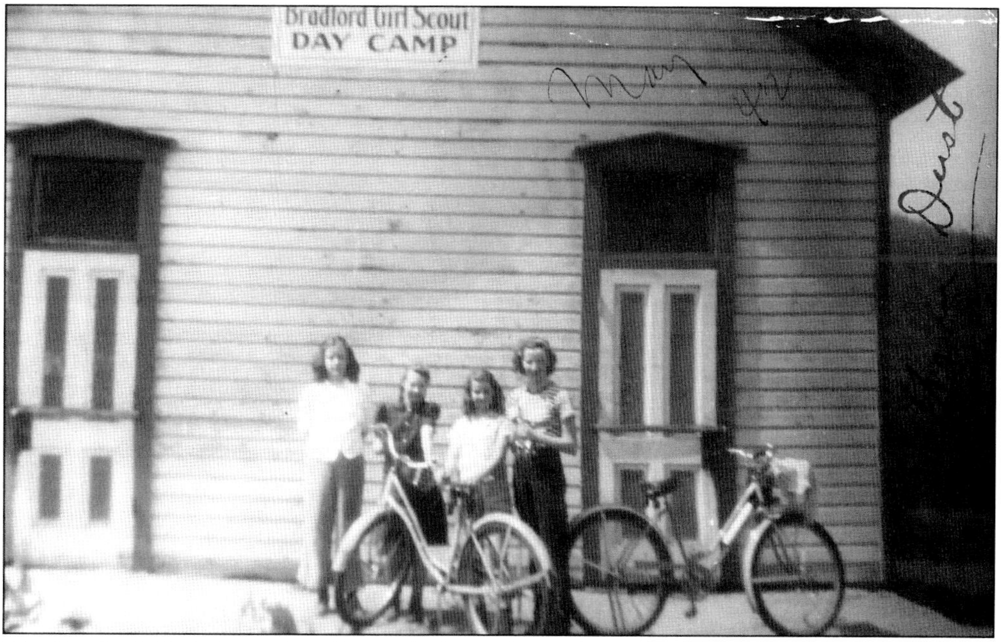

The Bradford Girl Scout Day Camp facilities, located in the old Crooker House School on West Corydon Street, 1942. This school building was moved to the Crook Farm on Seaward Avenue in 1975, and has been restored to its original condition. It is currently part of the Crook Farm Historical Farmstead.

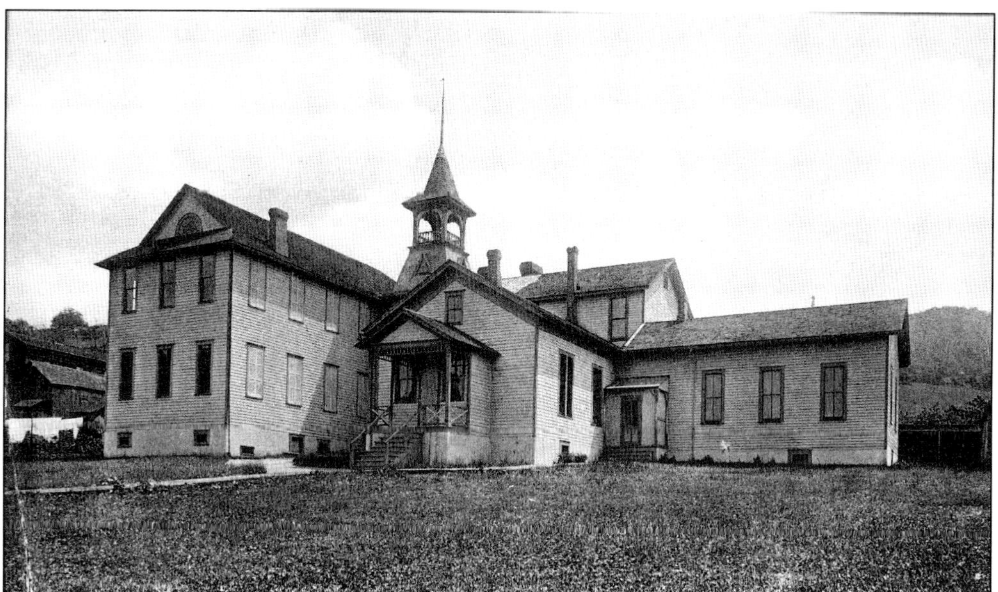

The Sixth Ward School. One of the last schools to be annexed to the Bradford school system, this original Sixth Ward School began as a one-room schoolhouse, and was added onto over the years.

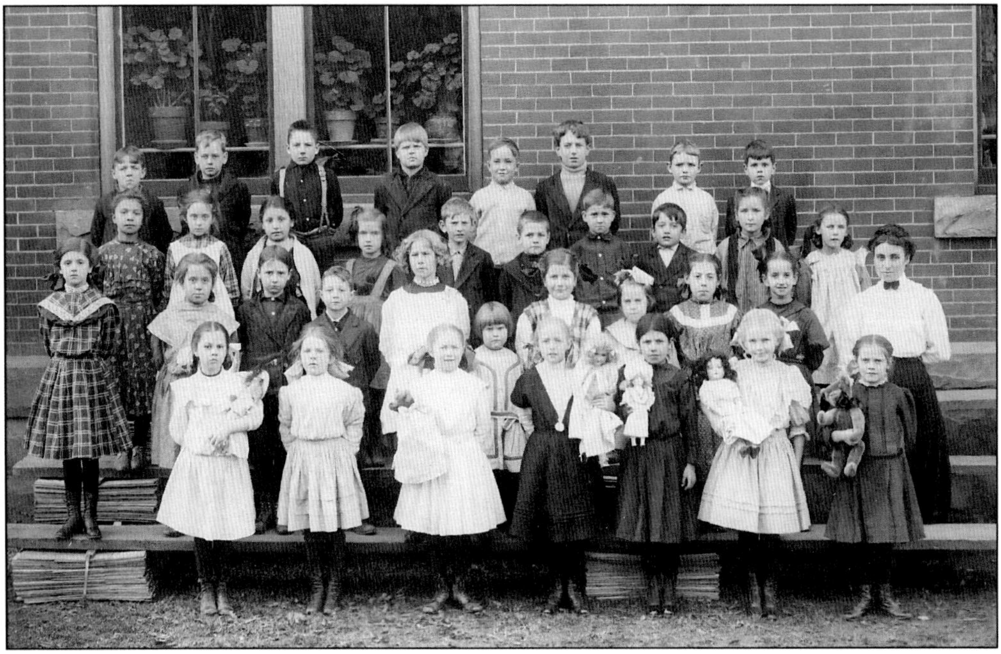

The Fifth Ward School, *c.* 1910. Like all school class pictures of this time period, this photograph was taken outside, where good light was available, all the children could line up on bleachers, and the school could serve as background. These children are probably in third or fourth grade. The girls in the front row have brought their favorite dolls and teddy bears for the day.

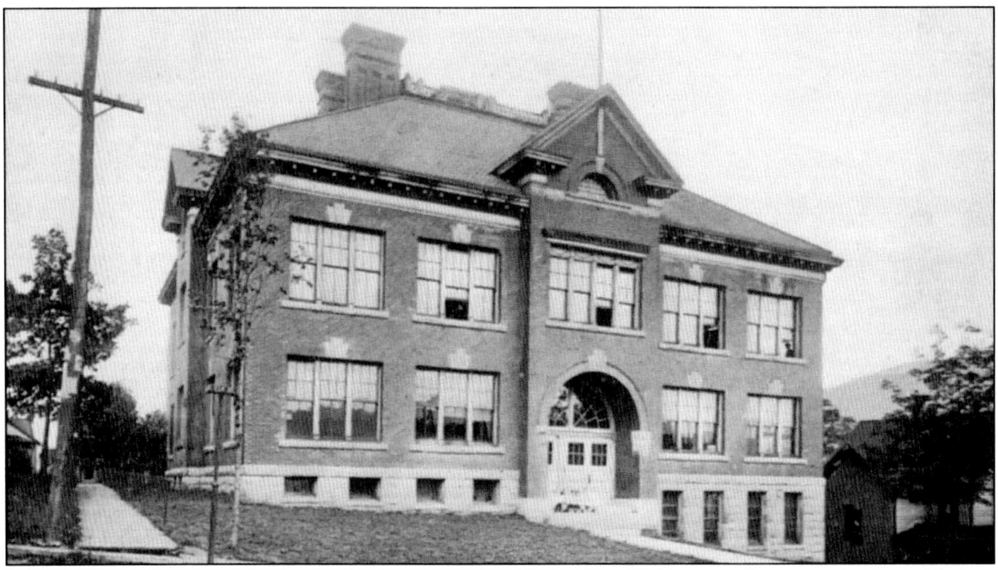

The Fifth Ward School, Elm Street, *c.* 1900. Originally, Bradford was divided into a series of districts, or wards, and five of the six wards inside the city limits had their own brick school building (the First Ward was the business district and had no school). The Fifth Ward School, located on Elm Street, has been demolished. The other four school buildings remain, although they are no longer used by the public school system. Opera singer and Bradford native Marilyn Horne attended this school in the 1930s.

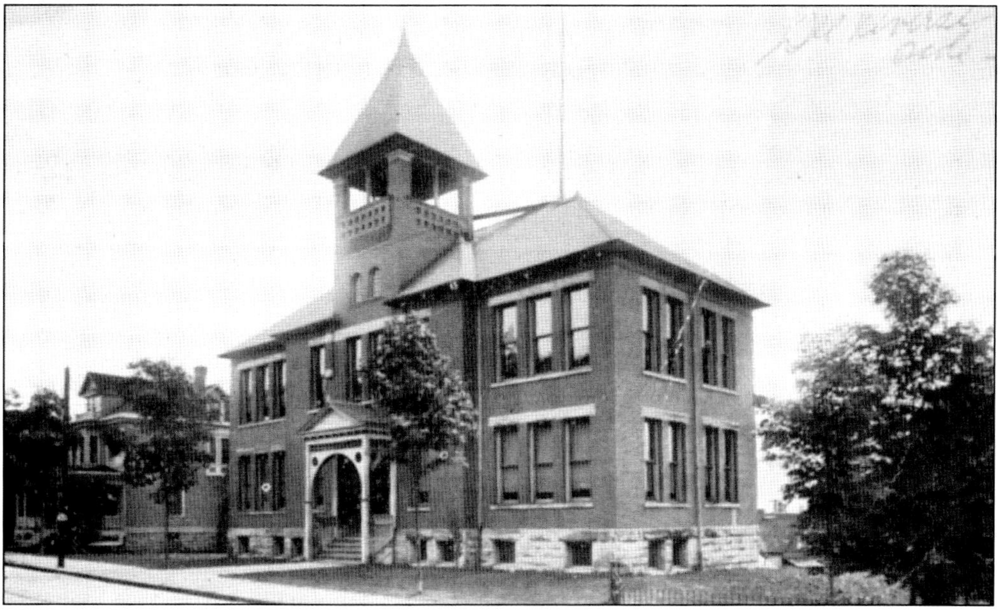

The Fourth Ward School. This, the second Fourth Ward School, was also the second to be destroyed by fire. On February 20, 1928, a blaze started on the upper floor and quickly spread, burning the school to the ground. Students were sent to other schools in the city for the remainder of the school year. The present Fourth Ward School was built in 1929.

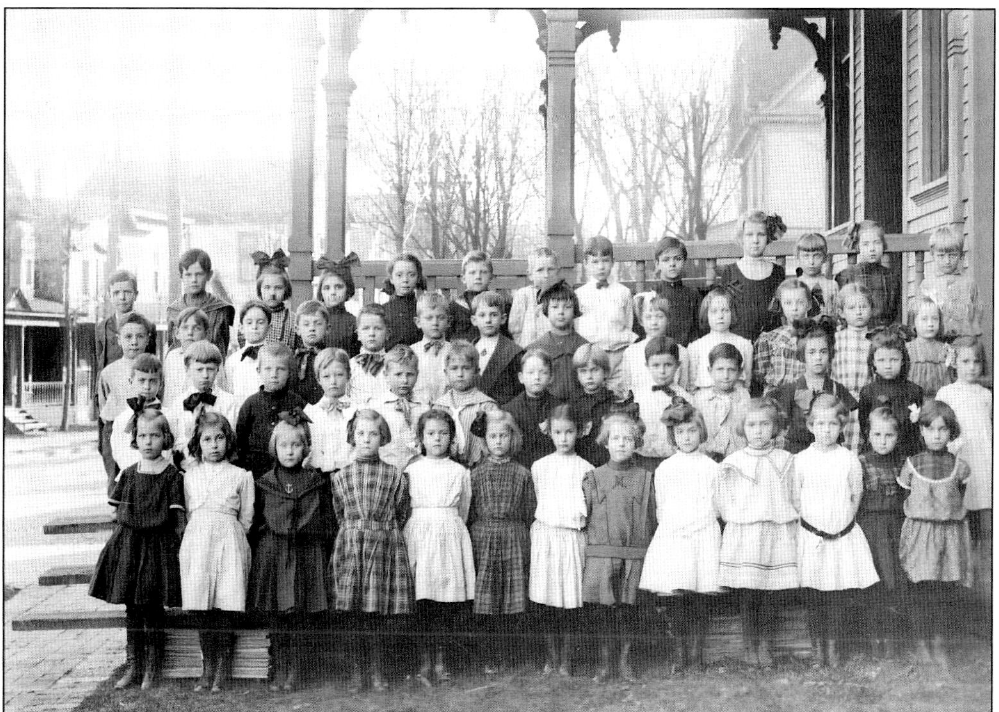

The Second Ward School, mid-1920s. The large number of students in this fourth grade class (fifty-two in all) was not unusual for this time period. Bradford's population stood at almost 20,000 in the 1920s.

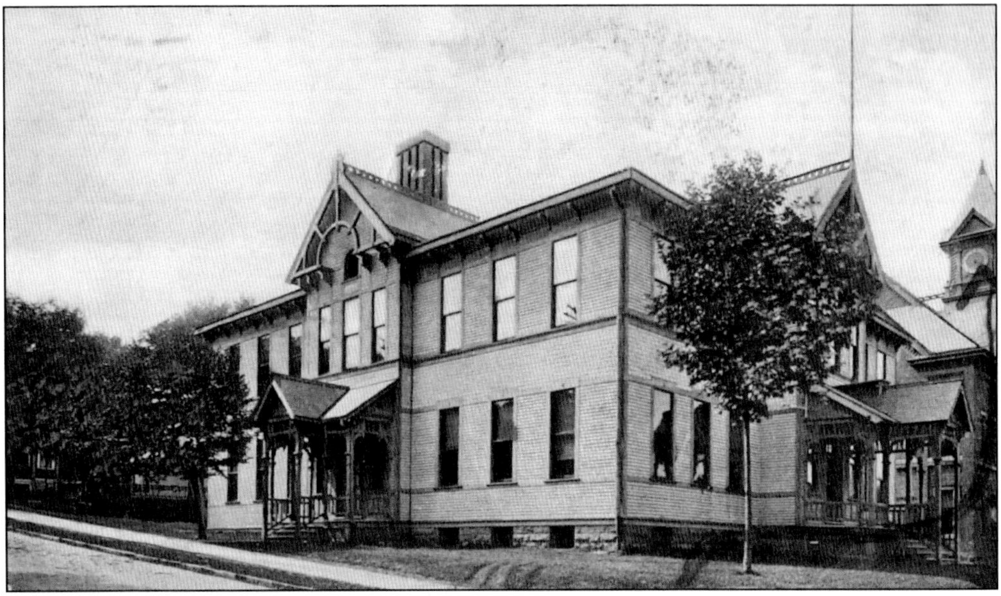

The Second Ward School, 1910, on the corner of Elm and Congress Streets. The first Second Ward was destroyed by fire on March 11, 1886. The present brick building was built in 1935.

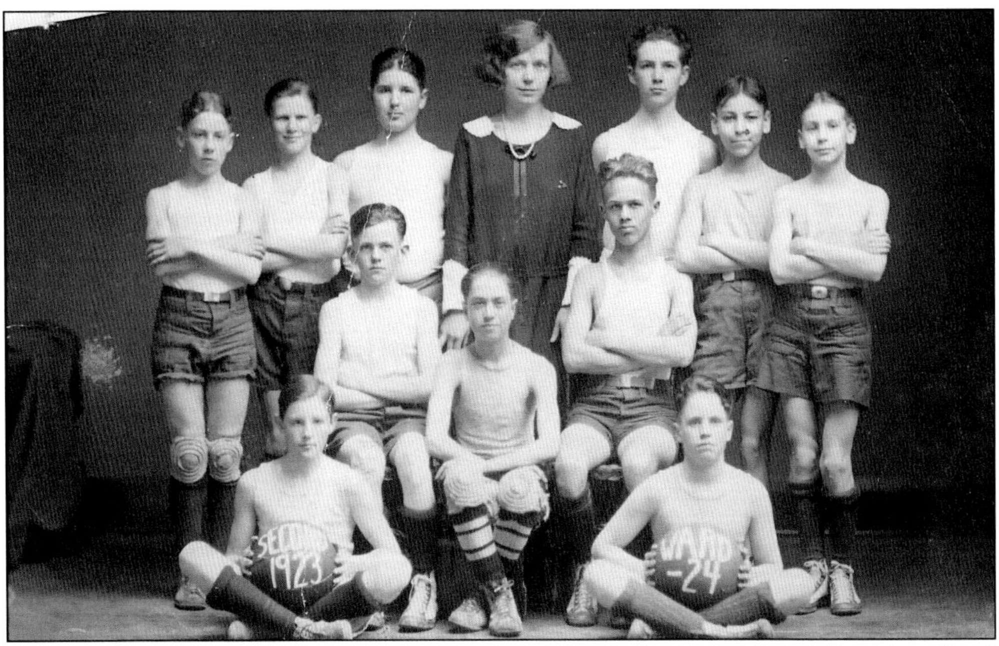

The Second Ward basketball team, 1923–24. From left to right are as follows: (sitting on floor) Robert Shaw and Jack Stewart; (second row) Bob O'Day, Elmer Taylor, and Jack Coit; (back row) A.J. Berry, Bob Harding, Chuck Corwin, Roberta Shaw, Ned Carr, Victor Kohn, and Dick (?) Glass.

Bradford High School, 1905. Located at the head of Mechanic Street from 1905 to 1925, this building was renovated into the present-day Third Ward, when crowded classroom conditions made the construction of the new high school on Interstate Parkway a necessity.

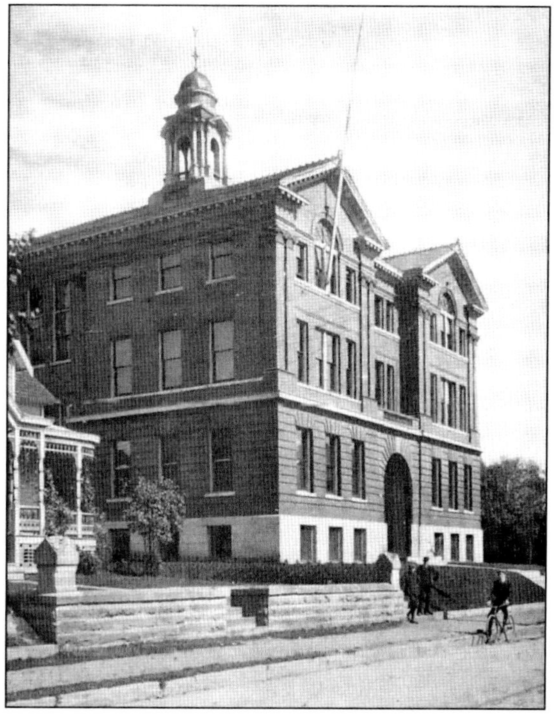

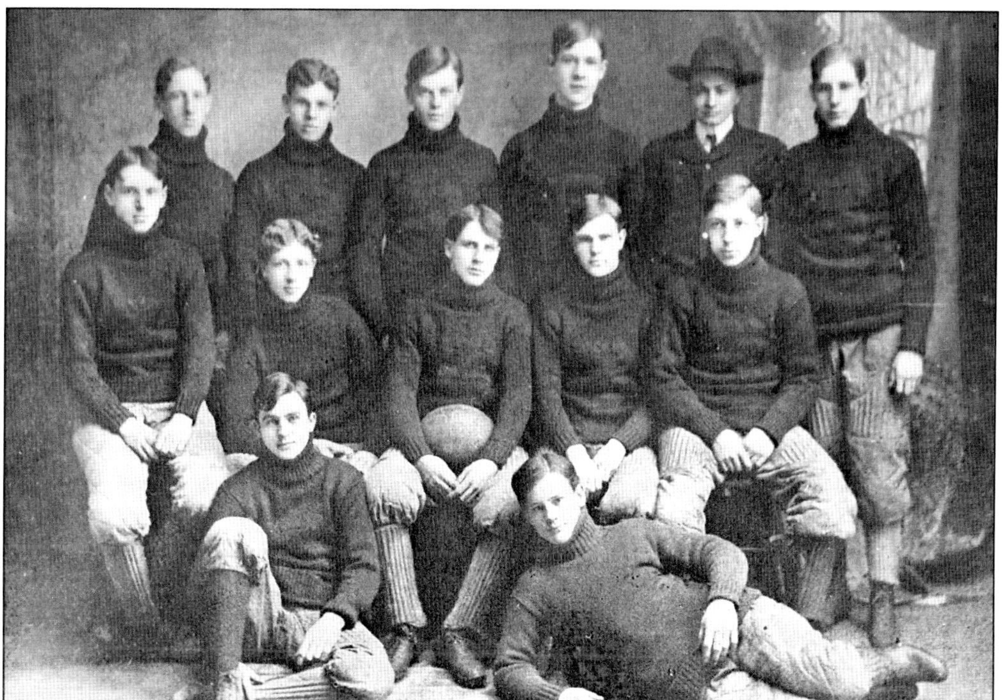

The Bradford High School football team, 1903. From left to right are as follows: (on floor, reclining) George Douglas and William Russell; (seated) Howard Coleman, Harry Goodrich, captain Fraser Sloan, Ralph Byles, and Pete Adsit; (standing) Joseph Pierce, Jid Dodge, Frank Bovaird, Ed Booth, coach Fred Heckel, and Paul Barrett.

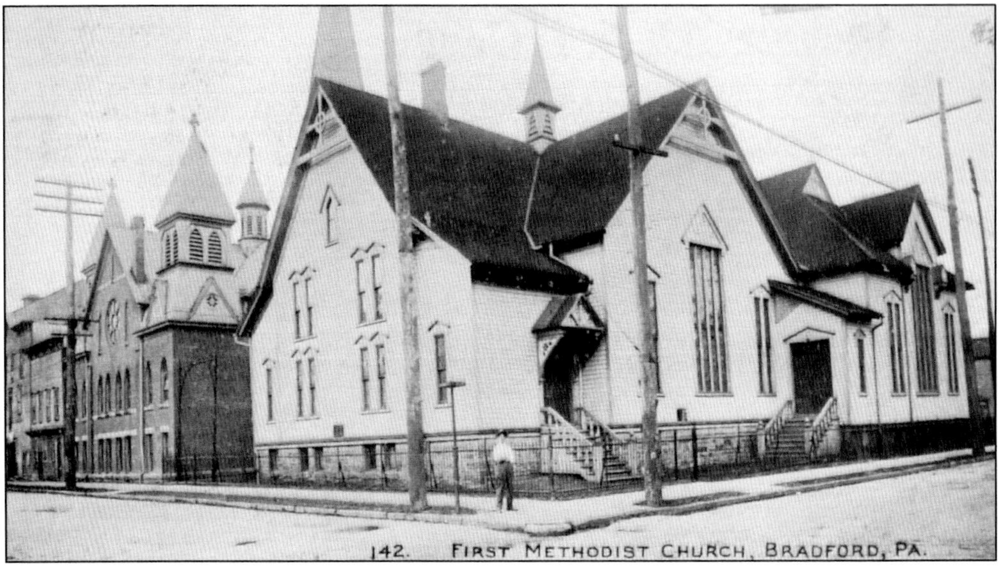

The original First Methodist Church on Corydon Street. Built in 1878, this church was replaced with the current stone church in 1927.

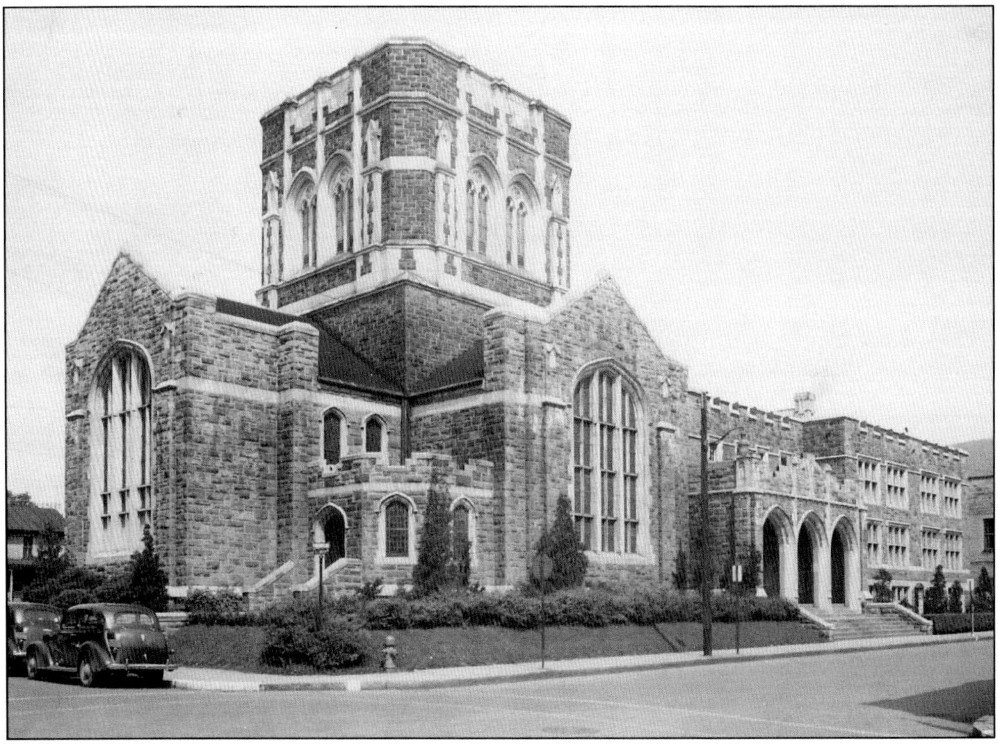
The First Methodist Church, June 1948. This impressive stone church was built in 1927 and is still located on Corydon Street. It was built of 35,000 square feet of stone found on the property of the Lewis Run Manufacturing Company. The stone was brought to the site in the rough and then cut on six sides; each piece was measured and cut for the particular place it was to fill. Enough stone was cut in the winter months to carry the masons through the following summer. In all, it took three years to complete construction.

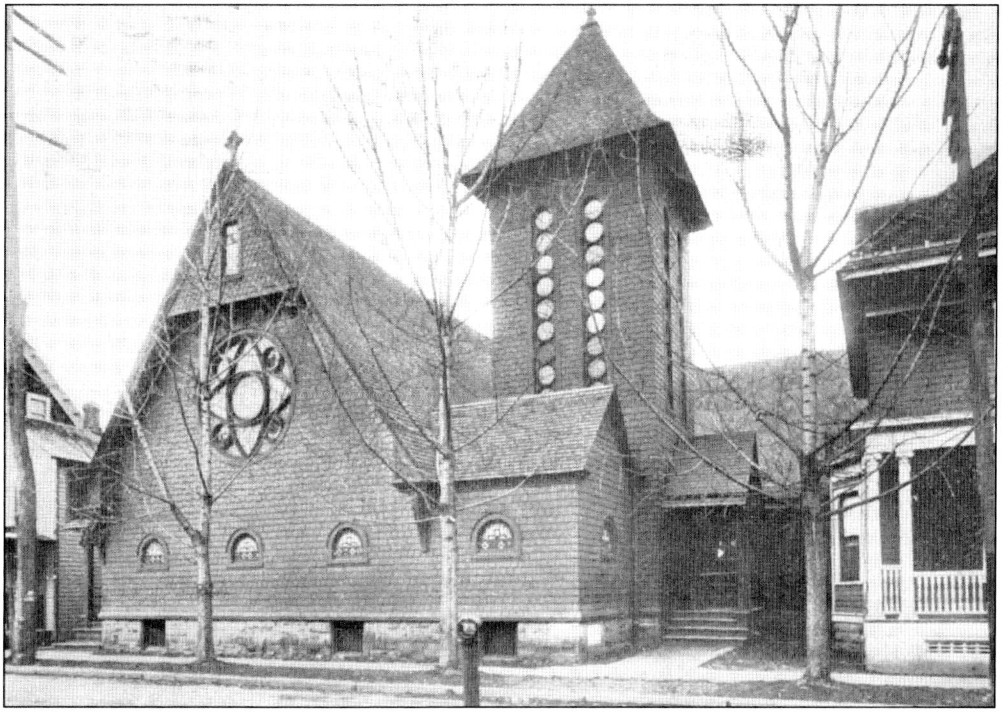

The Church of the Ascension, 1910. A disastrous fire caused by candles around the altar and Christmas wreaths destroyed the first church completely. The cornerstone of the second church (shown here) was laid on April 23, 1891.

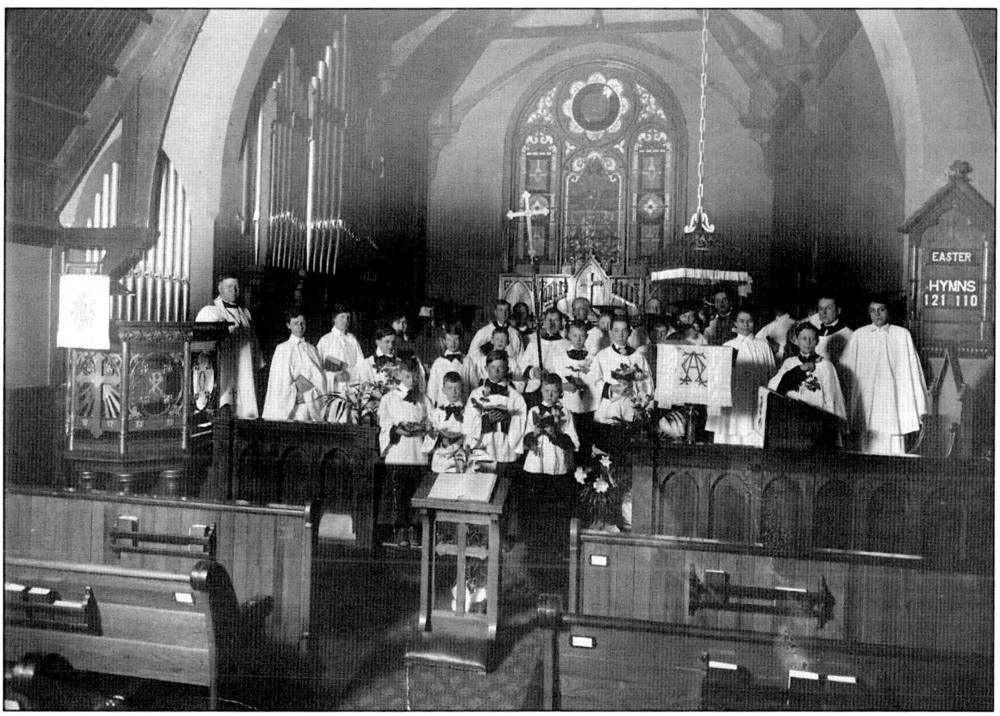

The interior of the Church of the Ascension, *c.* 1920.

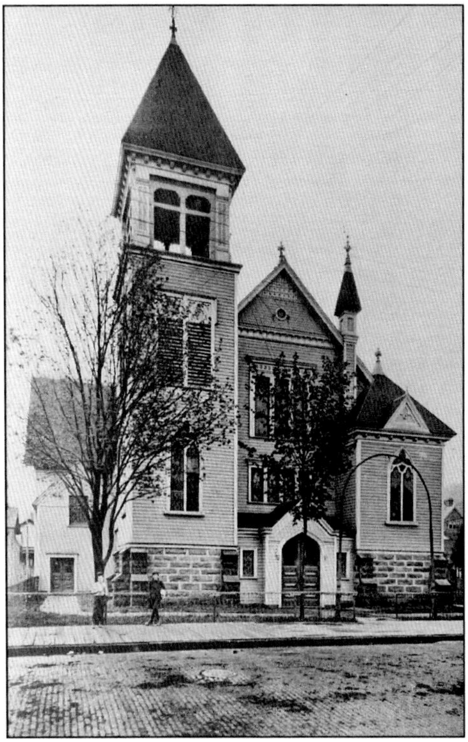

The First Presbyterian Church, Corydon Street, *c.* 1890s. This church, in existence from 1889 to 1917, was actually rebuilt from an older church structure which underwent extensive alterations and additions. The rededication ceremony was held on January 13, 1889. The growth of the congregation required yet another expansion in 1917, however, and this time an entirely new structure, the present church, was built. While construction was in progress, church services were held at the Y.M.C.A. on Boylston Street.

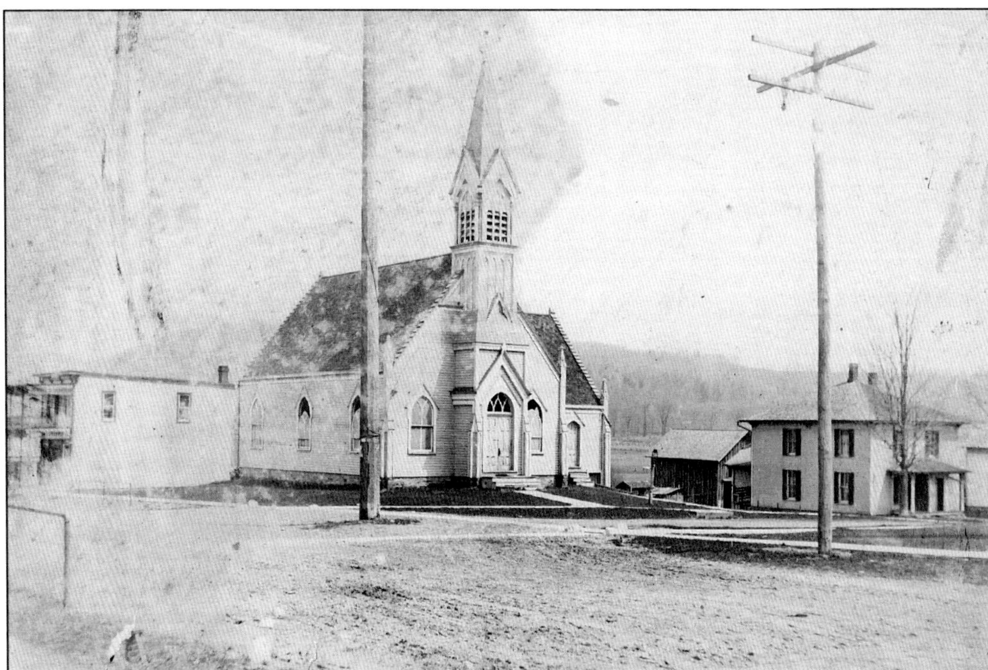

The First Baptist Church, 1881. On January 18, 1881, the formal dedication ceremony took place with Reverend Augustus H. Strong, president of the Rochester Theological Seminary, preaching the sermon. At this service, a sum of $6,000 was raised to help pay for the new building.

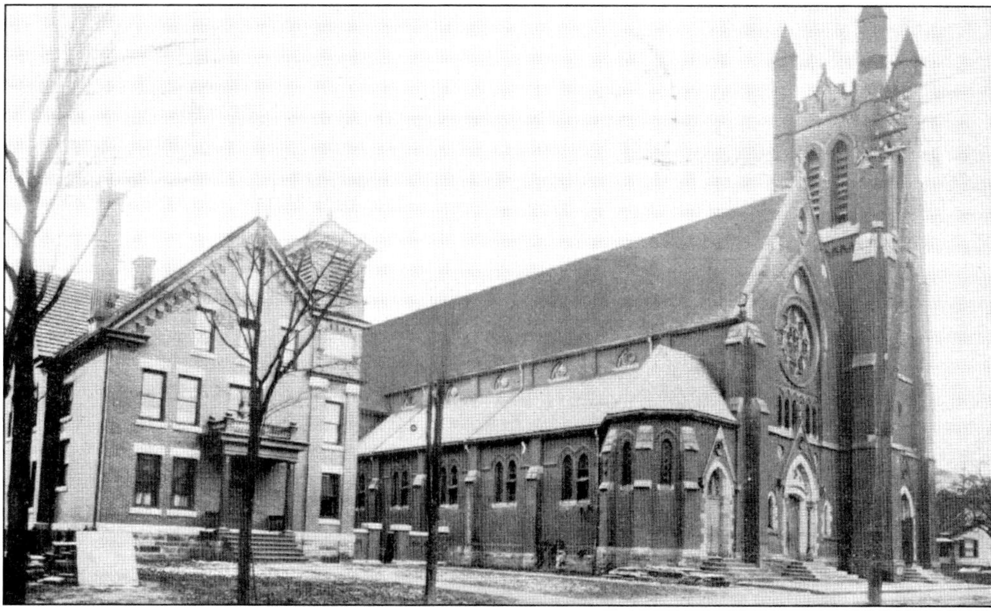

St. Bernard's Roman Catholic Church and convent, 1909. The cornerstone of the church was laid in 1892. Built of red brick with Ohio sandstone trim in a "modernized" Gothic style, the entire cost was $40,000. William Hanley was the contractor. The convent, built in 1906, was moved across the street and swung sideways to face Webster Street sometime between 1915 and 1923. Both are still standing and still in use.

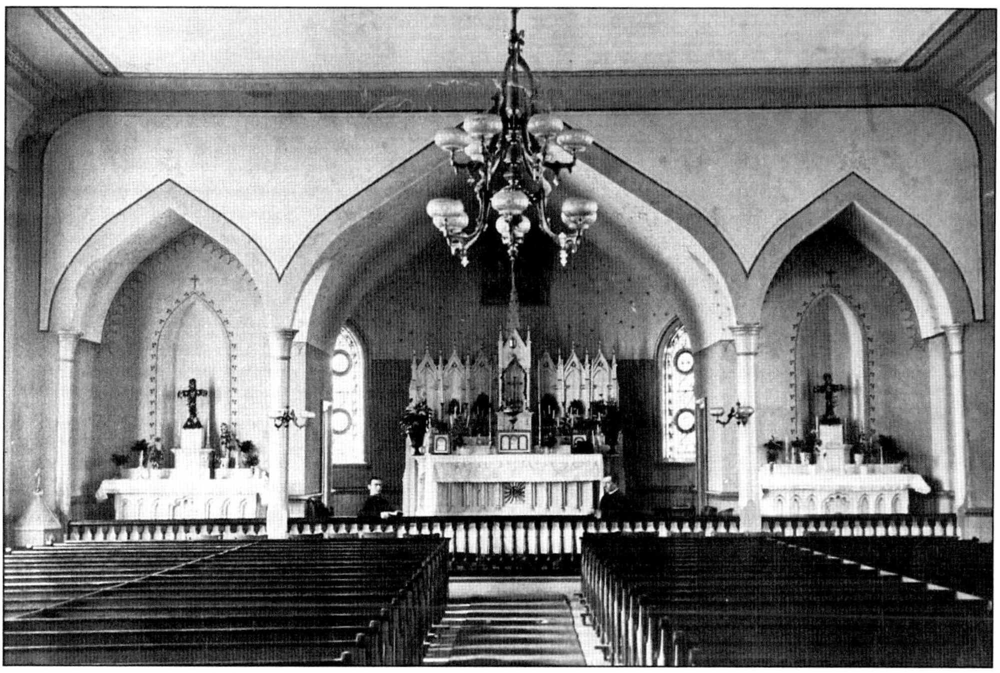

An interior view of the original St. Bernard's Church, 1890. The present church underwent renovations in the 1920s under the direction of Father Hickey, when the stenciled decorations were covered, a new marble altar rail was installed, and other structural modifications were made.

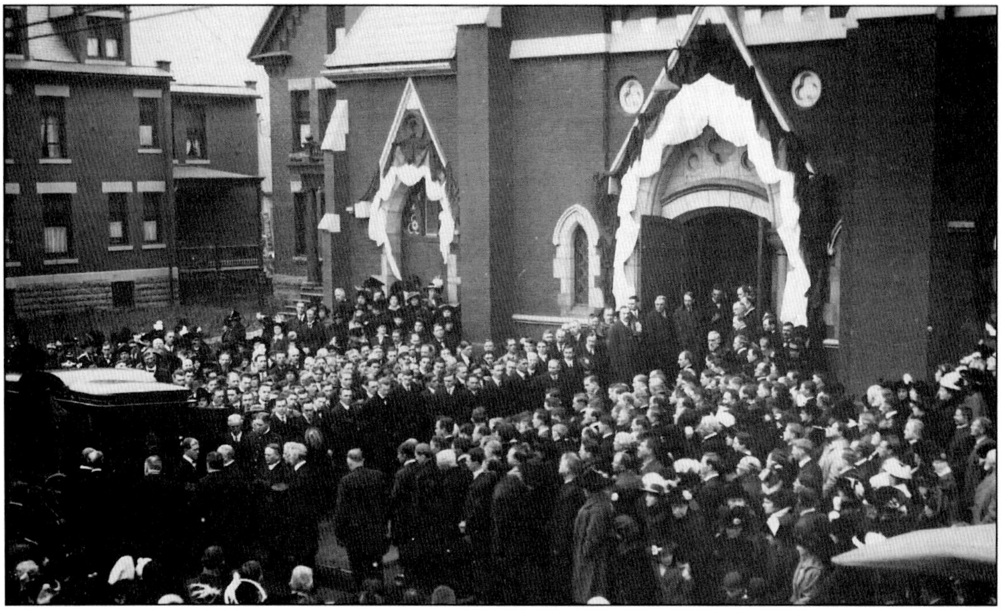

Father William Coonan's funeral, November 5, 1915. A beloved priest of St. Bernard's for thirty-eight years, he oversaw the construction of the present church in 1882, the building of the convent in 1906, the construction of the old school, and the purchase of St. Bernard's Cemetery.

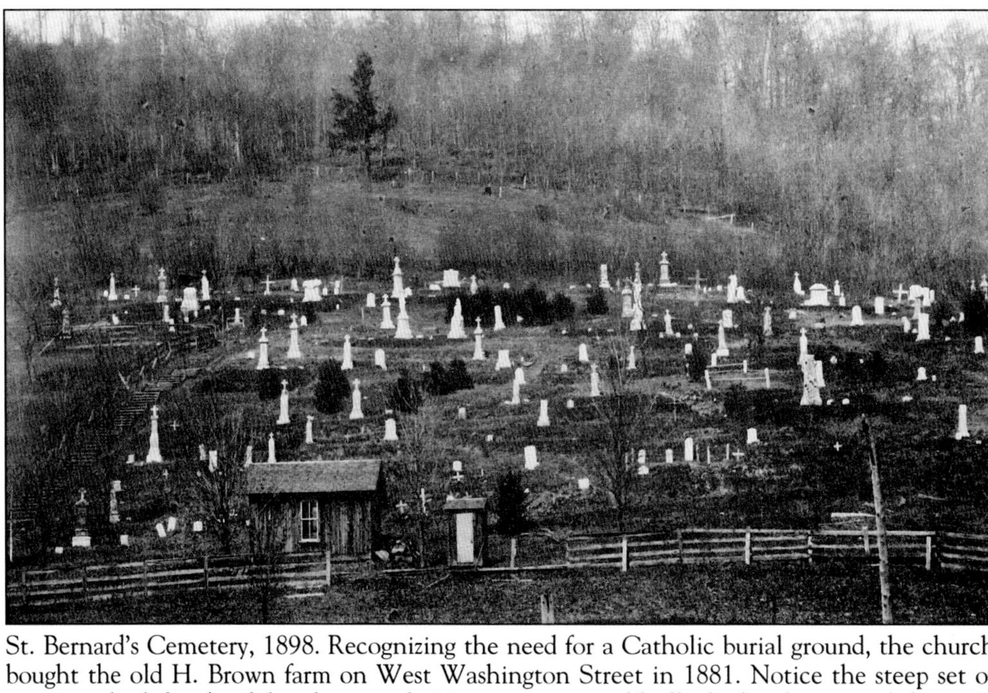

St. Bernard's Cemetery, 1898. Recognizing the need for a Catholic burial ground, the church bought the old H. Brown farm on West Washington Street in 1881. Notice the steep set of stairs on the left side of the photograph. Not everyone could afford a headstone and there are numerous unmarked graves.

Nine

Old Home Week, August 8–14, 1909

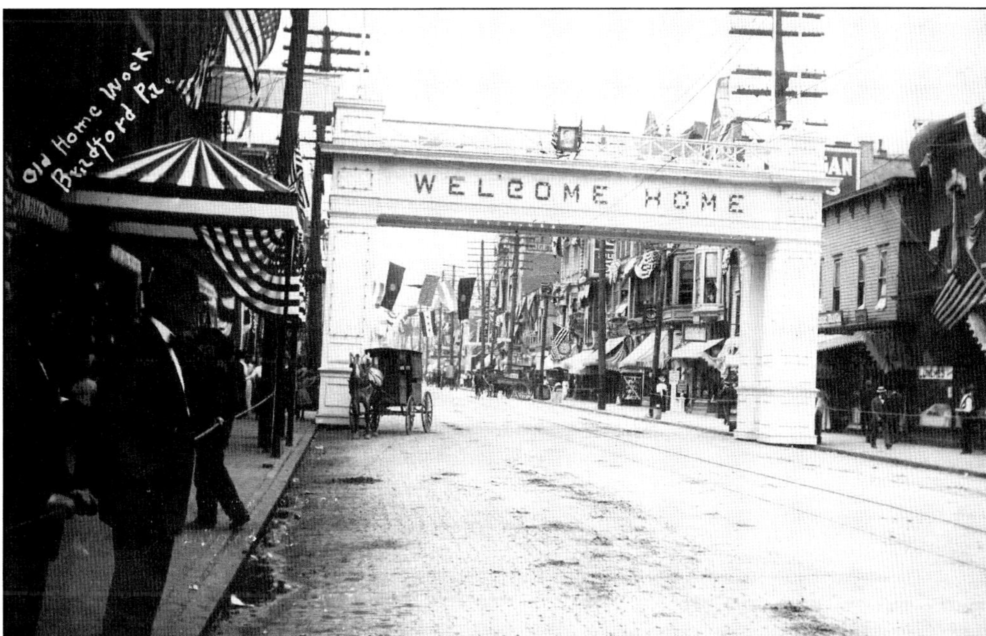

The first Old Home Week, designated to celebrate the 30th anniversary of the incorporation of Bradford as a city and to invite back early settlers and former Bradfordians. Parades were held daily and a huge wood and plaster arch was constructed over Main Street near the intersection of Main and Webster Streets. Large enough for trolleys to pass under, it provided a bridge (upper left of arch) for pedestrians wanting to view Main Street from above. Flags were hung on every building, commemorative flag pins with a tiny photograph of an oil derrick were sold, and a thirty-eight-page souvenir booklet was printed.

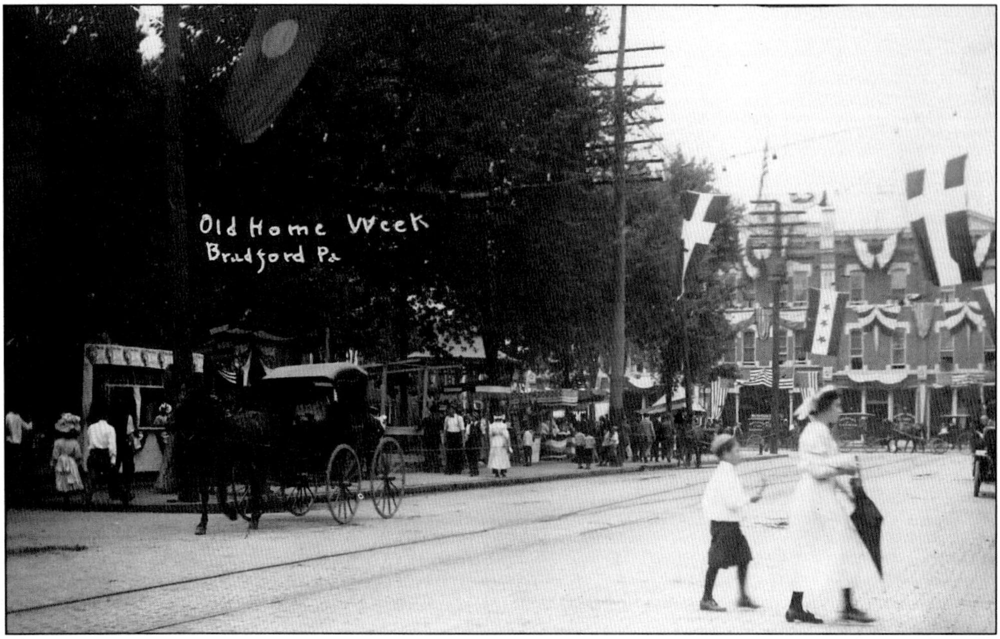

Old Home Week, August 1909. Festivities in the square included parades, ceremonies, dances, bands; hundreds of visitors enjoyed Bradford's Old Home Week.

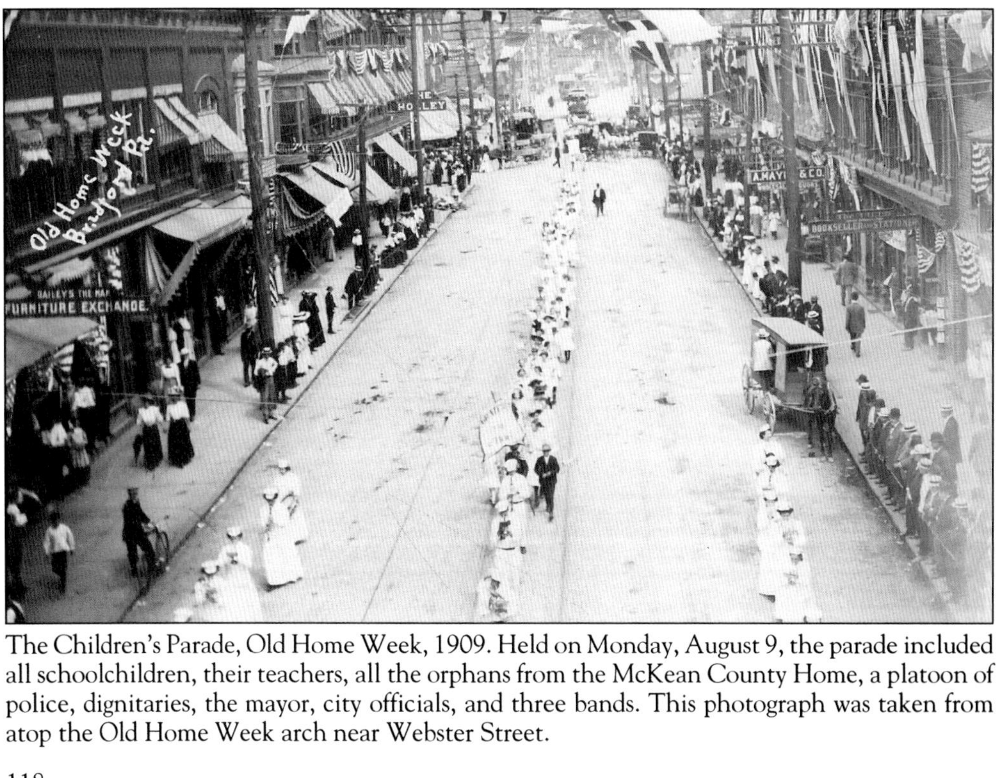

The Children's Parade, Old Home Week, 1909. Held on Monday, August 9, the parade included all schoolchildren, their teachers, all the orphans from the McKean County Home, a platoon of police, dignitaries, the mayor, city officials, and three bands. This photograph was taken from atop the Old Home Week arch near Webster Street.

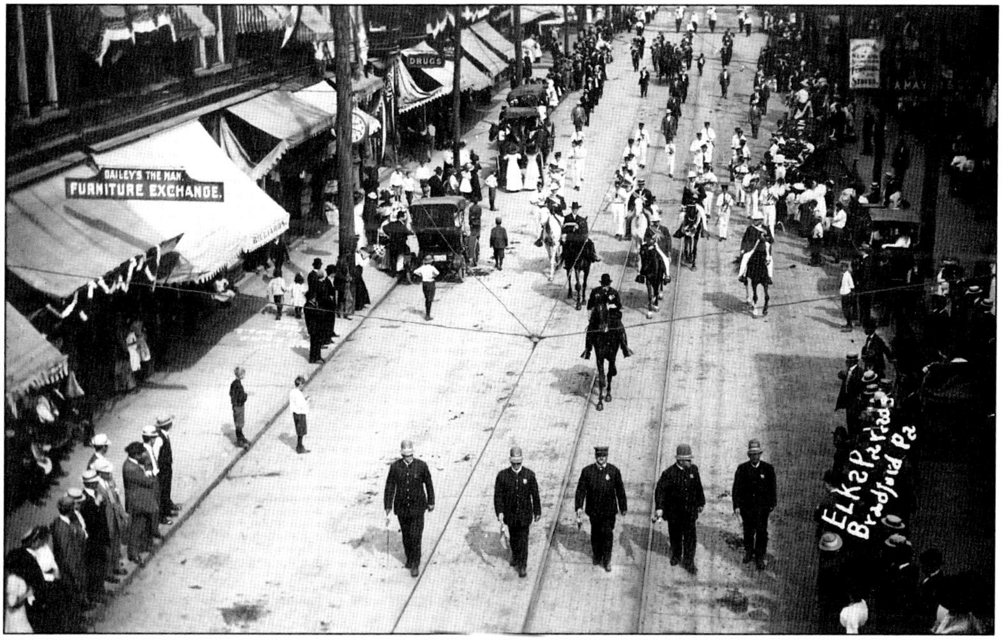

Wednesday, August 11, Old Home Week. The parade of the day featured railroad organizations, the military, and civic societies. Here, the Benevolent Order of the Elks marches down Main Street, led by Bradford's five-man police force.

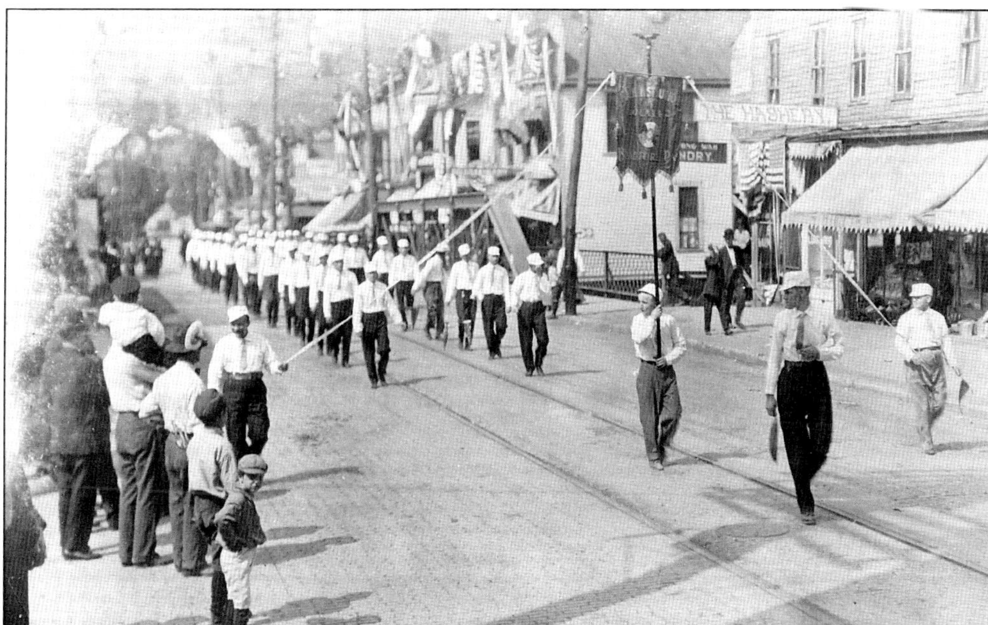

Labor and Industrial Day, August 13, Old Home Week. The Machinists Union of Bradford is shown here marching across the Mechanic Street Bridge on their way to Washington Street.

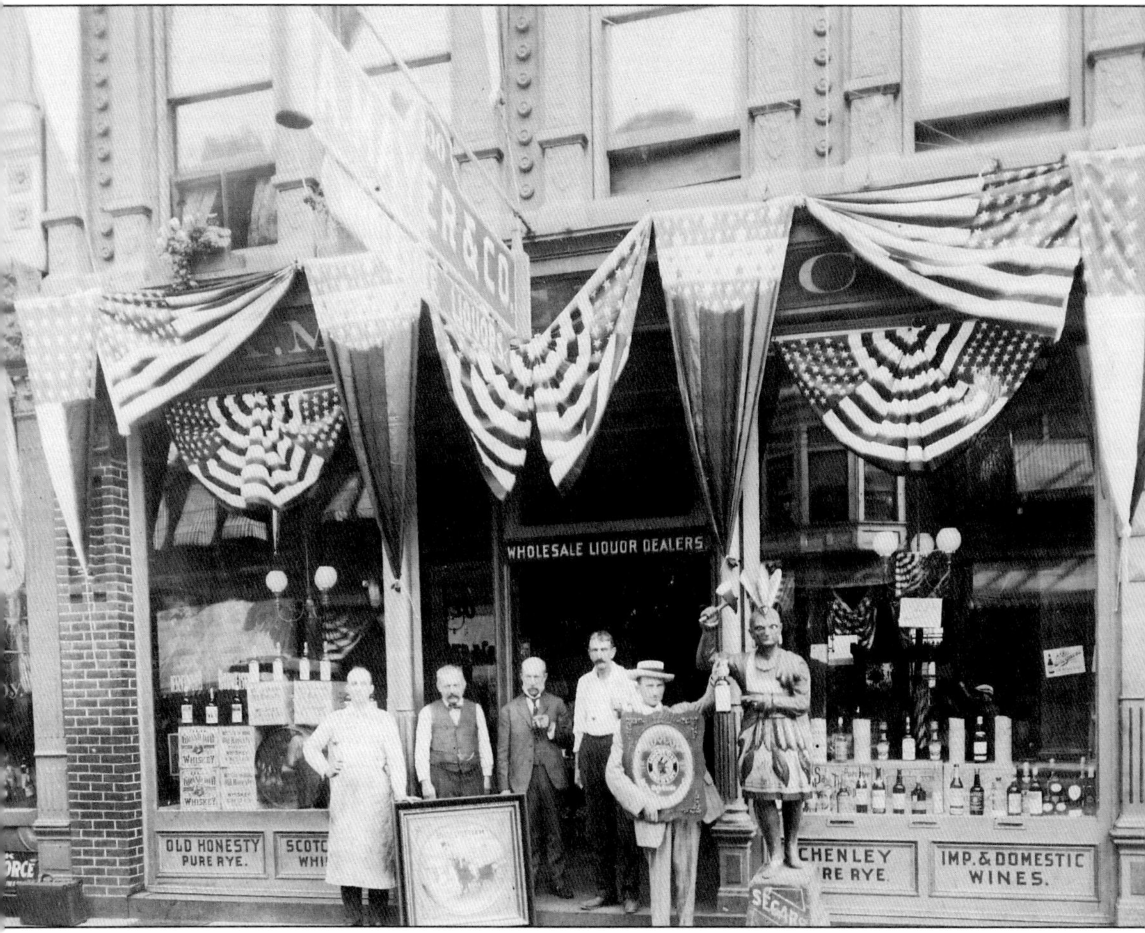

A.M. Mayer & Company, 1909. Dealers in wholesale liquors, tobacco, and cigars, the A.M. Mayer store was also the agent for the Iroquis Brewing Company of Buffalo. It was located where Tops Market is now. Here, employees are gathered outside in honor of Old Home Week. A. Marcus Mayer is the third man from the left, holding a cigar in his left hand. Born in Germany in 1836, he immigrated to the South, where he was drafted into the Confederacy during the Civil War. After the war he removed north, eventually settling in Bradford and establishing his store in 1878. He died in 1914, leaving behind a wife and five daughters.

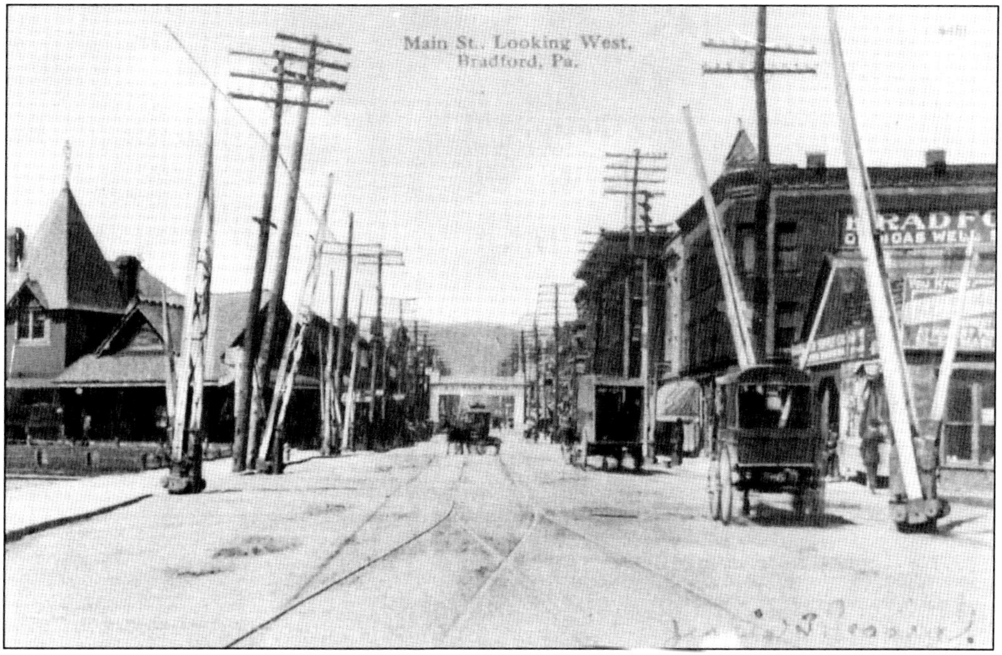

Looking up Main Street from near the train stations, 1909. The Old Home Week arch can be seen up near the Webster Street intersection. Trolley tracks in the street indicate the importance of streetcars as a mode of transportation.

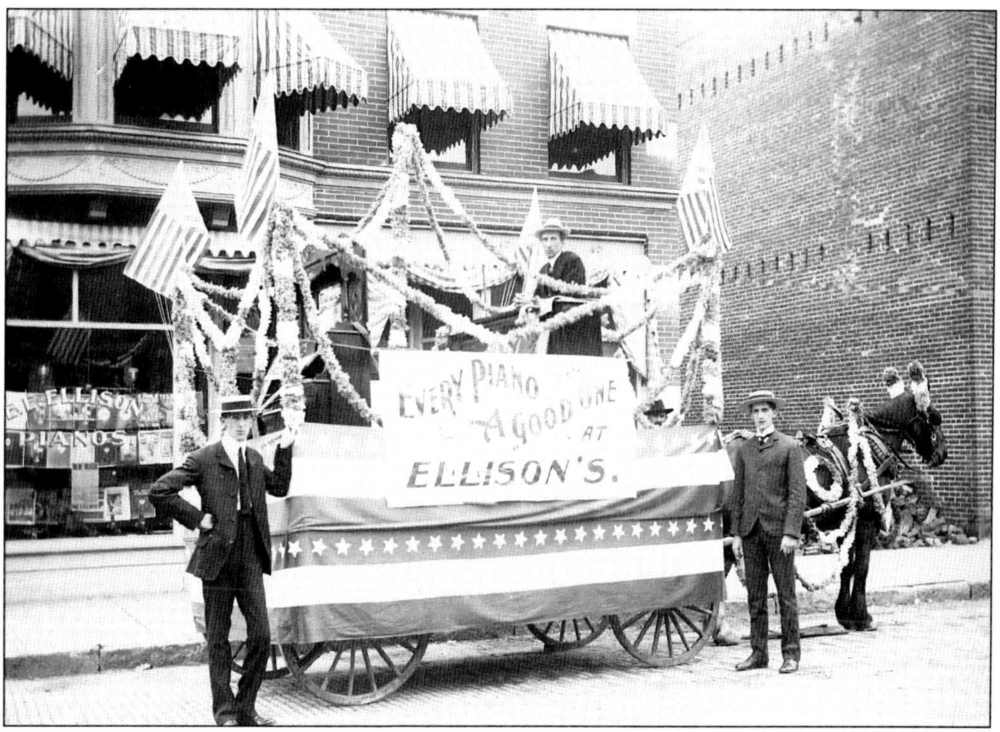

The Ellison's Piano parade float, Old Home Week, 1909. The Industrial and Labor Parade Day was held on Friday the 13th.

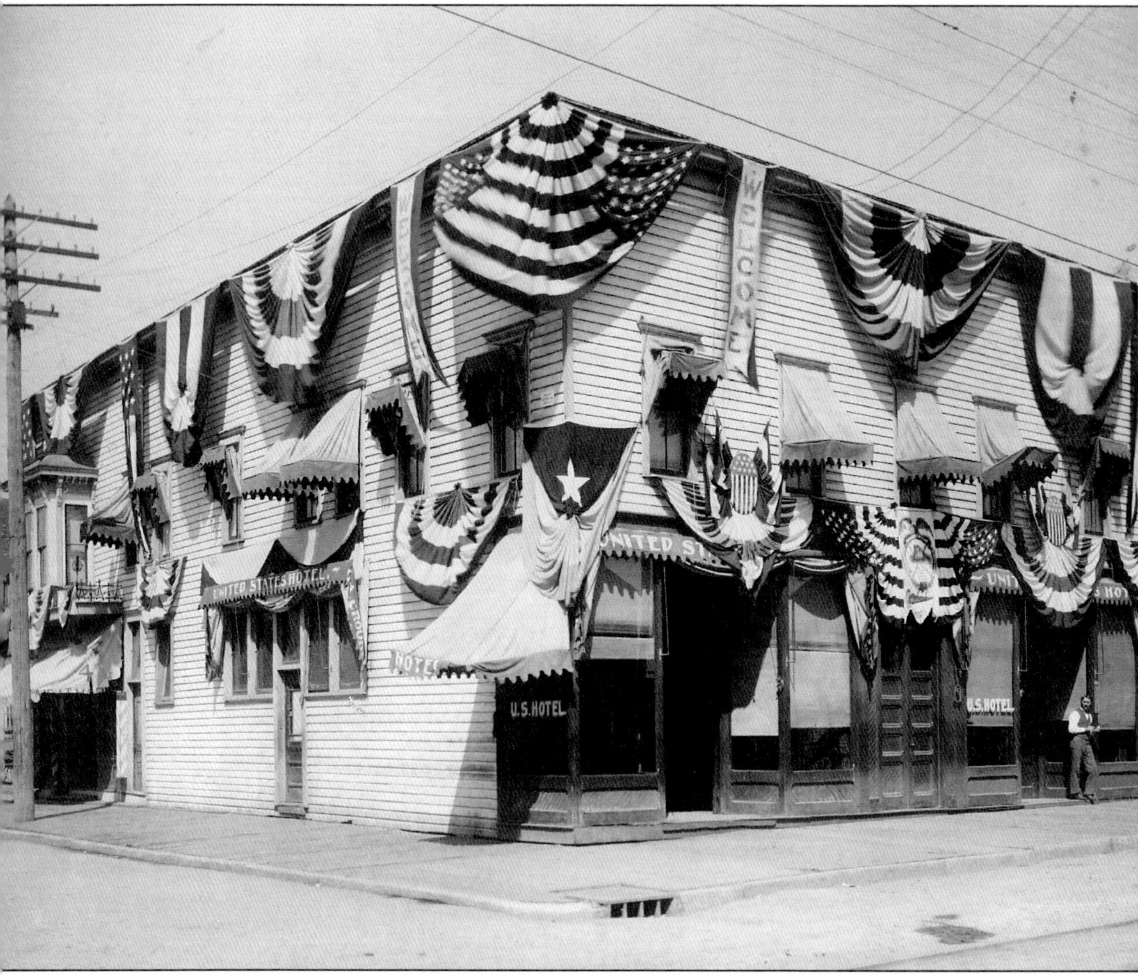

The United States Hotel (now the Star Restaurant), on the corner of Barbour and Mechanic Streets. With hundreds of Home Week visitors arriving daily, hotels in the city had a profitable week.

Ten

Floods

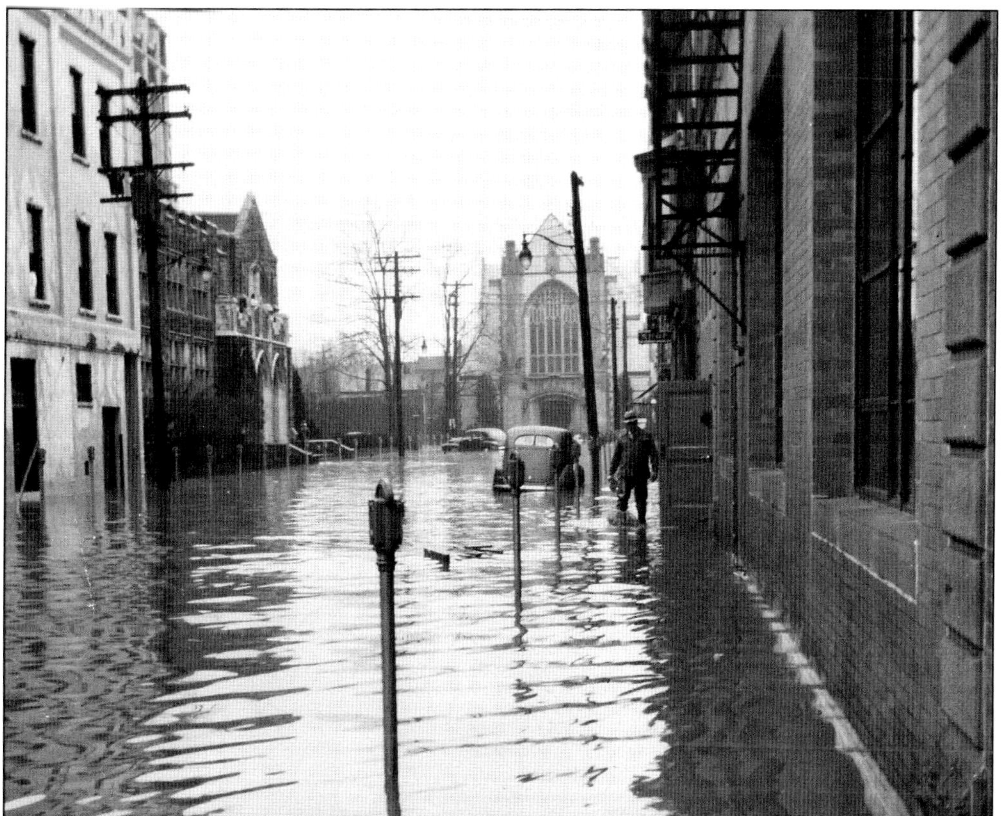

The spring flood of 1947, Chambers Street. Floods like this one did thousands of dollars of damage and prompted the establishment of citywide flood control measures in the early 1960s. Major floods occurred in 1901, 1910, and in several years during the 1940s.

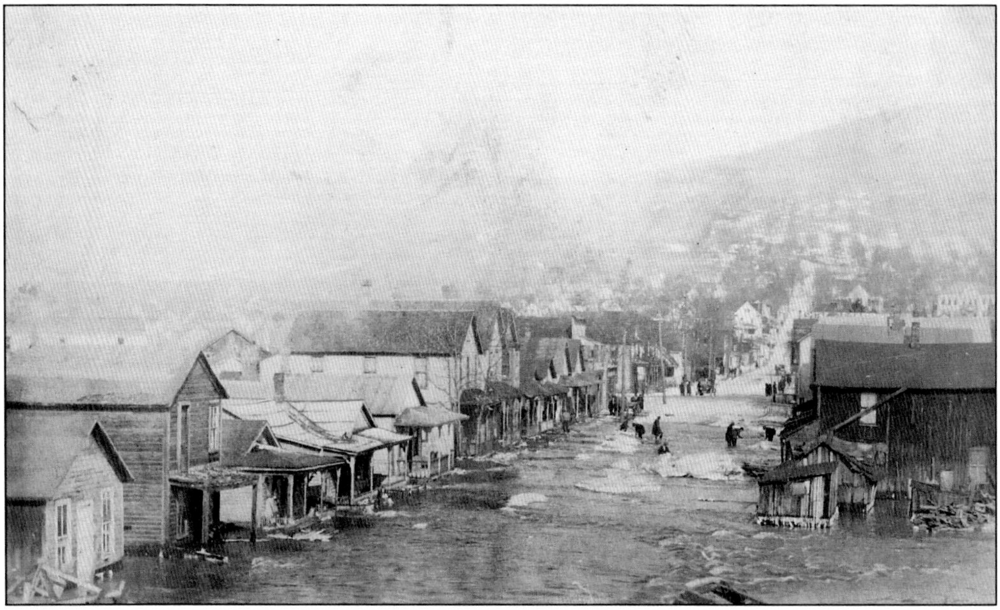

The 1901 flood, looking across the valley to Center Street from West Corydon Street. This flood occurred in early spring. Notice the ice floes in the streets.

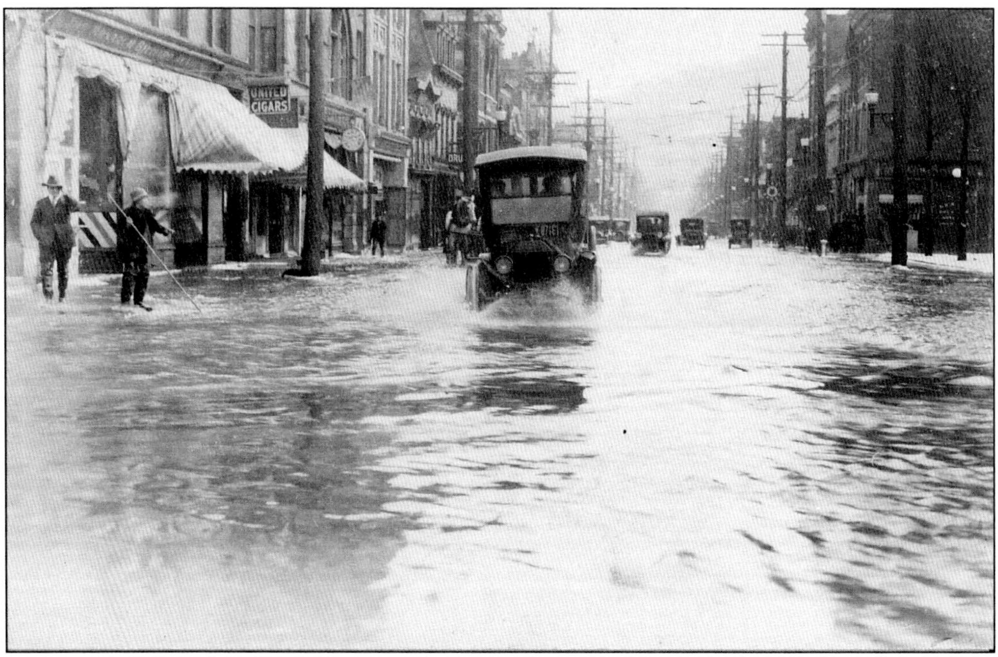

The 1918 flood. Here, automobiles attempt to navigate Main Street. This car is opposite the public square.

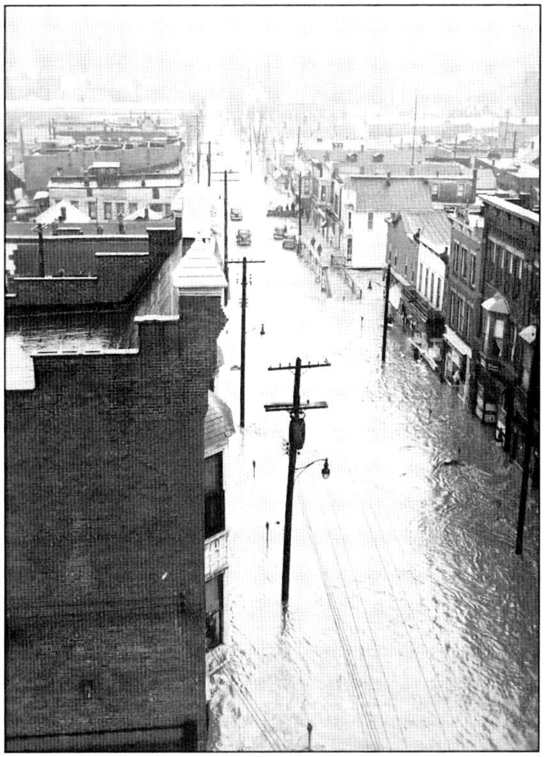

The 1947 flood. This photograph was taken from the roof of the Emery Hotel, looking up Mechanic Street.

The flood of April 5, 1947. The automobile is trying to turn the corner at Main and Mechanic Streets.

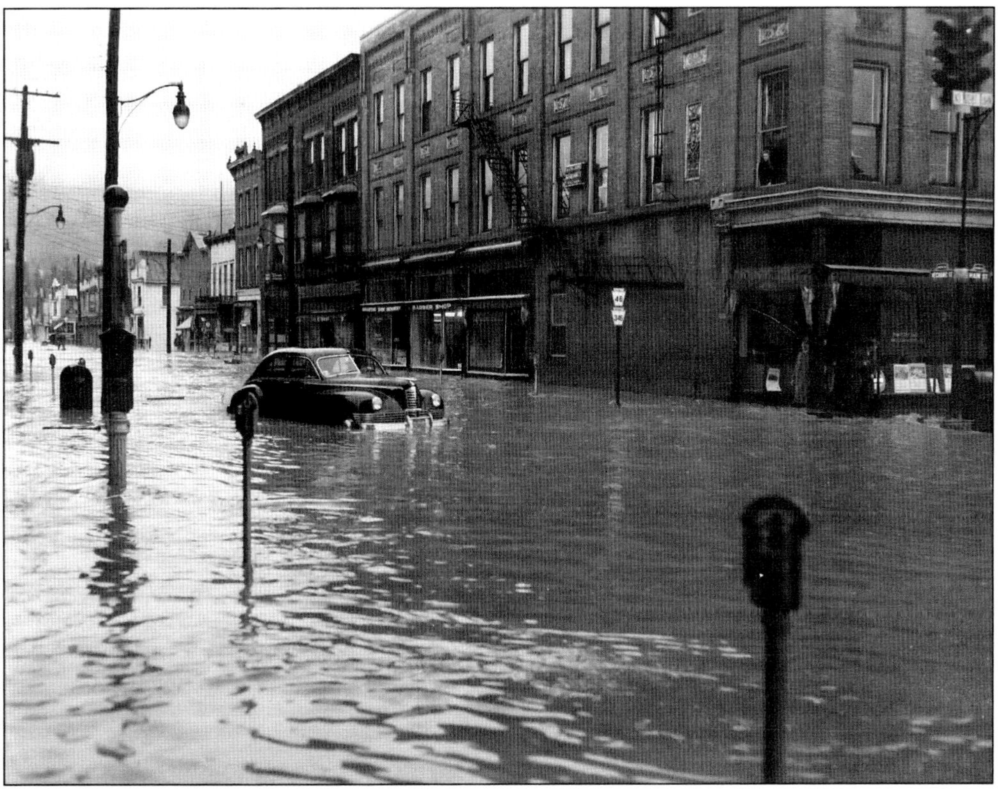

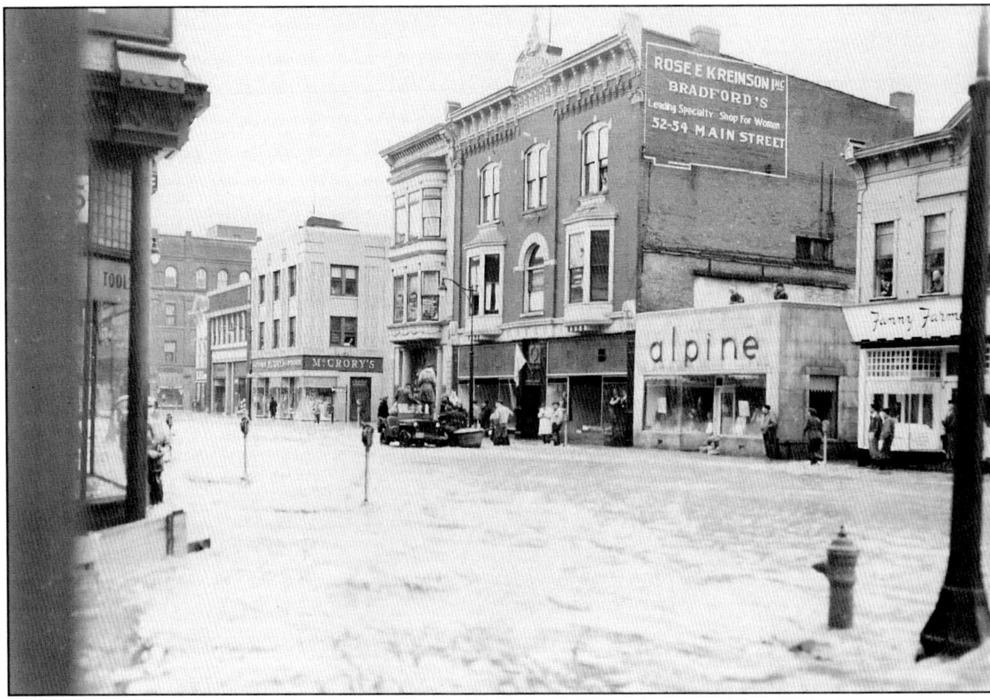

The 1947 flood, Main Street. A truck and boat on the opposite side of the street near the Alpine are picking up those stranded by the high water on the streets.

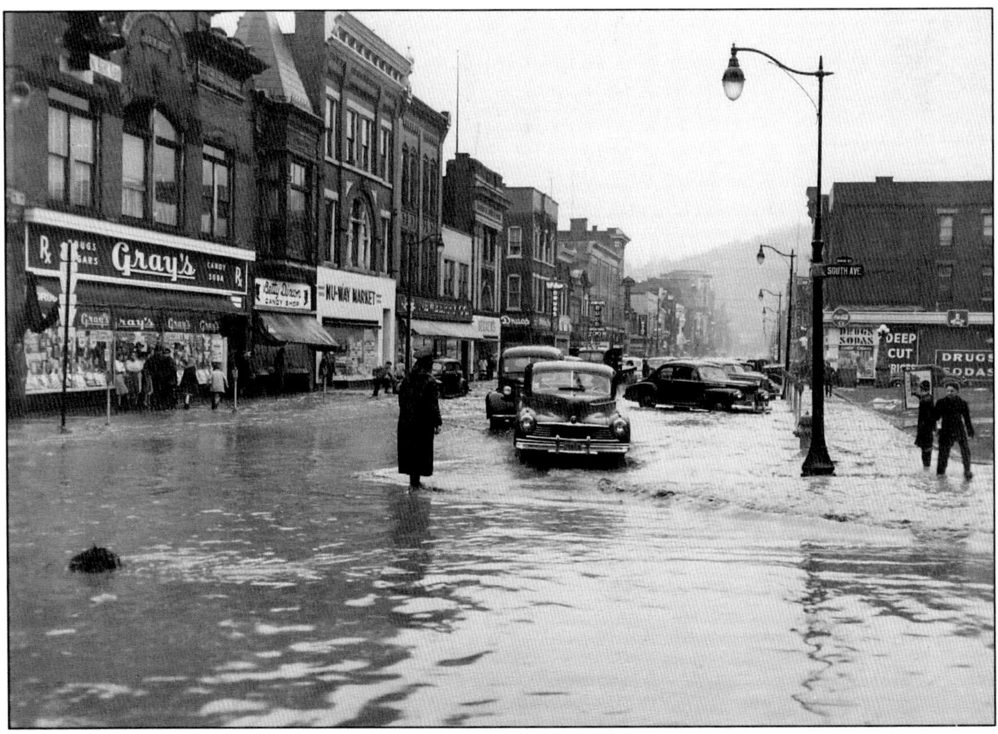

The 1947 flood, near the square. A policeman directs traffic as the flood waters recede.

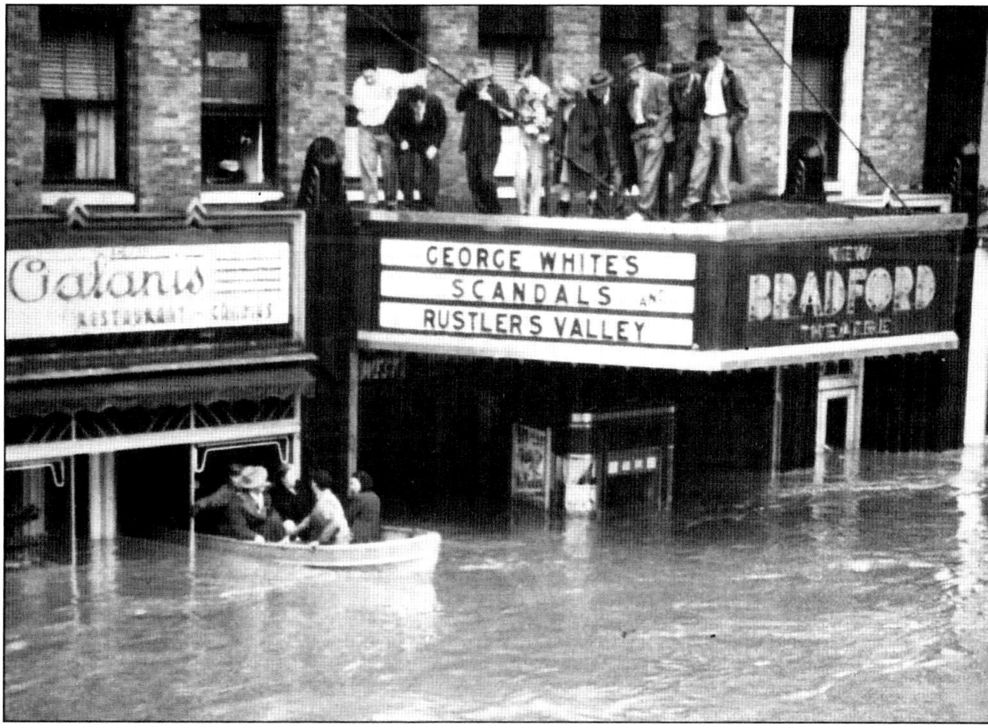

The 1947 flood. Stranded Bradfordians await rescue atop the marquee of the Bradford Theater.

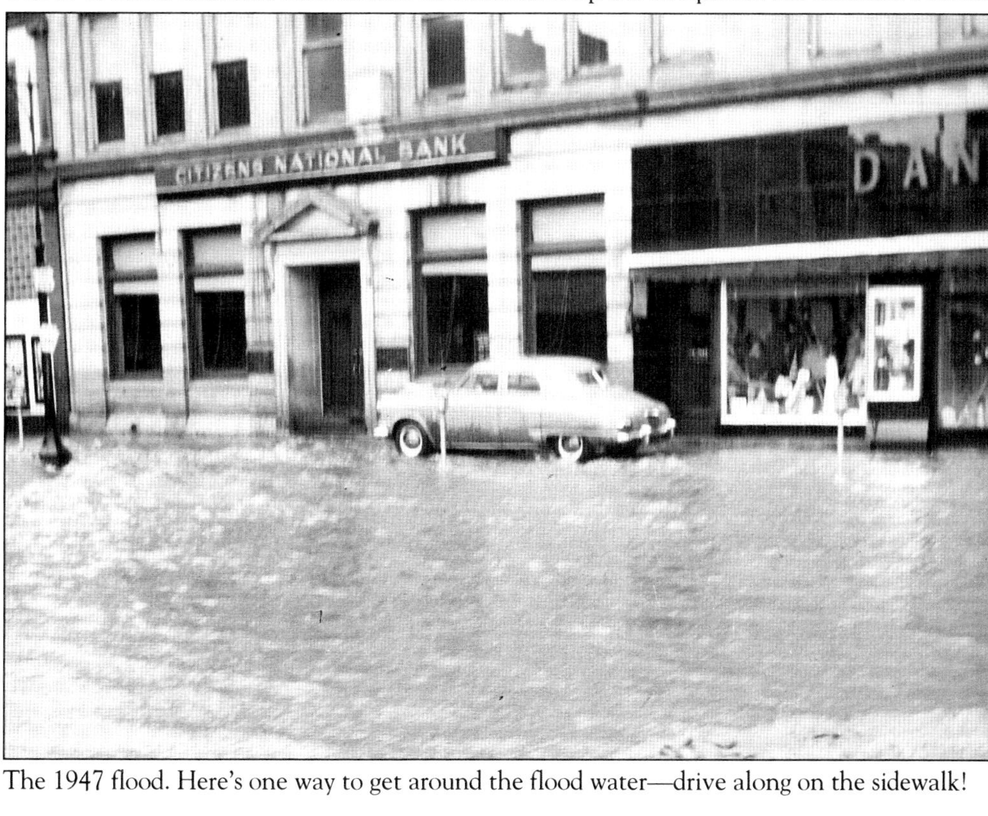

The 1947 flood. Here's one way to get around the flood water—drive along on the sidewalk!

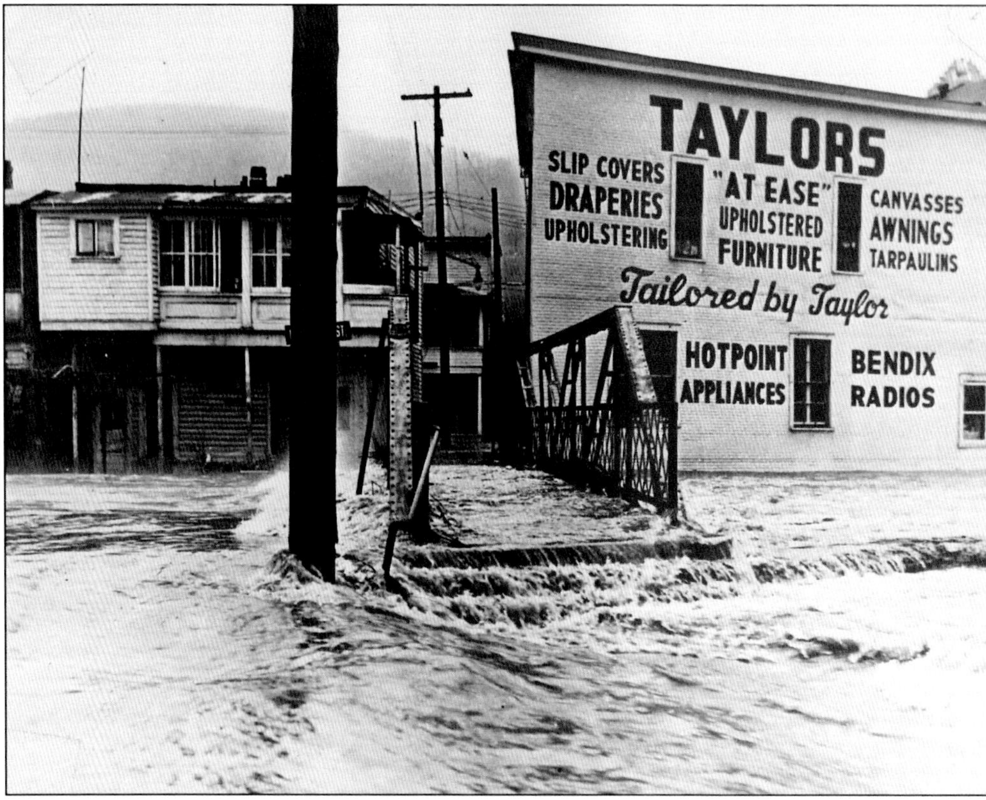

Flood waters over the Pine Street Bridge, 1947. This small footbridge between East Washington Street and Pine Street was completely inundated by waters. It was replaced after the flood, but at the present time it has been declared unsafe.

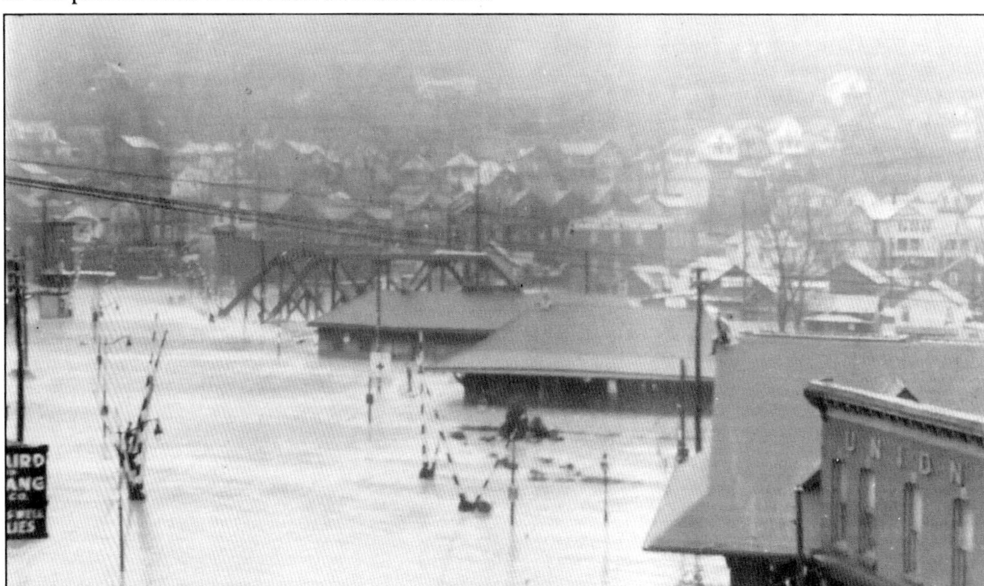

The 1947 flood. Major floods severely restricted the rail service into the city. This view is from the roof of the Hotel Holley.